ESSENTIAL
Tax Facts

Evelyn Jacks

**HOW TO MAKE THE RIGHT TAX MOVES
AND BE AUDIT-PROOF, TOO**

2019 EDITION

Published by Knowledge Bureau

WINNIPEG, MANITOBA, CANADA

ISBN No. 978-1-77297-087-6

Printed and bound in Canada

Canadian Cataloguing in Publication Data

Essential Tax Facts: How to make the right tax moves and be audit-proof too

Essential tax facts

Jacks, Evelyn - author

2019 Edition

Includes Index

C2006-904910-6 | ISBN: 978-1-77297-087-6

1. Income tax – Canada- Popular works. 2. Tax planning – Canada- Popular works.

HJ4661.J212 2006 | 342.7105′2

Published by: Knowledge Bureau, Inc.

187 St. Mary's Road, Winnipeg, Manitoba R2H 1J2

204-953-4769 Email: reception@knowledgebureau.com

Research and Editorial Assistance: Walter Harder and Associates

Cover and Page Design: Bruce Reimer, Reimer Communications

ACKNOWLEDGEMENTS

I would like to acknowledge and thank the excellent team that works with me at Knowledge Bureau; dedicated to providing world-class financial education.

Special thanks to Walter Harder, Bruce Reimer, and Christine Steendam for their help in producing this book.

I would like to dedicate this book to my sister, Kathy Rosato, who simply lights up my life.

Table of Contents

Introduction

Recent tax filing statistics from CRA confirm that 90% of all tax returns filed in Canada now use electronic processes, with the professional tax preparation industry winning significantly in the effort CRA has put into the digital process. EFILERs now prepare 57% of all tax returns filed in Canada; this compares to 42% in 2011. Back then 38% of all tax returns were still filed on paper, whereas today, about 10%—around three million returns—are filed on paper. In addition, CRA issued the vast majority of refunds electronically, through direct deposit to 79% of tax filers.

Yet, filing a tax return is an intensely human experience. Low income Canadians must use the tax system to apply for important tax benefits, like the Canada Child Benefit. Other important social benefits, like the Canada Learning Bond and Old Age Security, rely on the information reported on the return.

Most Canadians anticipate tax season with at least some glee—to get back overpaid taxes—over $1700 on average—for much needed help in paying down debt or shoring up retirement savings.

High income earners, on the other hand, have found themselves increasingly under siege with tax rates that confiscate more than 50% of their earnings over certain income levels, in some provinces.

Against that backdrop, CRA has become much more empowered to step up audit activities to go after "tax cheats". Yet, there have been many stories of overly aggressive tactics that have caused incredible stress to ordinary taxpayers who are simply trying to comply with their complicated tax laws under a self-assessment system.

These Essential Tax Facts have been written to empower you in your relationship with CRA—which is for life, by the way—so that you can keep more of your hard earned dollars working for your financial future. This is your legal right. Your obligation is to know and follow the tax rules, and keep records to back up your claims.

I hope these pages will help you make the right tax moves for your household and be audit-proof, too.

Sincerely,

Evelyn Jacks

PART I

TAX MATCHES
The Rules

1 WHY PLAY? This is About Your Keep

WILL I HAVE ENOUGH? HOW MUCH IS ENOUGH?

If you, like millions of Canadians have ever worried about these two common financial questions, I have some good news for you: you will likely have enough and you'll get there faster if you engage proactively in making the right tax moves. But that's going to require some stealth, in the form of "tax literacy".

By definition, tax literacy is about having the knowledge and skills to navigate your taxpayer rights so that you can control how much of your hard-earned money is left over for your own financial dreams, and how much of it must be given up to the Canada Revenue Agency—the CRA.

That's right. This is about your money and how much of it you get to keep, now and for your financial future.

That's the end game.

Here's the issue: you have to play the game. It's not optional. Your employer must take from the very top of your paycheque, the withholding taxes CRA requires you to pay. You will then file a tax return to get some of that back, or to pay up any additional balance required. Otherwise you will be penalized—heavily—by your opponent, the CRA. That's right, your opponent is also the referee.

That's the bad news. But, there is also good news. It is your right *to arrange your affairs within the framework of the law to pay the least amount of taxes legally possible.* You only have to pay the correct amount of tax—not one cent more.

That's how you start the game.

The more you know about the options you have in playing the tax game, especially how to use "tax preferences"[1], the faster you can increase your current standard of living, and the more empowered you will be to accelerate—and protect—your financial future from Canada's expensive tax system.

Put another way, by making the right tax moves, you can—*and should*—help yourself to the biggest refunds of your own top dollar as a first priority, by claiming the most tax deductions and tax credits you can, without attracting any penalties from the CRA.

Now, here's how you win: by positioning yourself to save the most capital in the most tax-advantaged investments, as soon as you can, you will score the most points to advance to your end goal—financial freedom: the day that your money works for you, *and you don't have to work at all!*

Make no mistake: the matches can get tough. The tax lingo is difficult, the rules change constantly and tax audits can be very time consuming and intimidating. But, as you get to be really good at understanding this tax game you will be engaged in for life, you will also be moving towards your personal financial goal line with purpose: you will get there faster, and you will worry less about your financial future, because you will actually have *more new money* to work with, after tax. You may, in fact, be able to retire much earlier than you thought.

So that's the game plan.

 Tax Moves

There's a lot to know to play the tax game with CRA, using all your tax moves. Just be sure to keep your eye on your mission: your healthy financial future. Tax savings are in the double-digits for most people. That's a more reliable return than the markets put out most years. So let's go get them!

---

2 THE COMMITMENT: Six Basic Strategies

THERE ARE SIX BASIC STRATEGIES TO paying less tax throughout your lifetime, so you can keep more, save more and worry less about your financial future:

STEP #1—FILE A TAX RETURN, ON TIME, EVERY YEAR.

Your financial freedom begins with a simple annual commitment: file your tax return on time—by midnight April 30—and make it your first mission to do so. Then do better: file those returns to your family unit's very best benefit.

Is there *a more correct way to file your tax returns?* That's a key question that should cross your mind with every entry you make in completing your returns. By taking advantage of perfectly legal tax deductions and credits that you may have missed out on in the past, you can in fact, accelerate your savings plans.

> **ESSENTIAL TAX FACT** ▶ **File to the Family's Best Benefit.** There are many ways to complete a tax return that is mathematically correct; the goal, however, is to file returns to your family's overall best tax benefit. By reducing family net income, and transferring available deductions and credits, you'll make more and save more money.

When you file your tax return to your family's very best benefit, you may find you'll also qualify for a greater share of lucrative refundable tax credits like the federal government's Canada Child Benefits, paid monthly to support the raising of a family, or for more of the Old Age Security payments you should get in your retirement years.

Most important, when you take advantage of more of your tax filing rights, you will learn that you can actually plan to help yourself to your own bigger tax refund *all year long.*

STEP #2—REDUCE YOUR WITHHOLDING TAXES AT THE START OF EVERY YEAR

Employers are required by law to deduct taxes from your pay and remit them on your behalf. That means the first dollars you earn every day go to the governments. Worse, the tax tables employers must use are skewed against you too. Consider how sizable the average tax refund in Canada is: about $1765 or approximately $147 a month. That's money you should be putting to use for your own financial future, rather than waiting until four or five months after the end of the year for it.

But can you do anything about this? The answer is yes. Start with the TD1 form your employer gives you at the start of your employment and usually annually after this. This *Personal Tax Credits Return* tells your employer about the personal amounts you will be claiming for yourself and your family when you file your return including claims for your spouse or disabled children or tuition for example. Don't just claim "single"—be sure you are accurate, so you can keep more money for savings with every pay period.

More good news: your claims for common deductions and credits—like your Registered Retirement Savings Plan (RRSP) contribution, child care or moving expenses, deductible employment expenses or interest on your investment loans, medical expenses, tuition fees or charitable donations—all can be used to reduce your withholding taxes, too. Most people don't know that. File form T1213 *Request to Reduce Tax Deductions at Source* to get those dollars included in your pay each pay period.

The result: even more money in your jeans every two weeks, to pay your bills or save for your future. Just fill out the second form and submit it to CRA, which will then give your payroll department permission to adjust your withholding taxes—downward—to account for your big deductions and credits.

Why does this matter so much?

Your tax refund is no small change, especially when most Canadians overpay their taxes throughout their working lifetime. Over 30 years, in fact, the average Canadian tax refund equates to just over $52,000 in capital that is not going into your retirement or lifestyle savings accounts, and that is before any investment earnings are considered.

Average Tax Refund $1765 x 30 years = $ 52,950
5% annual interest = $ 70,178
= $123,128 in a registered account

You can see what we mean. If the refund was saved in a TFSA—Tax-Free Savings Account—the earnings are sheltered from tax along the way. Plus, the earnings in this account will never be taxed. This can buy a lot of groceries, new clothes, and a few luxuries, like a much-needed holiday in the middle of winter.

Doing what most other Canadians do—cheerfully awaiting your big tax refund after filing in March or April—you are giving the government an interest-free loan. Playing the tax game as a pro, you will plan to receive and invest that money for your own future, and potentially, a six-figure retirement fund. That's the right way to win the tax game. But you'll need some tax tools to help:

> **TAX FORM FACT.** Check out tax forms *T1213 Request to Reduce Tax Deductions at Source* and *TD1 Personal Tax Credits Return* (federal and provincial) and make them work for you!

STEP #3. REPORT YOUR WORLDWIDE INCOME IN YOUR PROVINCE OF RESIDENCE AS OF DECEMBER 31.

In Canada, the tax filing year for most taxpayers is the "calendar year"; that is, income earned is reported for the period January to December. Canadian residents must pay taxes based on their worldwide income, reported in Canadian funds, and those taxes are payable to both the federal and provincial government. Your province of residence is based on where your permanent home is, as of December 31 of the tax year.

> **TAX FORM FACT.** Use the federal *T1 Income Tax and Benefits Return* to report your income, deductions and credits, attaching the applicable provincial schedules. If you live in Quebec, file a separate tax return, the TP-1, in addition to the federal return.

Provincial tax rates and credits do vary from one province to the next; so do the calculations of various refundable and non-refundable tax credits. In Quebec, some of the tax deductions differ as well. You can find out more about the federal tax rates and credits in the *Essential Tax Facts Appendices* in the back of this book; consult the website for the Finance Department in your province to keep up to date with the provincial tax changes.

> **ESSENTIAL TAX FACT** ▶ **Make Tax Smart Moves.** If you are thinking ahead, you will want to move in January rather than December, if your new province of residence has higher tax rates, so that your income for the whole year is taxed lower rates where you live this year. But do take into account what refundable tax credits are offered in your new province, too.

In the rest of our discussions throughout this book, we will refer to provisions relating specifically to the federal return, and the provinces that have a common definition of taxable income.

STEP #4 TAX ON INCOME DIFFERS, SO DIVERSIFY YOUR INCOME SOURCES TO ACHIEVE TAX EFFICIENCY.

Most Canadian tax filers will report income from multiple sources. The most common are reported on various information slips provided by your employer or financial institutions: T3—*Statement of Trust Income Allocations and Designations, T4—Statement of Remuneration Paid,* and the T5—*Statement of Investment Income.*

Because CRA receives this information directly from those employers and financial institutions, they will automatically match what you report on your tax return with the data in their own system. In fact, they can "push" out information directly to you, using an online portal called *"My Account".* It is a secure service that requires your logon information.

In addition, a telephone service for low income earners will ask for confirmation of the numbers they already have and, with your agreement, then process your return with just that information. It actually means for some people, no tax return is required! It's not a good idea, in general, as there are so many ways to miss your available tax preferences, but it may work in the simplest of cases.

Checking in with *MyAccount* is a must. Here, you can manage tax payments and authorize a representative to liaise with CRA on your behalf. You will also find out about valuable carry-forward amounts that can reduce your income of the previous three years or indefinitely into the future. Again, a great way to score tax points, is to make it your business to have the best tax knowledge possible.

Let's talk about some of the other income sources you have that may be self-reported. This includes income from investments, rental properties, or self-employment, as well as tips and barter transactions. It also includes the declaration of any gains you have on the sale of your principal residence, family heirlooms or other assets, like goodwill in a business. Yes, speculation in crypto-currencies and that business account on PayPal are included too.

Certain income sources, such as income from employment, pensions, and interest are fully taxable. They are known as "ordinary income." Dividends and capital gains earned in non-registered investment accounts attract more advantageous tax rates. Keeping track of the marginal tax rates attracted by various sources of income can help you make more tax efficient investment decisions.

That's important because the object of playing with tax efficiency can be better met when you diversify your income sources to pay the lowest possible tax rates on the next dollar you earn. To increase the tax efficiency of your investments, there is another tax move that can put you ahead: defer your taxes on income.

STEP #5. TO REACH YOUR FINANCIAL DESTINATION SOONER, BE PROACTIVE ABOUT YOUR TAX EFFICIENCY GAPS.

Where are the tax efficiency gaps in your savings? Could you be using the tax system to your advantage to get to your financial freedom sooner by deferring taxes on your savings?

Most Canadians have unused RRSP contribution room, unused TFSA room, unused RESP and unused RDSP room. Many have new opportunities to maximize their public pensions: CPP and OAS. But many don't understand these acronyms or where their money should be invested—or withdrawn from—first. This is where some investment "drills" are necessary: you need to know what comes first: an investment in a TFSA or an RRSP for example.[2]

You guessed it: there is an order to your investment strategies that can help you leverage the advantages available to you under the Canadian tax system. That order depends on a number of things: how old you are, what income sources you have and whether you have a spouse. You'll learn more about this in these pages.

STEP #6. BE AUDIT-PROOF.

This is the cloud to your silver lining as an empowered tax warrior: while it is every taxpayer's right to arrange their affairs within the framework of the law to pay the least amount of taxes possible, the Canadian tax system is based on self-assessment.

That means the burden of proof for what you claim on your tax return is on you and also, that CRA can audit your records. In fact, you are required to keep records by law. That essentially puts your opponent into the position of referee, too; an unequal and often confrontational relationship with the CRA, especially when there are grey areas in the law. That's a scary thought for many, and rightfully so.

Audit Check Point

- ✓ **KEEP RECORDS LONG ENOUGH** Even though you're not required to submit paper documentation with the tax return, you must keep those records for six years after the end of the calendar year to which your tax filings relate.

---

2 RRSP (Registered Retirement Savings Plan), TFSA (Tax-Free Savings Account), RESP (Registered Education Savings Plan), RDSP (Registered Disability Savings Plan), CPP (Canada Pension Plan), OAS (Old Age Security).

How to stay out of hot water with the CRA is discussed in further detail in the next chapter. It's an important first step in learning the rules of this game, because being offside with the CRA can be a significant wealth eroder, and that can set you back in your winning streak towards your bright financial future.

In fact, throughout this book you will learn little known tax facts and audit-busting strategies that support your mission to confidently take more control of your after-tax results, *so you can stop worrying about it,* because you know your rights, and are taking advantage of them.

 Tax Moves

The CRA has enormous powers. It can charge penalties and interest on money you owe and if you don't pay, it can garnishee your wages and tap into your savings to make sure you do. It can also disagree with your interpretation in the law, causing you to either accept theirs, and pay accordingly, or go down a variety of appeals routes.

But that's no reason to put your head in the sand (in fact, that's a very bad thing to do) or throw up a white flag (equally wrong and not very effective). The greater your tax knowledge, the more prepared you'll be for the unlikely chance of being chosen for a tax audit, and the more empowered you will be to maximize your taxpayer's rights and the professional dollars you spend with accounting or legal help to ensure them.

3 STAY CLEAR: Trouble with CRA

THE CRA HAS RECENTLY RECEIVED close to $1Billion dollars in new funding to review tax returns and collect on debts owed to it and other government departments. The goal is to track down "tax cheats" in Canada and abroad and collect the money CRA believes it is owed.

Every once in a while, you may come across someone who believes the *Income Tax Act* is part of a temporary law or that they are a "natural person" not required to file tax returns or pay taxes in Canada. Just to be completely clear: that's not only nonsense, CRA's successful convictions of tax delinquents is hard evidence of the reality. With all the new funding at the CRA, and a mandate to collect $7.5 Billion in overdue taxes, this is especially foolish.

Tax evasion—the willful intent to understate income or overstate deductions and credits—is a criminal offence and can attract penalties of up to 200% of the taxes payable (and jail in severe cases), plus a host of administrative penalties and interest.

This includes several layers of late filing penalties, a gross negligence penalty of 50% of the taxes owing. See the *Essential Tax Facts Appendices* for a chart of current penalties. Most expensive of all, can be the interest charged, compounding daily at the *prescribed interest rate* set by the government, plus 4%. As well, that interest is not deductible.

MANAGING CRA INTEREST COSTS. At the time of writing the prescribed interest rate was 2%. However, because the government *adds 4% to this prescribed rate* on outstanding amounts you owe them, the rate rises to 6%. Often, it is cheaper to borrow from the bank than to owe money to the CRA. You should enquire about this, do the math, and make informed choices about who your lender should be.

CRA charges interest starting on the day following *your tax filing due date*. Needless to say, it's important to file on time, even if you owe but can't pay. You'll avoid late filing penalties, upon which interest will be charged.

ESSENTIAL TAX FACT ▶ **Everyone Should File by April 30.** The filing due date is April 30 for individual returns and June 15 for those who file returns to report sole-proprietorship income or expenses. However, if proprietors owe money to the CRA, the interest clock starts ticking the day after the April 30 tax filing due date, just like for other taxpayers.

WHAT IF CRA OWES YOU? Unfortunately, the numbers and methodology on interest payments changes significantly when CRA owes you money. In fact, CRA will only pay you interest (it's taxable, by the way), at the prescribed rate *plus* 2%.

There's more bad news: interest is only paid on the latest of the following three dates:

- May 31
- the 31st day after you file your return
- the day after you overpaid your taxes

That means if you file 4 years late and the government owes you $7000, interest will be likely only be paid starting from the 31st day after you file to the time you get your refund.

It really never makes sense to leave your tax refund with CRA. Further, if you don't claim it and things change for you, you may never see it.

REFUND CONFISCATION. Be aware that CRA can also keep your refund in the following cases:

- You owe or are "about to owe" a balance to the CRA
- You have a garnishment order against you under the *Family Orders and Agreements Enforcement Assistance Act*
- You have any outstanding GST/HST returns from a sole proprietorship or a partnership
- You owe money to any other federal, provincial or territorial government, for example, on your student or immigration loans, or overpayments from Employment Insurance, social assistance or training allowances.

HOW TO GET YOUR MONEY, QUICKLY. For those who file on time, CRA will provide the fastest turn-around time if you file electronically and request direct deposit of the funds into your bank account. Their website stated, at the time of writing, that the goal is to issue your Notice of Assessment within two weeks of receiving your electronically filed tax return (or within eight weeks of receiving your paper filed returns). However, this is only so if you file your return by the filing due date; expect longer wait times if you file late.

> **ESSENTIAL TAX FACT** ▶ **It Often Pays To Have a Tax Pro.** Because the burden of proof for the numbers on your return is always on you, *even if CRA has made a mistake*, it is important to establish a relationship with a competent professional you can call on, should you have sudden trouble with the CRA.

Knowing your tax filing rights, together with what questions to ask of the pros—qualified tax accountant, financial and legal advisors—is a great defensive investment, especially when you need their help with the CRA. These people can go to bat for you in your relationship with the CRA, acting for you as a neutral and calm third party to enable important next steps, like negotiating payment terms and finding ways to maximize your filing rights over a period of years, if CRA makes adjustments to any of your tax returns.

This includes the opportunity to correct any prior errors or omissions to prior filed returns, and potentially offset or wipe out a bill CRA says you owe.

> **ESSENTIAL TAX FACT** ▶ **Do a "Tax—360."** Most people are not aware of their "carry-over" opportunities; that is, the potential to use certain tax provisions in previous or future tax returns to offset taxes payable.

Filing tax returns is never just a "one-year" affair. By taking a close look around you—ten years back and several years forward—you will often find opportunities to recover previously paid taxes; or position yourself to save money in the future.

To illustrate, you can make adjustments to:

1. the current tax return if you missed a slip or forgot to claim an important deduction or credit
2. prior filed returns filed up to 10 years back to recover refunds from missed tax provisions or up to three years back to apply capital or non-capital losses.
3. future tax returns to carry forward provisions like donations, medical expenses, political contributions or unused capital or non-capital losses.

More detailed information is available in the *Essential Tax Facts Appendices*. If you filed electronically, you can REFILE your return to do so; if not, request an adjustment to the previously filed return.

> **TAX FORM FACT.** Use form T1-ADJ *Adjustment Request* or use MyAccount to adjust online for up to 10 years back. Wait to get your Notice of Assessment first, however.

It always pays to be a model tax filing citizen; that is, to file your returns every year on time and to stay clear of trouble with the CRA (Canada Revenue Agency), especially if you run into financial hardship and have to appeal to CRA to consider giving you some time to pay your taxes.

Audit Check Point

✔ **APPLY FOR TAXPAYER RELIEF.** This special request for fairness and relief allows CRA discretion to grant penalty and interest relief in three specific cases, as described in Information Circular IC 07-1R1:

- Extraordinary taxpayer circumstances including natural or man-made disasters such as flood or fire, civil disturbances or disruptions in services, such as a postal strike, a serious illness or accident or serious emotional or mental distress, such as death in the immediate family
- Actions of the CRA including processing delays that result in the taxpayer not being informed, within a *reasonable time*, that an amount was owing, in errors in processing; or errors in material available to the public, which led taxpayers to file returns or make payments based on incorrect information, *incorrect information provided to a taxpayer*, e.g. where the CRA wrongly advises a taxpayer that no instalment payments will be required for the current year.

Also notable, especially in light of poor service levels at the CRA recently, is that taxpayer relief may be granted in the following cases:

- *delays in providing information*, so that taxpayer could not make instalment or arrears payments because the necessary information was not available or
- *undue delays in resolving* an objection or an appeal, or in completing an audit

INABILITY TO PAY OR FINANCIAL HARDSHIP. Interest or penalty relief is generally not allowed in these cases. However, when collection had been suspended due to an inability to pay and substantial interest has accumulated, or will accumulate, or when a taxpayer's demonstrated ability to pay requires an extended payment arrangement, CRA may waive all or part of the interest for the period from when payments start until the amounts owing are paid. But the taxpayer will need to make the agreed payments on time and continue to comply with filing obligations. Relief may also be possible when payment of the accumulated interest would cause a prolonged inability to provide basic necessities such as food, medical help, transportation, or shelter.

> **TAX FORM FACT.** A request for taxpayer relief may be made using Form RC4288 *Request for Taxpayer Relief—Cancel or Waive Penalties or Interest.*

JUST HOW FAR CAN CRA REACH BACK TO AUDIT? There is a limit to how far back CRA can go to check up on your returns. The normal reassessment period that CRA has for questioning your tax returns is three years from the date on the original Notice of Assessment. After this, the return is statute barred from CRA reassessments, unless CRA believes there is neglect, misrepresentation or fraud. There are other notable exceptions. For example, an unfiled return is never statute barred.

> **TAX FORM FACT.** You must file form T1135 *Foreign Income Verification Statement* by April 30 if you own offshore property with a cost base value of more than $100,000 Canadian.

> CRA has an extended audit period—from three years to six years—if the form was not filed on time, or where an eligible property was not identified properly on the form.

NEW VOLUNTARY DISCLOSURE PROGRAM (VDP) RULES, MARCH 1, 2018. A taxpayer may voluntarily comply with the Income Tax Act to correct errors and omissions on previously filed returns or to file omitted returns, as explained above. However, there is a special rule that allows taxpayers to request relief from penalties and interest under this general guideline: *if relief from penalties is possible, interest relief may be possible, too.*

As in the past, you can correct inaccurate or incomplete information, disclose information not previously reported, correct the claiming of ineligible expenses, correct your failure to remit source deductions, or your failure to file an information return, or to report underreported income.

Audit Check Point

✔ **YOU CAN APPLY FOR RELIEF FROM PENALTIES AND INTEREST.**

However, the amount of penalty and interest relief you are eligible for will depend on two claims categories:

- **GENERAL TRACK**—*Penalty Relief and Partial Interest Relief* is possible if the information is at least one year past due, the disclosure is voluntary; complete and involves the application or potential application of a penalty. *Note that the payment of the estimated tax owing is required before relief is extended.*

In this situation, there will be no penalties, and no criminal investigation will occur. However, only 50% of interest charges accrued will be paid—and then only for years prior to the 3 most recent years. *Full interest charges will be assessed for the three most recent years.*

- **LIMITED TRACK**—*Reduced Penalty Relief, but No Interest Relief.* In cases that include an element of intentional conduct by the taxpayer or a closely related person, some penalty relief may be applied for; specifically, relief from the 50% gross negligence penalty. But you should know that in severe cases of non-compliance, you will not qualify for relief at all—from either penalties or interest. No relief is possible if you are in receivership or have become bankrupt.

 Tax Moves

The income tax is the only type of tax you pay in which you can arrange your affairs to pay the least taxes possible. Be sure to know and exercise your taxpayer rights with confidence. But this begins with taking responsibility for them. Turning a blind eye can result in significant costs, and little or no leniency when penalties and interest are charged.

Tax Moves & Audit-Busters

TAX GAME DAY STRATEGIES

POSITION YOURSELF FOR CONTROL OF YOUR OWN MONEY. Do pay the correct amount of tax, but not one cent more.

SHOW UP AND FILE IT. Filing a tax return is required by law so buckle down and do it, on time, every year: midnight April 30. File earlier to recover your tax refunds as quickly as possible. File, even if you can't pay—you'll avoid late filing penalties and you can arrange to pay over time., with interest, however.

FILE TO THE FAMILY'S BEST BENEFIT. There are many ways to complete a tax return that is mathematically correct; but your goal, is to file returns to your family's overall best tax benefit. By reducing family net income, and transferring available deductions and credits, you'll make more and save more money.

REPORT YOUR WORLDWIDE INCOME IN YOUR PROVINCE OF RESIDENCE AS OF DECEMBER 31. Federal tax returns are required to be filed by all Canadians who have a balance due or file to recover overpaid taxes or refundable tax credits. Provincial taxes for the whole year are based on your province of residence on December 31.

Tax Tools of the Trade

- **REDUCE TAX WITHHOLDINGS AT SOURCE:** Check out tax forms T1213 *Request to Reduce Tax Deductions at Source* and TD1 *Personal Tax Credits Return* (federal and provincial) and make them work for you!

- **USE THE T1** *INCOME TAX AND BENEFITS RETURN* to report your income, deductions and credits, attaching the applicable provincial schedules.

- **USE FORM T1135** *Foreign Income Verification Statement* to report offshore assets with a cost base of more than $100,000.

- **USE FORM T1-ADJ** *Adjustment Request* or use *MyAccount* to adjust online for up to 10 years back

- **USE THE CRA TAXPAYER RELIEF PROVISIONS** if required. File Form RC4288 *Request for Taxpayer Relief—Cancel or Waive Penalties or Interest.*

Your Audit-Buster Checklist

- ✓ **KEEP RECORDS LONG ENOUGH.** You are required to keep tax records for six years after the end of the calendar year to which your tax filings relate. But, it's always best to keep documentation for 10 years, because you can adjust most federal tax provisions over a 10-year period.

- ✓ **LOOK BACK.** Do a "Tax—360": always maximize your "carry-over" opportunities reach back and forward to score. See the *Essential Tax Facts Appendices* for a list of provisions you can carry over.

- ✓ **CORRECT ERRORS AND OMISSIONS QUICKLY.** Tell CRA, before they tell you, that something is wrong and apply for taxpayer relief to receive missed refunds.

- ✓ **MANAGE YOUR INTEREST COSTS**—owing money to CRA is very expensive. Apply for relief from penalties and interest if you qualify under the Voluntary Disclosure Program.

PART II

THE FIELD OF PLAY
The Tax Return

4 AT THE STARTING GATE: Who Must File?

LET'S DIG A LITTLE DEEPER NOW and get onto the field of play. You will need to know some of the Essential Tax Facts to formulate your own tax-savvy approach to recovering overpaid taxes and then putting your money back to work for you.

> **TAX FORM FACT.** At the starting gate, you need to know this drill: you must file a T1 *Income Tax and Benefits* return every year by midnight April 30 to comply with your basic responsibilities as a taxpayer if you owe money to the CRA.

You've learned about the penalties and interest costs, and how far back CRA can go to charge them, so make filing your tax return on time one of those non-negotiable tasks on your list of things to do.

Schedule in time to start early to get ready for the task. Filing a tax return will definitely require some receipt keeping and sorting, something even the most organized humans have little time to integrate into their busy lives... but you must do it. In fact, doing it consistently throughout the year, will save you both time and money in the long run.

Next, you'll need to learn the tax jargon and more important, some important tax filing concepts which will improve your performance on the tax field of play. For example, take a moment and reflect on who *must file* a tax return, as opposed to those who will definitely *want to file*.

> **ESSENTIAL TAX FACT** ▶ **Required Filing** Individuals who are *resident in Canada, whether or not they are a citizen*, must file a Canadian tax return if they owe income taxes to the federal or provincial government on their balance due date.

WHAT IS THE BALANCE DUE DATE? This is April 30 for most people. Proprietors have until midnight June 15, but as you have learned, if they owe money, interest is charged effective May 1. Therefore, if that's you, you'll save money if you file by April 30. Also, don't forget to attach provincial calculations based on your province of residence on December 31.

REQUIRED T1 FILING. You will be penalized for not filing a tax return, regardless of your travel schedule, in these cases:

- You receive a request from CRA to file a return.
- You have an amount outstanding under the *RRSP Home Buyers' Plan* (HBP) or *Lifelong Learning Plan* (LLP).
- You are required to contribute to the *Canada Pension Plan* (CPP) because of self-employment income.
- You are self-employed and have opted to participate in the *Employment Insurance* (EI) program for self-employed taxpayers.
- You have disposed of your principal residence. You must file a return, even if the transaction is tax exempt. Starting with the 2017 tax year, you will need to also complete a really complicated form, the T2019 *Designation of a Property as a Principal Residence* and attach this to your return in these cases.
- You have disposed of other taxable property and earned a capital gain. (You should file to report losses, too, by the way, which can help you save tax dollars on prior or future capital gains.)
- You have elected jointly with your spouse to split *eligible pension income.*
- You have received an advanced payment of the *Working Income Tax Benefit (WITB)* (renamed the Canada Worker's Benefit after 2018).
- You must repay *Old Age Security* (OAS) benefits.

OPTIONAL—BUT LUCRATIVE FILINGS. The most common reasons taxpayers who are not required to file—that is, those with little or no income who are not taxable—will want to file include the following:

- To receive a refund of overpaid income taxes.
- To apply for federal refundable tax credits like the *Canada Child Benefit* (CCB), *GST/HST Credit* or the *Working Income Tax Benefit* (renamed the Canada Worker's Benefit after 2018).
- To qualify to receive provincial tax credits and benefits.
- To report capital losses for the purposes of reducing capital gains in the prior three years or to carry those loss balances forward to offset capital gains in the future.

- To use other carry forward provisions to save money: charitable donations, medical expenses, tuition amounts and so on.

It quickly becomes clear that filing requirements have a lot to do with your profile as a taxpayer, which can change over time, with your income, your personal relationships, your health and indeed, your travels.

That's one of two moving targets you always have to deal with in filing a tax return. The second is this: continuous change in our tax rules and interpretations.

Consider the excitement of buying a new home with your new spouse. Selling your old one will signify the end of one life chapter and provide new funds for your new home and this wonderful new life event. However, there are tax consequences to this common event, down the line.

Audit Check Point

✔ **TAX PENALTIES EXTEND TO AUXILLIARY TAX FORMS.** Even if you sell a tax exempt principal residence, you will need to know about a new requirement when you file your T1 tax return: you must file *form T2091 Designation of Property as a Principal Residence by an Individual* to report that principal residence disposition starting in 2017. Failing to do so can attract a penalty of up to $8000.

In short, to minimize costly consequences, you need to keep up with both—the financial changes in your busy life and in tax compliance and that's just one of the rules of the tax game!

ESSENTIAL TAX FACT ▶ **Review Annual Tax Changes.** Tax deductions, credits and brackets tend to change annually with indexing and federal/provincial budget changes. Check out the *Essential Tax Facts Appendices* for what's new in tax recently. Then, be sure to stay up to date as news happens by subscribing to the complimentary Knowledge Bureau Report or visiting often in the newsroom at knowledgebureau. com.

TAX FORMS FOR GLOBETROTTERS. Where you live for tax purposes is an obvious first consideration in assessing your tax filing obligations, but that's not always straight forward, especially when you have globetrotting boomers or free-spirited millennials couch surfing their way around the world.

What happens on your Canadian tax return when you have income offshore—from a rental property in Florida or an investment on the New York Stock Exchange? What if you have a foreign pension, from Europe or Asia? And what if you arrive here in Canada as a new immigrant or leave permanently for work or warmer climes?

Of course, you'll need to report your worldwide income in Canadian funds. However, if you are subject to tax in the foreign country, you can avoid double taxation by taking advantage of a special tax provision: a foreign tax credit, found on Schedule 1 of your personal tax return.[3]

> **ESSENTIAL TAX FACT** ▶ **Claim Foreign Tax Credits.** Where income is taxed in more than one country, tax treaties ensure that credit is given in the country of residence for taxes paid to the foreign jurisdiction. If you were subject to taxes in a foreign country, be sure to claim a *foreign tax credit* on your Canadian return.

There is another obligation for those with assets abroad. Recall that a separate tax form, one which contains its own late filing penalty, must be filed by April 30 to report information about the cost and income from the offshore assets themselves: form T1135 *Foreign Income Verification Statement.*

Know that international tax-sharing agreements now make it obvious to governments where your offshore assets lie and whether or not you are reporting the income or their value.

There are also requirements for financial institutions to share information on an international basis about your accounts and this will allow tax departments to audit your investment accounts.

Pensioners who receive *foreign social security and private foreign pension benefits* can also experience tax headaches. Translation of documents for each tax department involved is often an expensive challenge; so is communicating with each to recognize the foreign taxes withheld by the other.

Further, if you have *rental income from offshore assets*, you will be required to report this and in some countries, including Canada, there are withholding taxes on that rental income. In some cases, filing a tax return will result in a refund of taxes paid. For example, *gamblers* who are subject to a withholding tax on their winnings, may wish to file in the U.S. to recover some of those taxes.

 Tax Moves

Tax residency, both for people and their property, can become a thorny tax issue, that requires more attention by taxpayers. Wherever you work, live and play within our global economy; a tax liability will likely follow you. A short primer on the subject follows.

---

3 A foreign tax credit is credit against your Canadian taxes for income or profit taxes paid to a foreign jurisdiction with which Canada has a tax treaty.

5 RESIDENCY: In a Global Economy, It Matters

FOR MOST INDIVIDUALS, the question of tax residency is a straight-forward one. If you immigrate to Canada, you become a resident upon immigration. Also, even if you're just visiting, if you reside in Canada for *183 days or more*, you're deemed to be a resident for tax purposes, and you must file a Canadian tax return, if the taxes due on your worldwide income, less deductions, exceeds your credits.

But, the question of tax residency gets trickier when you spend part of the year outside Canada. It's especially common with university students who travel the world to take up gigs with NGOs (Non Government Organizations) in third world countries, or retirees who flit from place to place to find their nirvana in the sun.

Just where do they file their returns, or can tax filing be avoided entirely? Here's some background information to help you with this question:

DEEMED RESIDENTS. Some people are considered "deemed residents." This includes those who visit Canada for 183 days or more in the year, students studying abroad temporarily or members of the Canadian Armed Forces, those working in a foreign country under a program of the Canadian International Development Agency or those who work as a high commissioner, ambassador, officer or servant of Canada, for example. Also included in the definition are spouses or children of those taxpayers.

Deemed residents file a Canadian return as if they were regular residents of Canada. However, they will not be attached to a province of residence and so separate provincial forms are not required to be filed, unless there is business income from a province or territory. In that case, form T2203 *Provincial and Territorial Taxes for YEAR—Multiple Jurisdictions* is required.

TAX FORM FACT. Deemed residents will not be able to claim any provincial tax credits. In calculating their federal taxes, they will be subject to a surtax instead. (48% at the time of writing.)

IMMIGRANTS AND EMIGRANTS. Immigrants become residents once they establish their *permanent* residency in Canada. Emigrants become *non-residents* of Canada once they establish permanent residency in another country.

Immigrants and emigrants are often referred to as 'part-year residents' for tax purposes. Part-year residents are taxable on worldwide income *for the period in which they are resident in Canada*. See Immigrants in Chapter 36.

SEVERING TAX TIES WITH CANADA. Leaving Canada permanently has tax consequences.

ESSENTIAL TAX FACT ▶ **Departure Taxes.** Emigrants from Canada must file a "final return" to which a departure tax will be applied to the capital gains resulting from any increase in value of taxable assets, as of the date of departure. This is reversible if you decide to return to Canada in the future, so keep all your records.

Reportable property includes the Fair Market Value (FMV) of all assets that are not on an excluded list (see below) or personal property with a value of less than $10,000.

TAX FORM FACT. List reportable properties for departure tax purposes with your final T1 return: *T1161 List of Properties by an Emigrant of Canada.*

EXCLUDED PROPERTIES. The following properties will not have to be reported for the calculation of departure taxes should you leave Canada permanently:

- Canadian real estate, Canadian resource property
- Canadian business property (including inventory) if the business is carried on through a permanent establishment in Canada
- Pensions including Registered Retirement Savings Plans, Registered Retirement Income Funds, and Deferred Profit-Sharing Plans
- Registered Education Savings Plans, Registered Disability Savings Plans and Tax-Free Savings Plans
- Interests in life insurance policies in Canada (other than segregated funds)
- Benefits under employee profit sharing plans, employee benefit plans, employee trusts, and salary deferral arrangements, employee stock options

- Property owned at the time a taxpayer last became a resident of Canada, or property inherited after he last became a resident of Canada, if he was a resident of Canada for 60 months or less during the 10-year period before emigrating from the country

What happens next is actually paying the departure taxes, but there is some good news here: you do have some options to defer those taxes into the future.

TAX FORM FACT. If you owe money on departure, you may elect to defer paying taxes on your deemed disposition. Use form T1244 *Election, Under Subsection 220(4.5) of The Income Tax Act, to Defer the Payment of Tax on Income Relating to the Deemed Disposition of Property* and file it by April 30 of the year following emigration.

Where the amount owing exceeds $16,500, acceptable security must be provided to CRA. No penalty or interest is applicable to the amount owing, as long as sufficient security has been provided.

On a sailboat? Most people, and their money and property, belong to one taxing jurisdiction or another. While some board a sailboat and start travelling around the world, hoping to avoid tax altogether, governments tend to try to attach residency to your last taxing jurisdiction when you don't take up residence in another one. It's a grey area that is assessed on a case-by-case basis.

NON-RESIDENTS. Before you depart Canada for good, it pays to find a cross border expert who can help you determine with confidence what your tax filing status is. Knowing that will help you comply and avoid costly penalties and interest for failure to file, when you are compelled to do so, retroactively. You will also make better decisions about Canadian investments left behind: TFSAs, RRSPs, RRIFs, taxable Canadian real estate or business properties, for example.

You should be especially concerned about your tax ties if you are going to a country in which Canada does not have a tax treaty for the avoidance of double taxation.

Audit Check Point

- ✔ **ESTABLISHING PERMANENT RESIDENCY MATTERS.** Remember, that you must show that you have severed ties with Canada and have a permanent home elsewhere to avoid attachment to the Canadian tax system. However, taxable assets left in Canada will have tax consequences for non-residents upon their disposition.

In addition to taxing the worldwide income of residents, the government of Canada imposes income taxes on non-residents who earn income in Canada.

Except where there is an international tax agreement restricting the collection of such taxes, *anyone in Canada who pays income to a non-resident is required to withhold income taxes from those payments.*

In most cases, this is the only tax that the government will get on that income, as the non-resident will generally not be filing a Canadian income tax return. In fact, a departed non-resident of Canada may find that withholding taxes on Canadian income earned while a non-resident are cheaper than paying taxes in Canada.

However, in cases where there is little or no Canadian income, a non-resident may wish to file a tax return in Canada, in order to attempt a refund of the withholding taxes. There are three opportunities:

- *Under Section 216—Collection of rents and timber royalties.* These filings are not eligible for any personal amounts and so are subject to 48% non-resident surtaxes, the same taxes levied to deemed residents.
- *Under Section 216.1—Non-resident actors* may file a return in Canada under this section to report net Canadian-source acting income.
- *Under Section 217—Non-resident pensioners* receiving any of the following sources of income may file a return for amounts that include:
  - Old Age Security pension, Canada Pension Plan or Quebec Pension Plan benefits
  - most superannuation and pension benefits, deferred profit-sharing plan payments, RRSP or RRIF payments, certain retiring allowances or death benefits
  - Employment Insurance benefits or registered supplementary unemployment benefit plan payments, or amounts received from a retirement compensation arrangement (RCA), or the purchase price of an interest in a retirement compensation arrangement
  - prescribed benefits under a government assistance program

In these cases, if Canadian-source income is 90% or more of their worldwide income, the taxpayer will be allowed to claim full personal amounts. If Canadian-source income is less than 90% of world income, then their personal amounts are limited to 15% of their eligible income. The 48% non-resident surtax will apply but will be reduced by the factor of eligible income divided by non-eligible world income. Paying the 25% withholding taxes may be simpler and less expensive.

It's complicated, and that's why you may need help from a tax professional in making the right filing decision when life changes and takes you offshore. Expand your professional and referral network—it could pay off.

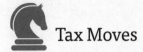 Tax Moves

The two moving targets you must navigate to maximize your tax moves—
your complicated life and the complicated tax system—can muddy the
waters in the tax filing games. However, both provide opportunities for
tax savvy planning. It all starts with this premise: you're in the game,
whether you like it or not, but you can learn to play with precision, to
your financial advantage.

6

NO TAX PAYABLE: Income That's 'Almost' Tax Free

A GREAT TAX MOVE IS TO PLAN TO EARN more tax exempt income. There are, in fact, many sources of exempt income which most people are unaware of. Once you understand more about this, you'll once again be in a position to accumulate more for your financial future, sooner.

ESSENTIAL TAX FACT ▶ **Don't Over-report Your Income.** As a general rule, exempt income sources are not entered on the Canadian tax return at all. If you reported these amounts in error, you may contact the tax department to have them removed.

The most common types of exempt income include the following. How many of them are you earning or about to receive?

- *TFSA (Tax-Free Savings Account) income earnings and withdrawals*
- *Inheritances*
- *Lottery winnings*
- *Capital gains* on the sale of a home used as a tax exempt principal residence (although you must file Form *T2091 (IND) Designation of a Property as a Principal Residence by an Individual* to report the disposition)
- *Capital gains* on publicly traded shares donated to a registered charity or private foundation
- Income exempt by virtue of a statute including the *Indian Act*
- Canadian Service Pensions, *War Veterans Allowance Act* Allowances
- Proceeds from accident, disability, sickness or *income maintenance plans* where the taxpayer has made all the (non-deductible) premiums

- Refundable provincial or federal *tax credits*
- Payments for *Volunteer Emergency Services*—up to $1000 if neither the Volunteer Firefighter Tax Credit or the Search and Rescue Volunteer Tax Credit is claimed.
- Social Assistance Payments received for providing *foster care*
- *Scholarships and Bursaries* for certain qualifying full-time post-secondary students or that relate to elementary or secondary programs
- *RCMP Pension or Compensation* received in respect of an injury, disability or death arising directly out of, or directly connected with, the service of a member in the RCMP
- *MLA and Municipal Officers Expense Allowances* but only until the end of 2018, when unaccountable allowances become taxable
- *Service Pensions from Other Countries* on account of disability or death arising out of war service received from a foreign country that was an ally of Canada at the time of the war service
- *Tax-free benefits of employment,* including transportation to a special worksite, certain transportation passes, uniforms supplied to the employee, education taken in order to benefit the employer, etc.

 Tax Moves

Most Canadians can significantly increase their wealth over their lifetimes by earning three tax exempt income sources: gains on the sale or disposition of their principal residence, investments in a TFSA and the private funding of wage loss replacement plans, which provide a tax-exempt income should something happen to your ability to earn a living.

7

THE T1 RETURN: A Walk Around the Field of Play

A BASIC UNDERSTANDING OF THE ELEMENTS of the T1 tax return is required to have a fruitful conversation about a successful and tax-efficient outcome for your income and capital. This is true even if it's your goal never to do your own tax return. Now that you've had a good primer on the basics of the field of play, it's time to get on it.

ESSENTIAL TAX FACT ▶ **There are Five Basic Elements in the T1 Return.** It helps to print out a copy of your tax return from your tax software or the Government of Canada website to become more familiar with them. Here they are:

1. **Total Income**
2. **Net Income**
3. **Taxable Income**
4. **Non-Refundable Tax Credits**
5. **Taxes Payable**

TOTAL INCOME takes into account the taxable amounts of all your income sources, for example:

- *Ordinary income.* The full amount of employment and pension income and interest earnings received or accrued every year. These income groups are also referred to as "ordinary income" because 100% of them are included in total income.

- *Grossed-up dividends.* These are the actual dividends you received, but for tax purposes they are "grossed up" to a higher amount which roughly represents the before-tax earnings of a corporation. Later on the return, a dividend tax credit offsets this grossed-up dividend for an advantageous tax result. However, the gross-up will reduce refundable and non-refundable tax credits.

- *Net rental income and net business income* from a proprietorship or partnership. This is what's left after reasonable expenses have been deducted from gross earnings.
- *50% of net capital gains*, calculated as the increase in value you have earned on your adjusted cost base, after outlays and expenses and available capital losses of the year are applied.

Social Assistance. It's worth mentioning that you'll find a list of non-taxable income sources on the calculation of total income:

- Workers' compensation benefits
- Social assistance payments
- Net federal supplements

While these amounts increase total and net income, they are not used in the calculation of taxes; rather the amounts reduce benefits from some other government programs because they increase net income, the figure on which most refundable and non-refundable tax credits are calculated. This income is later deducted so that it is not included in taxable income.

Audit Check Point

- ✔ **YOU MUST REPORT ALL YOUR INCOME** to avoid penalties. This includes barter transactions, your online activities and yes, those bitcoin transactions.

NET INCOME is probably the most important figure on the tax return. It is used in many ways: to determine the level of refundable tax credits you'll receive from lucrative credits like the Canada Child Benefit or the GST/HST Credit.

It will also determine the size of certain non-refundable tax credits a taxpayer is entitled to. Those non-refundable tax credits are found on various schedules; whereas the refundable credits are often simply calculated automatically for you by the government and sent/deposited directly to you.

In some cases, the net income figure can also affect provincial user fees, like per diem rates at nursing homes, for example, or determine the level of pharmacare deductibles in some provinces.

In B.C., for example, the pharmacare deductible is based on Net Income adjusted for income received from a Registered Disability Savings Plan (RDSP). In Manitoba, however, deductibles are based on Total Family Income. Ontario pharmacare for seniors seems to be based on net income after taxes (they ask for the Notice of Assessment).

ESSENTIAL TAX FACT ▶ **Take Steps to Reduce Net Income.** It's a critical marker in saving tax dollars both on the return, and off.

Efforts to reduce net income, in short, will determine how much you'll receive in income redistribution—refundable tax credits and social assistance. They also reduce your income taxes and certain costs you incur at the provincial government level that are income-tested.

The deductions leading to net income are therefore extremely valuable; increasingly so the higher your income rises. Often missed are lucrative claims for child care or moving expenses, employment expenses or carrying charges and of course, the deduction for your RRSP contributions.

Be sure to really dig for all the tax deductions you are entitled to reduce net income. By maximizing the deductions that reduce net income can save you tens of thousands of dollars over your lifetime.

TAXABLE INCOME is the figure upon which provincial and federal taxes are calculated. Federal taxes are reduced by non-refundable tax credits like the *Basic Personal Amount (BPA)* which is standard for everyone on the federal return, but this amount may vary on the provincial portions of the return, depending which province you live in.

NON-REFUNDABLE TAX CREDITS. From the BPA to the age and spousal amounts, amounts for infirm dependants under 18, medical expenses and charitable donations, and special credits for students and adult disabled dependants, these tax credits have the same value no matter what your income level is (although claims for the age amount and for medical expenses may be reduced as your net income rises).

ESSENTIAL TAX FACT ▶ **To Use Non-Refundable Tax Credits, You Must Have Taxable Income.** They are worth nothing to you otherwise and they cannot be carried forward to a future tax year if you don't need them.

With the exception of the donation credit, taxes are reduced on the federal tax return by 15% of the total of your non-refundable tax credits. Check out the *Essential Tax Facts Appendices* for the amounts anticipated for the current tax year and pay attention to the Federal and Provincial Budgets. They will change the tax credits—usually annually—and we'll keep you up on that!

Please subscribe to the complimentary Knowledge Bureau Report at knowledgebureau.com .

TAXES PAYABLE. This is, of course, the most interesting number of all... total taxes payable to federal and provincial governments. Are you aware of the total taxes you are required to pay? If you think that number should be lower, now is the time to plan how to do it, all year long.

 Tax Moves

Everyone should try to file their own tax return at least once. It's a life skill for a financial activity that's not bound to disappear any time soon: you will be paying income taxes for the rest of your life, so learn about the structure of the tax system and the elements of your tax return, so you can exercise your rights and make better decisions all year long.

8 KEEPING WHAT'S YOURS: Understanding Tax Rates

NOT EVERY DOLLAR YOU EARN is subject to tax; every Canadian tax filer can take advantage of a Tax Free Zone, also known as the Basic Personal Amount (BPA).

The BPA usually changes annually on the federal return, as it is indexed with inflation, although that's not guaranteed. There have been periods in Canada's tax filing history where indexation of personal amounts stopped; the result was a hidden tax known as "bracket creep." The BPA also offered on provincial tax calculations but may differ from the federal amount. Depending on the province, it may or may not be indexed.

Because everyone has their own BPA, which currently is just over $12,000, on the federal return, smart tax players will quickly see that one person making $48,000 will pay a lot more tax than 4 people in the family making $12,000 each. That's why income splitting is so attractive; but unfortunately, the government has made it difficult to do that. More on this later.

Because our tax system features "progressive tax rates" over and above the BPA, computing your "effective tax rate" on combined income sources can be a useful measure in family tax planning. Not all income sources enjoy those progressive rates. Some income sources are subject to flat tax rates at 50% or more, depending on where you live.

ESSENTIAL TAX FACT ▶ **Manage your Effective Tax Rate.** This is the final rate paid on all your income, when you take tax free zones and progressive tax rates into account.

As you plan your tax game strategy, however, you should consider five questions:

- How much can each family member make before paying any taxes?
- How much can income be reduced with deductions and credits?
- What is the combined or effective tax rate on all my income sources?
- What is the tax rate on the next dollar I make?
- Is the tax rate the same on all my income sources?

Check out the current federal tax brackets and rates in the *Essential Tax Facts Appendices*.

 Tax Moves

The object of tax planning is to plan to pay the least average tax legally possible on all your earnings, over your lifetime. If you know how high the tax rate will be on the next dollar you earn—information you can glean by estimating your tax calculations—you can consider whether you have any opportunities to change your income sources or the timing of your income receipts more advantageously.

By deferring income to the next tax year, income splitting or withdrawing more money at the same tax rate, you'll better manage your Effective Tax Rate (ETF) over your lifetime.

9 DIFFERENT: Income & Rates

AS YOU DEVELOP MORE TAX-EFFICIENCY skills, you will learn that there are different tax attributes attached to different types of income.

ESSENTIAL TAX FACT ▶ **Active and Passive Income.** There are two categories of income we generally report for tax purposes: active income and passive income.

The third category, exempt income, is not generally reportable, but as you have learned, there are some exceptions. Tax-exempt principal residence dispositions, workers compensation, social assistance and federal supplements, for example, require reporting on the T1 but are ultimately not subject to tax.

ACTIVE INCOME. There are two types of "active earnings": employment and self-employment.

Employment Income. Most Canadians will have employment income at some point in their careers. Employers must issue T4 slips by the end of February of the following year. On the T4 slip the employer will indicate the taxable amount of wages or salaries in Box 14, but also the taxable perks or benefits of employment which may not have been received in cash. An employer-provided vehicle is a common example.

The T4 slip also lists amounts that have been withheld from the employee's paycheque for which a tax deduction or credit is available. This can include Statutory Deductions the employer is required to make: CPP contributions, EI premiums and Income Taxes. Employer-sponsored pension plans (or Registered Pension Plans (RPP)), union dues and work-based charitable donations are examples of non-statutory deductions.

The following amounts are claimed as non-refundable credits on the tax return:

- CPP contributions through employment, but a portion will be deductible starting in 2019.
- Employment Insurance premiums paid
- Donations made through the employer

Other amounts withheld from your pay; employer-sponsored Registered Pension Plan (RPP) contributions and union dues, for example, are claimed as deductions on the appropriate lines.

ESSENTIAL TAX FACT ▶ When you have employment income, you may qualify to claim a variety of additional tax deductions on the tax return, but many of these require additional tax forms to be filed with the return and the keeping of tax receipts in case of audit.

Deductions that will reduce employment income include the following:

- **RRSP Contributions**
- **Child Care Expenses** incurred to earn that employment income.
- **The Disability Supports Deduction** if the disabled taxpayer requires assistance to earn that employment income.
- **Moving Expenses** if he or she moved at least 40 km closer to their work location in Canada.
- **Employment Expenses** where out-of-pocket expenses are incurred in order to earn that employment income.
- **Clergy Residence Deduction**
- **Canadian Armed Forces and Police Deduction**
- **The Securities Option Deduction** for employees who report a taxable benefit as a result of exercising an option to purchase shares in the employer's company.
- **A Northern Residents Deduction** if they live in a prescribed northern zone for at least six months beginning or ending in the taxation year.

Remember that claiming some of these deductions is a trigger for completing form T1213 *Request to Reduce Tax Deductions at Source.*

At the time of writing, employees were also eligible to claim certain non-refundable tax credits; notably, the *Canada Employment Amount*. This credit of approximately $1,200 has been in place to acknowledge the costs of driving to and from work, lunches, clothing and other expenses of working.

Self-Employment. Self-employment income is income from a business owned by a proprietor. That unincorporated tax filer will compute taxable business income on the personal tax return. Not so for an incorporated business.

> **TAX FORM FACT.** As a corporation is a separate legal entity, it must file a separate *T2 tax return*. Shareholders can receive income from the private corporation in a variety of ways; generally, as employment income or as "non-eligible" dividends.

In either case, business income is self-reported, for the most part. That is, the taxpayer is required to prepare a statement of income and expenses for the business and, in the case of the proprietor, adds the *net business income* to his or her other income for the year. In some cases, self-employed agents may also receive T4A Slips or royalty statements.

> **TAX FORM FACT.** The proprietor will file Form T2125 *Statement of Business Activities* with the T1 Tax Return to report net business income.

All reasonable expenses that were incurred to earn income from the business may be deducted in computing the "net *profit*" from the business. This is quite different from employment income, where any expense not specifically *allowed* by the *Act* may not be deducted from employment income.

In addition, deductions may be taken, at your option, to account for the cost of wear and tear on business assets. The tax jargon for those deductions is *Capital Cost Allowance* or *CCA*.

Some business expenses are *restricted*, for example, the personal-use components of home office or auto expenses are common.

In addition, aside from the business statements, the tax return contains deductions and credits for certain expenses specific to the proprietor. For example, the most common deduction is the "employer's portion" of Canada Pension Plan premiums. The most common non-refundable tax credits on the T1 return include:

- CPP contributions. Starting in 2019, more of these costs are deductible.
- Employment Insurance premiums paid if the taxpayer elects to participate in the EI program to be eligible for special benefits.

Net income from self-employment will also be used in claiming other provisions on the tax return; it is considered to be qualifying *"earned income"* for the following provisions:

- Making and deducting contributions to an RRSP.
- Claiming child care expenses incurred to earn that self-employment income.
- Claiming the disability supports deduction for disabled proprietors who need assistance to earn that net income.
- Claiming moving expenses for moves at least 40 km closer to a business location in Canada.
- Claiming the "employer's portion" of CPP contributions payable on self-employment income as a deduction, as noted above.

This topic is a large one and the subject of the book *Make Sure It's Deductible* by Evelyn Jacks, as well as a certificate online course, both available at knowledgebureau.com.

PASSIVE INCOME. This is income from property—it's not actively earned by the taxpayer like employment or self-employment income; rather it results from the investment of money in a property. The most common types of income from property are:

- Interest
- Dividends
- Rents
- Royalties

Special rules apply to certain types of income derived from property, specifically dividends from taxable Canadian corporations and rental income. These rules will be discussed in detail later.

Claiming expenses against income from property. Similar to the computation of taxable business income, the *Income Tax Act* defines the taxable income from property as the "profit" from that property.

In general, this is interpreted to mean that in calculating income from property (or from a business), the taxpayer may deduct any reasonable expense that is incurred in earning that income, to arrive at the profit, unless an amount is specifically restricted by the Act. Most recently, for example, the claiming of *safety deposit box fees* ended in the 2013 tax year.

ESSENTIAL TAX FACT ▶ The most common expenses deducted from income from property are carrying charges such as:

- Accounting fees
- Investment counsel fees
- Management and safe custody fees
- Interest paid on money borrowed to make the investment.

CAPITAL GAINS ARE A SEPARATE INCOME SOURCE. Note that, for tax purposes, capital gains—the increase in the value of the property—are neither active nor passive income. The expenses that offset income from property may not be claimed against assets that increase in value unless *a potential for income exists*.

CAPITAL GAINS. A capital gain occurs when an asset, whose value has increased over its cost base, is sold or deemed to be sold. More specifically, a capital gain is calculated as:

Proceeds of Disposition — Adjusted Cost Base — Outlays and Expenses

Capital gains are given preferential income tax treatment in that the taxpayer is not required to include the full capital gain in income. The capital gain is multiplied by an inclusion rate (currently 50%) to determine the taxable capital gain. In later chapters, we'll go into detail about each of these terms as well as the special rules that apply to specific types of capital property, and what happens when there is a loss.

ADVENTURES OR CONCERNS IN THE NATURE OF TRADE. Briefly, an "adventure or concern in the nature of trade" is a term used by CRA to describe a source of income that it considers to be business income, even though a business has not been set up by the taxpayer. It is essentially the recharacterization of a capital gain (50% income inclusion) into business income (100% income inclusion) for tax purposes.

Audit Check Point

✔ **BEWARE OF THE POTENTIAL FOR INCOME RECHARACTERIZATION.** This can occur when CRA reviews a single transaction or a series of transactions which may appear to be capital in nature, but because of their relation to the taxpayer's other sources of income or because of the number of similar transactions, CRA considers them to be business income (100% taxable).

What results is an unwelcome and expensive change on reassessment of taxes after a tax audit. You'll want to seek the help of an experienced tax professional to determine whether you have a good case for a reversal of CRA's opinion.

TAXABLE RETIREMENT AND EDUCATION BENEFITS. Other types of taxable income that result from the combination of your pursuits of active income and your savings activities are your retirement and education benefits. This includes:

- *From Public Pensions:* Canada Pension Plan Benefits (contribution-based) and the Old Age Security (a social benefit paid to all Canadian residents but subject to income-tested clawbacks)
- *From Private Registered Investments:* The following income sources are commonly withdrawn from "registered savings accounts":
  - RPP (Registered Pension Plan) income
  - Foreign pension income
  - RRSP or RRIF income
  - RDSP (Registered Disability Savings Plan) income
  - RESP (Registered Education Savings Plan) income

These topics will be covered in more depth later.

MARGINAL TAX RATES—CONNECTING THE DOTS. Now that you understand some of the categories of income you'll be reporting on your return, you can think about some tax planning opportunities. For example, you will want to keep a close eye on what type of income attracts the lowest *Marginal Tax Rates*.

> **ESSENTIAL TAX FACT** ▶ **Understand Your Marginal Tax Rate or MTR.** This is the tax rate you pay on the next dollar you earn. It measures its tax cost based on the source of the income and the tax bracket it will fall into.

Recall that after considering the Basic Personal Amount or tax free zone, tax rates are applied to a series of incremental income ranges (i.e.: tax brackets). The Federal Tax Brackets at the time of writing are shown at the back of the book in the *Essential Tax Facts Appendices*.

The highest marginal rates will apply to "ordinary income": employment income, interest income, net rental or self employment income as well as public and private pension sources, such as RRSP or RRIF withdrawals.

Other income sources, such as dividend income and capital gains income resulting from increases in value of capital assets upon disposition, attract lower marginal tax rates. An example for illustrative purposes follows; check out the rates for the current tax year as budget and indexing changes occur. Be sure to subscribe to *Knowledge Bureau Report* to keep up with such changes at knowledgebureau.com.

COMBINED MARGINAL TAX RATES, 2019, FEDERAL AND B.C.

Taxable Income Range	Ordinary Income	Capital Gains	Small Bus. Corp. Div.	Eligible Dividends.
Up to $10,682	0%	0%	0%	0%
$10,683 to $12,069	5.06%	2.53%	3.56%	-9.58%
$12,070 to $40,707	20.06%	10.03%	10.43%	-9.60%
$40,708 to $47,630	22.70%	11.35%	13.47%	-5.96%
$47,631 to $81,416	28.20%	14.10%	19.79%	1.63%
$81,417 to $93,476	31.00%	15.50%	23.01%	5.49%
$93,477 to $95,259	32.79%	16.40%	25.07%	7.96%
$95,260 to $113,506	38.29%	19.15%	31.39%	15.55%
$113,507 to $147,667	40.70%	20.35%	34.17%	18.88%
$147,668 to $153,900	43.70%	21.85%	37.62%	23.02%
$153,901 to $210,371	45.80%	22.90%	40.03%	25.92%
OVER $210,371	49.80%	24.90%	44.63%	31.44%

 Tax Moves

You will get the best after-tax results if you can arrange to earn a variety of different income sources, thereby "averaging down" taxes payable each year because different marginal tax rates apply to different income sources. Earning active income will also help you to fund future retirement income sources.

10 RATE BOOSTERS: Beware of Clawback Zones

READY TO LEARN MORE? There is one more wrinkle you need to know about in calculating your taxes and understanding how the next dollar of income you make will affect what remains in your pocket.

ESSENTIAL TAX FACT ▶ **Clawback Zones Boost Your Tax Rates**—for example where a portion of a social benefit like OAS (Old Age Security) or EI (Employment Insurance) benefits must be repaid; or a refundable tax credit such as the Canada Child Benefit is reduced, your marginal tax rate could be significantly higher.

That's because as income rises, not only do your taxes increase, but your eligibility for certain benefits decrease, too. Taken together, that "double whammy" hits low to middle income earners harder than other taxpayers, whose incomes exceed the clawback zones.

Two clawbacks are particularly vexing to taxpayers in the middle income brackets: the clawback of the EI benefits and the clawback of the Old Age Security Benefits. They are based on the individual's net income.

EI BENEFITS REPAYMENT. Taxpayers who receive *regular* EI benefits more than once in any 10-year period are required to repay the lesser of 30% of the benefits received and their income in excess of the base amount. This is generally the case for seasonal construction workers or others who work part of the year only.

For 2019, the base amount for EI repayment is $66,375. This means the taxpayer, who may be paying tax at a marginal tax rate of say 32%, will pay taxes at a whopping 62% if they are required to repay EI because they have income near the clawback threshold.

ESSENTIAL TAX FACT ▶ **More RRSP; More EI.** An RRSP contribution can be very valuable for middle income earners subject to clawbacks of their EI payments. The RRSP deduction will decrease the net income upon which the clawbacks are determined.

REPAYMENT OF OAS BENEFITS. Taxpayers who receive Old Age Security benefits and have income in excess of the annually adjusted "base amount" must repay the lesser of the Old Age Security benefits received and 15% of their net income (before adjustments) in excess of the base amount.

For 2019, the base amount is $77,580. For a taxpayer with net income above this, let's say at a marginal tax rate of 35%, would be paying an effective rate of 50% on any additional income. The OAS is completely clawed back when income is over approximately $125,696.

However, these seniors with higher incomes have another problem: the age amount, a non-refundable tax credit for those over 65, will be clawed back with incomes between $37,790 and $87,750 in 2019... another 15% increase in federal taxes as well as an increase in provincial taxes.

Therefore, seniors with incomes between about $37,000 and $125,696, marginal tax rates, including clawbacks, often exceed those paid by the top taxpayers in Canada.

An RRSP contribution will not be an option for those age 72 or over, unless there is RRSP contribution room available and the money is invested in a spousal RRSP for a younger spouse. Some tax planning strategies are addressed later.

REFUNDABLE TAX CREDITS. Refundable tax credits like the GST/HST credit and the lucrative monthly Canada Child Benefits are income-tested, too. As your *family net income* rises (yes, that's the net income of both spouses in the family), a clawback of benefits will occur once income start rising above $31,120 (indexed).

Remember, the RRSP is a great defence in reducing net income so that you can maximize these benefits. It will also help you secure your future in retirement. And this rings true for taxpayers at low income levels too. Therefore, sound tax planning is important for people at most income levels. Check out the income ceilings and the clawback rates in your *Essential Tax Facts Appendices*.

 Tax Moves

Clawbacks of social benefits and tax credits increase your marginal tax rates significantly. You'll want to learn at what level of income this happens. Then plan not to cross over the clawback zone by organizing your income sources and their timing for tax purposes to stay within income levels that are less punitive.

Tax Moves & Audit-Busters

TAX GAME DAY STRATEGIES

KNOW YOUR EFFECTIVE AND MARGINAL TAX RATE: The ETF is the final tax rate paid on all income sources after deductions and credits, and the application of progressive tax rates, while the MTR, is the tax rate paid on the next dollar of income you earn.

PLAN YOUR INCOME SOURCES. Earning a variety of different income sources with different tax attributes can help you to "average down" the taxes you pay.

USE TAX FREE ZONES. Everyone in Canada qualifies for the Basic Personal Amount (BPA). These days, you can earn close to $1000 every month tax-free. Planning family income to maximize the BPA for each person can help reduce the overall tax your household pays.

DON'T SKIMP ON YOUR RRSP CONTRIBUTION. An RRSP contribution will increase your credits and your after-tax cash flow, too, because it will help you reduce clawbacks of important social benefits you'll receive all year long.

FILE FAMILY TAX RETURNS TOGETHER. Because many credits are based on "family" rather than "individual" net income, you and your spouse need to file tax returns together. a smart start for a focus on family tax planning.

Tax Tools of the Trade

- **OWN A PRIVATE CORPORATION?** *File a T2 corporate tax return.*
- **SOLD OR TRANSFERRED YOUR HOME?** *Form T2019 Designation of a Property as a Principal Residence*
- **LEAVING CANADA FOR GOOD?** List reportable properties with your final T1 return: *T1161 List of Properties by an Emigrant of Canada.*

Your Audit-Buster Checklist

- ✔ **GET ORGANIZED:** Keep meticulous tax records—in order—all year long to save time & money on filing your audit-proof tax return. This is your first defence in the tax filing requirement.
- ✔ **PRESERVE YOUR APPEAL RIGHTS.** Take note of the date on your Notice of Assessment or Reassessment—CRA's response. This is used to determine your further appeal rights. Keep a hard copy of this form with your permanent tax records.
- ✔ **GLOBETROTTERS:** A departure tax is payable if you leave Canada permanently, but it's reversible if you change your mind. Keep all your tax records.

✔ **INVESTORS:** Understand the different definitions of income—both active and passive—and the power for CRA auditors to challenge their tax attributes. On an audit, you may need to prove why an investment should be considered passive rather than active in nature, to save tax dollars.

✔ **BEWARE OF THE POTENTIAL FOR INCOME RECHARACTERIZATION.** CRA can view a single transaction or a series of transactions to be business income (100% taxable), although you filed them as a capital transaction (50% taxable). The burden of proof is on you to convince CRA why you are right. Keep detailed records about the reasons for the transaction, its relationship to your regular line of work and other criteria set out by CRA in its Interpretation Bulletin 459.

PART III

THE PLAYERS
Filing With Family

11 YOUR FAMILY: Scoring as a Team

Economic decisions—including spending and investing—are generally made as a household; yet in Canada, taxation is based on the individual. It follows, that there is a lot of complexity in accounting for taxation of family units in our tax system. Yet, there are significant tax advantages when households file and plan their after-tax results together.

ESSENTIAL TAX FACT ▶ **Progressive Tax Rates Work to a Family's Benefit.** When individual incomes are taxed, each earner is subject to progressive tax rates. That is, you pay more as you earn more.

This ensures that the income of the household, is not bumped into one large tax bracket that is quickly subject to top tax rates. Clearly, when income earned as a family unit is equally distributed, the unit as a whole will pay less tax on total income.

However, when certain tax refundable credits are calculated, *family net income* (your income and that of your spouse) will be considered together. In other cases, both spouse's net incomes must be compared to determine the best claim or transfer of non-refundable tax credits. You and your spouse can even choose between you, who will claim certain income sources and deductions.

ESSENTIAL TAX FACT ▶ **Leaving Single Life? File Returns Together.** To achieve better results for the family, individual filers need to shift focus at tax filing time. The opportunity is to file your family returns to the *household's overall best benefit*.

When you live in a household with others, winning the tax game is about how much money you will save and keep as a *financial team*. You will lose points if you treat it as an individual sport.

However, the game becomes more challenging. That's because modern family life, like the tax system itself, is complicated.

For example, today we have a much broader definition of what a *"conjugal relationship"* is for tax filing purposes, than when the foundations of our current tax system were developed back in the period 1962-1972. We have traditional unions, same sex units and households headed by singles who support others.

Consider scenarios where supporting individuals take care of an infirm adult dependant; a healthy sibling takes care of a disabled one; or a granddaughter lives with her dependent gramma.

New types of households are forming with our aging population and new immigration, and each has a common tax thread: claiming tax benefits requires attention.

There are two reasons for this: claiming your rightful tax "preferences"—Finance Canada's lingo for your available deductions and credits—is not straightforward; and second, your burden of proof goes beyond the numbers on your return. You may be asked to prove your marital status or that your children, in fact, are yours.

This can be tricky in common law situations or where relationships are on again, off again, or in joint custody arrangements. You may have heard media reports of divorced or separated adults who have trouble justifying changes in their households to disbelieving CRA auditors, who have the power to withhold child tax benefits until you do.

Audit Check Point

MODERN FAMILY LIFE IS SUBJECT TO A UNIQUE AUDIT RISK. Because CRA distributes generous income-tested tax credits to households based on the combined net incomes of supporting individuals, it wants to be sure that your family net income is right, and that you are not claiming more kids than you actually support.

Family business owners have further headaches with the taxman. The federal government has recently altered the tax reporting rules for family members who receive income from a private family business.

New *Tax on Split Income* provisions took affect January 1, 2018; they are in place to curtail the splitting of income between high earners and family members who are inactive in a private family business to reduce tax rates paid overall. These rules are extremely complicated and the reasonableness tests they invoke will invite detailed scrutiny by CRA of potentially all family returns.

Savvy taxpayers will not let these tax obstacles deter them; rather they will step up their game and really dig for all the tax advantages family filing has to offer.

HOUSEHOLD FILING BASICS. In approaching your family tax filing strategies, it's also important to consider that your top tax advantages can be planned when you consider tax season to be a year-round sport. There are two main goals:

1. *Your Tax Season Focus.* Your focus at tax filing time needs to be on reducing taxes on income earned by *each family member*; then on making sure you prepare the family tax returns in a way that maximizes both refundable and non-refundable tax credits for the family unit. *Combined family net income* will have a major impact on your results.

2. *Your Year-Round Family Management Focus.* Family life change throughout the year should be considered from a tax viewpoint—in advance: the purchase of a new home or rental property, a career change, marriage, divorce, incapacity, retirement or death of a loved one all have tax consequences.

It's important to plan your affairs within the framework of the law to build and protect income and savings from tax erosion for each member in the family, but also, for the family unit as a whole.

Consider: Is money being saved at all? By whom? Is it in the right accounts—registered or non-registered—to set up tax efficient results now and on withdrawal? Which accounts should be funded first? Are there any tax incentives to support your financial goals, like education or retirement?

THINKING AHEAD. Your annual tax filings present an opportunity to develop a *family wealth management strategy*, with a focus on *tax efficiency*. That makes good sense because the taxes your family will pay over each individual's lifetime can be one of the largest eroders of your wealth.

To keep things simple at tax time, try to maximize every family member's tax filing advantages individually first; then develop your savvy tax moves as a team to secure your future.

Start by understanding everyone's position on the tax field of play. Put some numbers on the financial drawing board: what are the sources of income, capital and debt specific to each family member? It may look something like this:

ANNUAL FINANCIAL SUMMARY

Financial Facts	Spouse 1	Spouse 2	Child 1	Child 2
Active Income				
Employment				
Self-Employment				
Casual Employment				
Scholarships & Grants				
Other				
Passive Income—Registered Account Balances:				
RPP				
TFSA				
RRSP				
RESP or RDSP				
Passive Income—Other				
Non-registered Accounts				
Rental Income				
Royalties/Other				
Capital gains or losses				
From asset dispositions				
Debt				
Home	( )	( )	( )	( )
Other	( )	( )	( )	( )

ESSENTIAL TAX FACT ▶ **Financial Accounting Matters.** Compiling a simple *net worth statement* for the family as a whole before filing a tax return, will help you think about your best filing advantages, but more importantly, will refocus the financial decisions you should be making throughout the year to maximize *everyone's* tax opportunities.

TARGET TAX EFFICIENCY GAPS. This exercise will help you identify *tax efficiency gaps* to understand your tax filing rights, like what tax deductions and credits you might be missing out on. But in addition, it's important to connect the dots between better tax filing results and the investments your family should consider making to maximize take-home pay and invest wisely for your future.

It is true that many Canadians under-contribute to tax-advantaged registered accounts like their RRSP, TFSA or RESP accounts every year, at the expense of building family wealth. Others miss maximizing important deductions, like the interest expenses they are paying on their operating lines, which are used to fund investments in their non-registered savings accounts.

By improving your *tax literacy*, you and your household can make more confident and responsible financial decisions, get a better return on the investment you make in professional fees paid to accountants, lawyers or other financial advisors and most importantly, pay only the correct amount of tax.

FILE AS A HOUSEHOLD. The tax system offers several opportunities to take advantage of income redistribution. Even if you have little or no income, your family should a tax return file to receive money back. Specific federal provisions to claim include:

- The GST/HST Credit (GSTC)
- The Canada Child Benefit (CCB)
- The Climate Action Incentive (for carbon tax relief in SK, MB, ON and NB).

 Tax Moves

It is your legal right to arrange your *family's tax affairs within the framework of the law* to pay the least taxes possible, and that includes the opportunity to defer and split income, claim all the tax credits and deductions your household is entitled to, and transfer assets within the family, to get better after-tax results throughout various life stages and at the end of life, too.

12 THE WARDS: Tax Moves for Your Dependants

WHEN LIVING TOGETHER AS A FAMILY UNIT, it's important to define who your family members are for tax purposes. Here's what you need to know:

Your Spouse. This is the person with whom you have a "conjugal" relationship:

- A spouse, for tax purposes, is someone to whom you are legally married.
- A common-law partner, for tax purposes, is someone who is not your spouse but is:
  - a person of the same or opposite sex with whom you lived in a relationship throughout a continuous* 12-month period, or
  - someone who, at the end of the tax year, was the actual or adoptive parent of your child.

*Note that separations of less than 90 days do not affect the 12-month period.

For income tax purposes, all rules that apply to a spouse apply equally to a common-law partner, and for the purposes of this book, when we refer to a spouse we include the common-law partner in the term.

ESSENTIAL TAX FACT ▶ **Reduce Your Taxes with a Spousal Amount.** You may be able to make a claim for your spouse but only if your spouse's net income is low enough.

Computing Your Spouse's Net Income. You'll find the details for claiming the Spousal Amount in the *Essential Tax Facts Appendices*. The amounts change, depending on the indexing rate, from year to year. Essentially, the federal government lets you claim a second Basic Personal Amount (BPA) for your spouse, less the amount of the spouse's net income.

Singles with Dependants. If you are single, widowed, separated or divorced and support a dependant who lives with you, you will be able to claim the same spousal amounts as an equivalent-to-spouse amount, again depending on the size of your spouse's net income.

This is officially known on the tax return as the *Amount for Eligible Dependants.* To qualify the dependant must be your child, grandchild, brother, or sister by blood, marriage, common-law partnership, or adoption, and either

- your parent or grandparent by blood, marriage, common-law partnership, adoption or
- either under 18 years of age or wholly dependent on you because of mental or physical infirmity.

AMOUNT FOR AN ELIGIBLE DEPENDANT. An equivalent-to-spouse or amount for "eligible" dependant is possible if you were single, separated, divorced, or widowed and supporting a dependant if these rules are followed:

- only one person can claim the amount for an eligible dependant in respect of the same dependant,
- no one may claim the amount for an eligible dependant if someone else is claiming the amount for spouse or common-law partner for that dependant,
- only one claim may be made for the amount for an eligible dependant for the same home,
- where more than one taxpayer qualifies to make the claim, the taxpayers must agree who will make the claim or no one will be allowed to,
- if a claim for the amount for an eligible dependant is made in respect of a dependant, no one else may claim the "Canada Caregiver Amount" in respect of the same dependant.

Audit Check Point

ALWAYS **AUDIT-PROOF YOUR TAX CREDIT CLAIMS.** To claim non-refundable credits for your spouse or equivalent, use the dependant's individual net income. However, you will have to combine net income levels for the purposes of claiming refundable tax credits like the *Canada Child Benefit.*

If you do the wrong thing and file for refundable credits by claiming them based on one income only, it will cost you: repayment, with interest, can create hardship; so, it's always best to file correctly at the outset. See the next chapter for more details.

Spouses who split income—from a higher earner to a lower earner—are also subject to very strict rules. Some income splitting is possible under specific rules, and you'll want to know them and take advantage of them. However, shifting income from a higher earner to a lower earner to save tax dollars is circumvented by CRA through *Attribution Rules* and a *Tax on Split Income*.

You will learn more about this later in this section.

Two Spouses, Multiple Assets. When it comes to your assets, know that the family unit will also be allowed one tax-exempt family residence, not two, and so valuations are required when spouses who each have a residence, cohabitate. One of those properties will become a taxable residence when you start living together. You will learn more about family assets in the next section.

OTHER DEPENDANTS. Taxpayers who support minors (under 18) or adult dependants, or both, may qualify for additional tax benefits. A dependant is generally defined as:

- a child of the taxpayer or their spouse,
- the taxpayer's (or spouse's) parent or grandparent or
- a person related to the taxpayer or their spouse who is under 18 years of age or if over 18, wholly dependent on the taxpayer because of mental or physical infirmity.

These qualifications need not be met throughout the whole year but must be met *at some time* during the year.

> TAX FORM FACT. **THERE IS NO LINE ON THE T1 TO CLAIM HEALTHY MINORS.** But, if your child is infirm, some additional tax support is available under the *Canada Caregiver Amount* and the claim for *medical expenses*.

There is no form to claim the refundable *Canada Child Benefit, either*. But you must file a tax return so that the government can calculate it for you. You will learn more about all of this in the next chapter.

♞ Tax Moves

Claiming available tax benefits for your dependants can be tricky, because not all of them appear on the tax return. Every family should file tax returns annually to claim Canada Child Benefits and GST/HST credits. To receive the most, pay attention to how much each spouse can contribute to an RRSP: bigger tax refunds and tax free benefits may be the happy result.

13 NEW MONEY: Maximizing Family Tax Credits

FAMILIES QUALIFY FOR A SERIES OF TAX CREDITS—both refundable and non-refundable—which create new money for spending or investing for your dependants' futures. Both the federal and provincial governments offer tax credits—although they vary in size and scope. We will run you through some of federal government's credits, in this chapter.

CANADA CHILD BENEFIT (CCB). The refundable *Canada Child Benefit (CCB)* is the most lucrative; available on an income-tested basis for children under 18, it is completely tax free.

The CCB is a refundable tax credit that is based on family net income and the number and age of eligible children. In most cases the CCB is paid to the mother of the children although it may be split between parents when parents are separated and share joint custody. The CCB must be applied for, generally when a child is born (or when a family immigrates).

The amount of the CCB is not shown on the tax return at all; rather CRA calculates this automatically for you.

> **TAX FORM FACT.** **YOU MUST FILE A RETURN TO GET THE CCB.** In order to continue receiving the CCB, *both spouses must file a tax return each year* so that family net income can be determined.

The size of your family net income will determine how much you get; the more you earn over the income thresholds set by the government, the less you get.

How much is the CCB? Upon its introduction in 2016, the maximum monthly CCB was $533.33 ($6,400 per year) for each child under age 6 plus $450.00 per month ($5,400 per year) for each child between ages 6 and 17. The rates have since been indexed, starting with the July 2018 benefit year.

CCB for Disabled Children. If a child is disabled, the Child Disability Benefit of $2,832 in 2019 ($2,771 in 2018) is also paid; reduced where family net income exceeds $67,426.

Understanding Income Testing. As you can tell, the tax savvy family needs to beware of the "clawback zones"—net income ceilings that limit your benefits. Once family net income gets just over $30,000 ($31,120 in 2019), your family's tax benefits will start to decrease. Check out the numeric details in your *Essential Tax Facts Appendices.*

ESSENTIAL TAX FACT ▶ **Clawbacks Cause High Marginal Tax Rates.** Clawback rates can be as high as 23% for low income families. That results in marginal tax rates of 50% or more, as income rises. An important tax move therefore, is your RRSP contribution, which reduces net income levels, and cuts the impact of the clawback zones.

The RRSP contribution can be made throughout the year and within 60 days after the end of the tax year. This makes it possible to create higher refundable tax credits in the next CCB "benefit year," which runs from July 1 to June 30. If it's too late for this year, be sure to get a handle on those clawback zones for next year and plan now to contribute to an RRSP.

Tax Deductions Reduce MTRs. Another strategy for reducing net income and your overall marginal tax rate is to make sure you have indeed claimed every tax deduction that your family is entitled to. Check out the list below:

Checklist of Deductions that Reduce Net Income

- ☐ Contributions to employer-sponsored Registered Pension Plans (RPPs). Check your T4 Slips for these numbers.
- ☐ Contributions to RRSPs
- ☐ Elected split pension amounts (from eligible pensions)
- ☐ Union and professional dues
- ☐ Child care expenses
- ☐ Disability supports deduction
- ☐ Business Investment Losses
- ☐ Moving expenses

- [ ] Spousal support payments
- [ ] Carrying charges and interest expenses
- [ ] Deductions for the CPP contributions on self-employment income
- [ ] Exploration and development expenses
- [ ] Clergy residence deductions
- [ ] Other deductions like certain legal fees or social benefit repayments of Employment Insurance (EI) and Old Age Security (OAS) benefits

CLAIM MORE REFUNDABLE CREDITS. Families focused on reducing net income may also qualify to claim other refundable tax credits offered by the federal government: the *GST/HST Credit* and the *Canada Workers Benefit* are good examples. See the *Essential Tax Facts Appendices* for numeric detail. In addition, some provinces have their own refundable tax credits.

LEVERAGE REFUNDABLE CREDITS FOR EDUCATION SAVINGS. If you can, be sure to save the refundable credits you receive for your children in a separate account in the name of each child.

> **ESSENTIAL TAX FACT** ▶ **You Can Split Investment Income with Children.** Investment income from deposits of refundable tax credits received for the child can be reported by that child, usually tax free.

But, don't taint the account by transferring in money from sources; you will learn more about that, and some exceptions, later.

Leveraging your tax free refundable credits into education savings is a fantastic opportunity. It's also a great way to instill financial literacy lessons in children.

I remember taking my small sons to the bank every month with their monthly "bonus," showing them not only where and how to save money for their futures regularly, but also instilling in them the non-negotiable goal of a post-secondary education. These savings were the impetus for parent-child contributions and discussions about the role of education in a secure financial future.

NON-REFUNDABLE TAX CREDITS. While most refundable tax credits are automatically calculated by government and sent directly to Canadian homes, (or you can choose to have them deposited electronically into your bank accounts after you file family tax returns), non-refundable tax credits must be proactively chosen and claimed on your tax return. These credits will reduce your taxes payable, so they are of no benefit to you unless you have taxable income.

TAX FORM FACT. **Claim Non-Refundable Tax Credits.** On the federal tax return, you'll find your non-refundable tax credits on Schedule 1. (For provincial credits[4], look for Form 428 for your province of residence; e.g. Form ON428 for Ontario).

You should be familiar with many of the non-refundable tax credits, especially if you are an employee, because your employer will require you to indicate which ones you qualify for so that he or she can reduce your tax withholdings to reflect the costs of supporting family members.

What are they worth? To get the real dollar value of your non-refundable credits, total them and then multiply them by the lowest federal tax rate (15%). That's the number that will reduce your federal taxes payable. Your provincial non-refundable credits also reduce your taxes so multiply the total of your provincial non-refundable credits by the lowest provincial tax rate to determine the additional savings.

CARING FOR INFIRM DEPENDANTS. For 2017 and later years, the federal government introduced a new *Canada Caregiver Credit* (CCC) for those looking after infirm dependants. This is a complicated provision that combines several claims for dependants—your spouse, your minor child and an infirm adult dependant—into one. The numeric detail for making the claim is in your *Essential Tax Facts Appendices* (and will be calculated by your tax software); however, you will want to be aware of the following tax rules:

- Only one claim will be allowed for the Canada Caregiver Credit for a dependant, although the claim could be shared amongst two or more taxpayers.
- The Canada Caregiver Credit may not be claimed by a taxpayer who is required to pay a support amount for the dependant.

Who is an Infirm Dependant? The rules for the *definition of infirmity* can be confusing. In CRA's Interpretation Bulletin IT-513, it means "lacking muscle or mental strength or vitality."

A child under 18 will be considered to be infirm only if they are likely to be, for a long and continuous period of indefinite duration, dependent on others for significantly more assistance in attending to personal needs compared to children of the same age.

It's also important to draw the distinction between "infirm" and "disabled."

A disabled dependant is one who has a "severe and prolonged impairment in mental or physical functions." To qualify as disabled, a *Disability Tax Credit Certificate* (Form T2201) must be completed and signed by a medical practitioner

---

4 For Quebec, see the TP1 return.

to certify that the individual is disabled for tax purposes. Detail about filing the Disability Tax Credit is available in the *Essential Tax Facts Appendices*.

> **ESSENTIAL TAX FACT** ▶ It is no longer a requirement that a dependant reside with the taxpayer in order to claim the *Canada Caregiver Credit*. CRA also does not have specific documentation requirements but may ask for a letter from your medical professional to verify infirmity.

JOINT FILING FOR DEDUCTIONS AND CREDITS. When you file family tax returns at the same time, starting with the lowest income earner and working your way up to the highest, you'll ensure that income is taxed at the lowest possible rates and the family net income is as low as possible to maximize eligibility for available tax credits.

Transfers of unused credits from spouse or common-law partner. If your spouse's income is too low to claim any of the following credits to which they are entitled:

- Age Amount
- Pension Income Amount
- Disability Amount
- Tuition Amount
- Canada Caregiver Amount for an infirm child

You may transfer the portion they do not need to reduce taxes to your return.

Amount for Adoption Expenses. If you adopt a child, in the year that the adoption becomes final, you may claim a credit for the adoption expenses. This amount may be claimed by either spouse.

Medical Expenses. You may claim medical expenses for your family members on your return, or the return of your spouse. Generally, whoever has the lower net income should make this claim, as the total medical expenses must be reduced by 3% of the claimant's net income up to a specific threshold amount, as outlined in your *Essential Tax Facts Appendices*.

Audit Check Point

✔ **MEDICAL EXPENSES ARE OFTEN MISSED—AND AUDITED.** Save all your receipts for these common expenditures so often missed by taxpayers. Check out this partial list of claimable amounts and the *Essential Tax Facts Appendices* for new additions.

COMMON MEDICAL EXPENSES CLAIMABLE ON THE T1 RETURN

Payments to Medical Practitioners	Other Eligible Expenses
• a dentist, medical doctor or practitioner, or optometrist • a pharmacist • a psychologist, a speech-language pathologist • an osteopath, chiropractor • a naturopath • a therapeutist (or therapist) • a physiotherapist • a chiropodist (or podiatrist) • a Christian science practitioner • a psychoanalyst who is a member of the Canadian Institute of Psychoanalysis or a member of the Quebec Association of Jungian Psychoanalysts • a psychologist • a qualified speech-language pathologist or audiologist • an occupational therapist who is a member of the Canadian Association of Occupational Therapists • an acupuncturist • a dietician • a dental hygienist • a nurse, practical nurses or a Christian science nurse • an audiologist (after Feb 18, 1997)	• attendant or nursing home care • ambulance fees, transport, travel • eyeglasses, dental work, hearing aids and batteries • guide and service animals • transplant costs • alterations to the home to accommodate disabled persons • lip reading or sign language training, sign language services • training a person to provide care for an infirm dependant, cost of deaf-blind intervening services • drugs obtained under the Special Access Program (not yet approved, but authorized) • Cannabis—with a "medical document" issued by a medical or nurse practitioner as of October 17, 2018. • tutoring services for those with a learning disability or mental impairment • private health plan premiums, group insurance premiums paid through employment, Blue Cross premiums including travel costs • a wheelchair, crutches, spinal brace, brace for a limb, an ileostomy or a colostomy pad, truss for a hernia • a wig made to order for abnormal hair loss due to disease, treatment or accident.

Transfer of Disability Amount or Tuition Amount from Children. If your child is eligible to claim the Disability Amount or the Tuition Amount but does not need those credits to reduce taxes payable, you may claim them on your return.

For the Disability Amount, you may claim whatever portion your dependant does not need, with no additional documentation (other than the Disability Tax Credit Certificate).

For the Tuition Amount, your child must complete the back of the T2202A slip they receive from their educational institution. This transfer is limited to $5,000 less the amount used by the child.

Tax Planning with Tax Credits. Keep these transferrable provisions in mind when you plan investment activities throughout the year and account for them at tax time. You will be in a position to ask better questions about the tax and investment planning decisions you would like to make; for example:

- How can we increase the Canada Child Benefits we receive?
- Will an RRSP help? Who should contribute?
- Should we pay down the mortgage first, then invest in the RRSP?
- How should we invest the Canada Child Benefits received? In whose account? In whose hands will the income be taxed in the future?
- How can we split income between family members to reduce taxes?
- Who should own a TFSA? Should we invest our tax refund there?
- Is an RESP a good idea for education savings for our family?
- Should we borrow money to invest? If so who should do this?
- Should we consider buying life insurance and how should we fund this?

The following chart will help you identify transferrable provisions to use to your best benefit to minimize tax for the family unit.

 Tax Moves

Stop filing as a "single" when you have a new spouse and/or family. Start claiming all the non-refundable tax credits you qualify for on your TD1 *Tax Credit Return*, which can reduce your withholding taxes. Then increase your tax refund by claiming all deductions and credits to your top advantage as household, reducing family net income with an RRSP contribution to increase benefits.

TAX SAVERS FOR SPOUSES

Tax Provision		Claimed By
Passive Income	Taxable Dividends	Dividends can be transferred by lower earner to high-earning spouse if, by doing so, a Spousal Amount is created or increased.
Pension Benefits	Canada Pension Plan Benefits	After age 60, split CPP income by applying for benefits sharing through Service Canada.
	Eligible Pension Income from RPPs, RRSPs and RRIFs	Up to 50% can be transferred to your spouse, by election, on form T1032 if you are age 65 in the case of RRSPs and RRIFs; at any age for RPPs.
Non-Refundable Credits and Deductions	Spousal Amount	Higher earner claims. Reduce lower earner's net income with an RRSP contribution, if that spouse has RRSP room, to increase the spousal amount, a possible transfer of other tax credits, bigger medical expense claim.
	Age Amount, Pension Income Amount, Disability Amount, Tuition Amount CC Amount*	These amounts are transferable to the higher earner if the lower earner is not taxable. For the Disability Amount and Tuition Amount transfers from other dependants may also be made.
	Claims for Eligible Dependant	Claimed by a single, separated, divorced or widowed spouse who is living with and supporting a dependant under 18 or infirm.
	Canada Caregiver Credit, Charitable Donations, Adoption Expenses, Home Buyers Amount, Political Contributions	Can be claimed by either spouse or shared between them.
	Medical Expenses	Family expenses are usually claimed by spouse with lower net income for best benefit (if that spouse is taxable). Medical expenses for other dependent adults can be claimed by either spouse.
	Deductions: Moving expenses and child care	Moving expenses can be claimed by either spouse as long as there is income earned at the new location; child care is usually claimed by the lower earner; some exceptions apply.

*Canada Caregiver Amount for minor child.

14 NEW HURDLES: Family Income Splitting

FAMILY INCOME SPLITTING IS THE PROCESS of shifting income from one family member who has a fairly high marginal tax rate to be reported and taxed in the hands of family members who have lower marginal tax rates.

There are several methods of income splitting such as contributions to spousal RRSPs, the election to split eligible pension income, drawing up inter-spousal loans or transfers to non-arm's length minor children, and the timing of the transfer of assets, which are acceptable. We'll discuss those in this chapter.

But, because of the significant tax savings families may realize from income splitting attempts, the *Income Tax Act* has many rules that restrict them. The test for the vast majority of these restrictions is whether a transaction was between someone you deal with at arm's length (unrelated) or non-arm's length (related).

The *Attribution Rules*, for example, clearly set out what's allowed and what isn't when it comes to non-arm's length transfers of income and assets; that is, transfers amongst family members. Onerous new rules have also recently been introduced to thwart "dividend income sprinkling" with family members by professionals and private family business owners. Details follow:

ATTRIBUTION RULES. The Attribution Rules are triggered by "non-arm's length" transactions, that shift income or capital from high earners to low earners. Here's what you can't do:

- *Transfers and loans to spouse or common-law partner.* If you transfer or loan property either directly or indirectly, by means of a trust or any other means to a spouse or common-law partner for that person's benefit, any resulting income or loss or capital gain or loss from that property is taxable to you.

- In addition, where one spouse guarantees the repayment of a loan to the other spouse, made for investment purposes, attribution will apply to any income earned from the loaned funds.

- *Transfers and loans to minors.* Where property is transferred or loaned either directly or indirectly to a person who is under 18 and who does not deal with you at arm's length or who is your niece or nephew, the income or loss resulting from such property is reported by you until the transferee attains 18 years of age. Capital gains or losses do not, however, attribute back to you.

  In other words, income resulting from assets transferred to a minor child will trigger attribution of rental, dividend or interest income, but not capital gains.

These rules thwart an otherwise perfect plan: the transfer of assets from the higher earner to the lower earners in the family that would result tax on income being paid at lower tax rates, leading to lower overall family taxes payable.

ESSENTIAL TAX FACTS ▶ **The Attribution Rules Can Be Avoided.** There are several legal ways to get around the Attribution Rules to meet the goal of splitting income with family members.

CIRCUMVENTING ATTRIBUTION RULES. The following are examples of transactions you can undertake to split income and put assets into the hands of various family members, all within the framework of the law:

- *Inheritances.* Attribution does not apply to inheritances. If possible, invest the money in separate savings accounts to verify the origin of the capital.

- *Tax-Free Savings Accounts.* If you make contributions to a Tax-Free Savings Account for your spouse or adult children they will earn income on those deposits with no income tax payable. The contribution must be made by the TFSA holder; but you can make a gift of money to do so. These earnings will have no effect on your ability to claim the Spousal Amount.

- *Spousal RRSPs.* Attribution does not apply to contributions made to a spousal RRSP, unless there is a withdrawal within three years.

- *Interest income from Canada Child Benefit (CCB)* payments. If CCB payments are invested in the name of a child, the income will not be subject to attribution. In other words, interest, dividends and other investment income may be reported in the hands of the child. Be sure this account remains untainted by birthday money and other gifts.

- *Joint accounts.* T5 Slips are issued by banks in the names of the account holders to report earnings on investments including interest and dividends. This does not mean that the income on those slips is taxable to those whose names are on the slips. Instead, report income on the return of the individuals who contributed the funds to the account in the proportion that the funds were supplied. For example, if only one spouse in a family works and is the source of all of the deposits, then all of the interest earned on the account is taxable to that person, no matter whose name is on the account.

- *Property transfers to a spouse.* A special rule applies when property is transferred to a spouse. Normally, such property transfers at tax cost, so that no gain or loss arises. This is true even if the spouse pays fair value for the property. The property will not transfer at tax cost, but at fair market value, provided the transferor files an election to have this happen with the tax return for the year of transfer and the spouse has paid fair value consideration.

- *Transfers for fair market consideration.* The Attribution Rules will not apply to any income, gain or loss from transferred property if, at the time of transfer, consideration was paid for the equivalent of fair market value for the transferred property by the transferee. The person acquiring the property must use his or her own capital to pay for it.

- *Transfers for indebtedness.* The Attribution Rules on investment income will not apply if the lower income spouse borrowed capital from the higher earner, and the parties signed a bona fide loan that bore an interest rate which is at least the lesser of:

  o the "prescribed" interest rates in effect at the time the indebtedness was incurred and

  o the rate that would have been charged by a commercial lender.

Note that the prescribed interest rate used in establishing bona fide inter-spousal loans is set quarterly by the CRA. It is based on average yields of 90-day Treasury Bills for the first month of the preceding quarter.

Payment of interest on inter-spousal loans. Interest must actually be paid on the indebtedness incurred by the spouse, under a formal loan agreement described above, by January 30 of each year, following the tax year, or attribution will apply to income earned with the loaned funds.

- *Second generation earnings.* While the income earned on property transferred to the spouse must be reported by the transferor, any secondary income earned on investing the earnings is taxed in the hands of the transferee.

- *Spousal dividend transfers.* One spouse may report dividends received from taxable Canadian corporations received by the other spouse if, by doing so, a Spousal Amount is created or increased.

- *Assignment of Canada Pension Plan Benefits.* It is possible to apply to split CPP benefits between spouses, thereby minimizing tax on that income source in some cases.

- *Pension income splitting.* The election to split pension income between spouses does not involve the actual transfer of funds from one spouse to another but is an election to have the split pension taxed as if it were the other spouse's income. As such, the attribution rules do not apply. (However, if funds are actually transferred from one spouse to the other, the attribution rules will apply to any income earned on the transferred funds).

TAX FORM FACT. **OPTIMIZE PENSION INCOME SPLITTING ON FORM T1032.** Elect to split pension income with your spouse on Form T1032 *Joint Election to Split Pension Income.*

- *Investments in spouse's business.* Investments in the spouse's or common-law partner's business venture are not subject to Attribution Rules as the resulting income is business income rather than income from property.

- *When spouses live apart.* If spouses are living separate and apart due to relationship breakdown, they can jointly elect to have the Attribution Rules not apply to the period in which they were living apart. The Attribution Rules do not apply after a divorce is finalized.

- *Wages paid to spouse and children.* Where a spouse or children receive a wage from the family business—in other words, earn active employment income—the attribution rules won't apply if the wage is reasonable and is included in the recipient's income. It's important to track all of the hours family members work in the business and to actually pay the wages for the work done. You'll need to make statutory deductions for income tax, the Canada Pension Plan, and in some cases, EI (Employment Insurance). This will have a bearing on new Tax on Split Income Rules, discussed below.

- *Property transferred to an adult child (over 18).* This will, in general, not be subject to attribution. However, when income splitting is the main reason for a loan to an adult child, the income will be attributed back to the transferor. An exception again occurs when *fair market value (FMV)* consideration is paid, or a bona fide loan is drawn up with interest payable as described above, by January 30 of the year following the end of the calendar year.

Audit Check Point

✔ Always pay interest on inter-spousal investment loans. This must happen within 30 days of the calendar year end.

TAX ON SPLIT INCOME—MINORS. The Attribution Rules will not apply when an amount is included in the calculation of Tax on Split Income (TOSP) on Schedule 1 of the tax return. This special tax is assessed on certain income sources earned by minor children from their parents' or other relatives' ventures. It's also known as the "Kiddie Tax". Specifically, dividends or shareholder benefits earned either directly or through a trust or partnership, from a corporation controlled by someone related to the child, are extracted from the normal tax calculations and top marginal tax rates are applied.

The result is the elimination of any tax benefits of such an arrangement. Capital gains on the sale of shares in the business are also subject to the Kiddie Tax.

TAX ON SPLIT INCOME (TOSI)—ADULTS. New Tax on Split Income Rules (TOSI) will extend the existing "Kiddie Tax" provisions to adults who are related to the business but do not make a "reasonable" contribution. There are particularly onerous rules for young adults between the ages of 18 to 24.

TAX FORM FACT. **CALCULATE THE TAX ON SPLIT INCOME ON FORM T1206** Look for the calculation on Schedule 1 of the T1 return.

Exclusions. The best way to understand the new rules is know what's not caught in this tax web. Non-residents are excluded from the rules, for example. In addition:

- For anyone under 25 years old, income or gains from the disposition of property resulting from the *death of a parent* will be exempt.
- The under-25-year-olds, will also escape TOSI if they are entitled to the *Disability Tax Credit* or are a *full-time student* in a post-secondary institution and received the money from someone other than a parent.
- Property transferred, at any age, due to a separation agreement or judgement due to *marriage or common-law relationship breakdowns.*
- Taxable capital gains resulting from deemed disposition on *death of a taxpayer.*
- Taxable capital gains resulting from dispositions of *qualified farm or fishing enterprises or qualifying small business corporation shares.*
- *Active Engagement in the Business.* There will be specific exceptions from the TOSI for those who are "actively engaged" in an "excluded business."

- *Appropriate Shareholding.* Also excluded are those who hold shares that represent at least 10% of the votes and value of the private corporation. In this case, income and capital distributions will qualify for regular tax rates.

- *Dividends received as a retirement income* by the spouse or common-law partner of the source individual (the active spouse) if the active spouse has attained age 65 before the end of the year, or the amounts were received as a result of the active spouse's death.

Fortunately, these more relaxed rules on splitting dividends with spouses in retirement provide a key benefit compared to the pension income splitting rules in place for recipients of matured RRSPs, RRIFs, or employer-provided pensions: they are not limited to a 50% rule.

- *For estate planning.* A specified individual—that is, someone who receives income subject to TOSI—will not be subject to top tax rates on income that was an excluded amount of the deceased.

At the time of writing further clarification of these rules and rules surrounding the taxation of passive investment income in a private corporation were pending.

 Tax Moves

Family income splitting in not easy in Canada, as it is governed by Attribution Rules and starting in 2018, onerous reasonableness tests for when splitting income from a business.

But there are some savvy tax moves to consider, like having the higher-income spouse pay household and personal expenses, while lower earners use their own-source savings to acquire investment assets. Income tax refunds and refundable tax credits are "own source" capital, so that resulting earnings, if invested, are reported by lower earners, too.

15 RUNNING DEFENCE: The Family RRSP

LIKE MANY TAX SAVINGS OPPORTUNITIES, the RRSP, is not well understood by most Canadians. You have now learned how powerful it is for the vast majority of families. The *Registered Retirement Savings Plan (RRSP)* will reduce marginal tax rates and clawbacks of important tax benefits that multiply into thousands of dollars of new money *every year*.

ESSENTIAL TAX FACT ▶ **The RRSP is a Key Defender of Your Financial Future.** Running defence to put a bigger refund in your pocket when you file your return, the RRSP also reduces clawback zones that limit your refundable and non-refundable tax credits. That's golden.

But, the RRSP can cause tax headaches upon withdrawal. While you get a deduction for your principal when you invest it in the RRSP, that principal and the earnings on it while in the plan are taxed then. That means you will need a tax strategy for both contribution and withdrawal to make it work for you. The object is to use the RRSP to *average down* the taxes you pay over your lifetime.

TOP TEN RRSP BENEFITS. Here's what you need to know to get the most out of your RRSP investment now and in the future:

1. *Increase your refund.* The RRSP investment results in a tax deduction which provides an immediate return in tax savings.

2. *Reduce withholding taxes.* It can help reduce withholding taxes, throughout the year, so you have more to invest with.

3. *Reduce net income.* It will also reduce net income, the figure on which your refundable tax credits like the *Canada Child Benefit* and the clawbacks of social benefits like the *Old Age Security* and *Employment Insurance* are based. That creates and preserves income for you throughout the year.

4. *Earn tax deferred income.* The income earned on the principal invested in the RRSP loses its identity within the plan and all the earnings are tax deferred until withdrawal. This means you'll accumulate exponentially more money for your retirement, because there is no tax bite along the way.

5. *Tap in—tax free.* The RRSP is not just for retirement—you can tap into the money on a tax-free basis if you buy your first home (under the *Home Buyer's Plan*) or go back to school (under the *Lifelong Learning Plan*), although, this may interrupt your retirement savings.

6. *Split income with spouse.* Upon withdrawal to create a regular retirement pension benefit, both principal and earnings are taxed as "ordinary income"—100% is added to income, but income splitting is possible with your spouse once you turn 65.

7. *Use the savings for debt management.* Given higher costs of servicing debt vs. the lower returns on investments in recent times, you will want to review using the tax savings generated by the RRSP to pay off debt that results in high, non-deductible interest costs.

8. *Risk management.* Life or critical illness insurance can be secured with the tax savings from the RRSP.

9. *Tax leveraging.* The tax savings generated by the RRSP contribution will be in the double-digit zones, depending on the taxpayer's marginal tax rates. For example, if your Marginal Tax Rate is 50%, each dollar invested in an RRSP will increase your tax refund by fifty cents. These large tax savings can be leveraged into other tax-efficient investments.

ESSENTIAL TAX FACT ▶ **Leverage Tax Savings From Your RRSP Into a TFSA.** Deposit your increased tax refund to a TFSA to grow your investment income tax-free forever without any upper age barrier.

10. *Contributions to RRSPs can be carried forward indefinitely.* If your income will be higher in the future than it is in the current tax year, make your RRSP contribution this year, but carry forward the use of the deduction to a future year, when the tax deduction gets better results. That's a powerful tax reduction tool in your back pocket if your income fluctuates, or for taxpayers who will be withdrawing pension income at high tax brackets in the future.

RRSP ELIGIBILITY CRITERIA. To participate, you do need to be age-eligible (under age 72—or have a spouse under 72) and have the required "unused contribution room."

This room can only be created by filing a tax return, and the taxpayer must earn the requisite "earned income" sources; most commonly, income from employment or self-employment. The actual contribution is limited to 18% of earned income *in the previous tax year* up to an annual dollar maximum.

Calculating Your RRSP Room. You'll find your RRSP Contribution room on your Notice of Assessment or Reassessment from CRA. It's not always right, though, especially if you missed filing a tax return on which you had qualifying "earned income" in the past 10 years.

> **TAX FORM FACT.** **USE FORM T1ADJ** *Adjustment or REFILE for electronic adjustments.* Be sure to request adjustments to errors or omissions in your filings and be ready to show documentation to justify your request.

Especially if you are a late filer, get caught up to create RRSP room and reduce penalties and interest if you owe money.

> **ESSENTIAL TAX FACT** ▶ **Your RRSP Contribution Room Never Expires.** If you don't contribute, the unused RRSP contribution room may be accumulated and carried forward for use in the future... indefinitely. But it's better to use your RRSP room sooner, as it's not indexed to inflation, and therefore erodes in value over time.

Check it out, you may have a large number there now—it's ready for you to fund anytime in your future. When you do, you'll get access to a tax deduction.

RRSP Age Limitations. You now know there is no lower age limit for contributing to an RRSP; but, that there is an upper age limit. The RRSP accumulations you have must be collapsed by the *end of the year in which you turn 71.* You will not be able to make further contributions to your own plan after this time.

Upon collapsing the fund, most people receive a periodic pension benefit from a RRIF (*Registered Retirement Income Fund*) which requires minimum annual payments to be added to income, or an annuity, which generally provides for equal payments throughout the term of the annuity. The benefits will qualify for the $2000 *Pension Income Amount*, as well, if you have reached age 65.

Unused RRSP contribution room can, however, still be an important bonus in reducing net income for retirees who are no longer age-eligible for RRSP contributions if they have a spouse who is under age 72.

SPOUSAL RRSP CONTRIBUTIONS. Consider funding a Spousal RRSP when you have unused RRSP room—at any age. The benefit of doing this is that *you take the tax deduction*, but you also get to plan retirement income accumulations with your younger spouse, and potentially tap into that person's plan earlier.

ESSENTIAL TAX FACT ▶ **Two RRSPs Are Better Than One.** If you have all the money in your plan, you'll have to wait to age 65 to split RRSP accumulations with your spouse.

More Benefits: Reduce Clawbacks of Old Age Security (OAS). A sound RRSP tax strategy between spouses can also preserve your indexed *Old Age Security* pension as an added benefit.

> *TRUE-TO-LIFE EXAMPLE 1.* Jason is 72 with a net income of $80,000 after pension income splitting. He is subject to a clawback of part of his *Old Age Security* income because his income level exceeds the OAS income threshold. Jason's wife Ella is 69.

> Because Jason has unused RRSP contribution room of $10,000, he can make a spousal RRSP contribution and reduce his net income and eliminate all of the OAS clawback. All things being equal, this technique could be used again in the following year, using up his available contribution room and eliminating the clawback next year.

Three Year Restrictions for Spousal RRSP Plans. Assets transferred to the spouse using a spousal RRSP become the spouse's income when they are removed from the RRSP, but any contributions made in the same or prior two calendar years are income to the contributor.

Therefore, to accomplish pension income splitting with a spouse at his or her age 60 using a spousal RRSP, contributions must be made before the spouse is 57 years old.

> *TRUE-TO-LIFE EXAMPLE 2.* Ken has contributed $3,000 annually to a spousal RRSP for his wife Fiona for the past ten years. This year he made no contribution and Fiona withdrew $10,000 from her RRSP.

> Because Ken had contributed a total of $6,000 in the current and prior two calendar years, Kenneth would have to report $6,000 of the withdrawal and Fiona would report the remaining $4,000. All subsequent withdrawals from the RRSP would be Fiona's income so long as Kenneth makes no more contributions.

Should Fiona want to convert the spousal RRSP into a RRIF, within the three year restriction period, she can report the minimum withdrawal payments, but Ken must report anything above this. So it's best to plan your retirement withdrawals with the spousal contribution restriction period in mind.

Tax averaging necessary in retirement. As mentioned, the whole amount of your withdrawals from the RRSP—principal and earnings—will be taxed as income on withdrawal in retirement. That means you will need to plan to be tax-efficient with this income source. The way to do that is to withdraw the money out of your "RRSP Bucket" over a longer period of time to "average down" tax rate exposure.

Two exceptions on withdrawal. Taxpayers can withdraw from their RRSPs on a tax-free basis in two cases: under the *RRSP Home Buyer's Plan (HBP)* which has recently been enhanced (see appendices) or the *RRSP Lifelong Learning Plan (LLP)*. However, in each case a repayment schedule must be met, or the unpaid instalments are added into income in each year the repayment is missed.

Audit Check Point

- ✔ **BEWARE OF OVERCONTRIBUTIONS.** Taxpayers who are at least 18 may over contribute to their RRSP above their contribution room, but only by $2000. Above this, excess contributions are subject to a 1% per month overcontribution penalty and failure to file Form T1-OVP *Individual Tax Return for RRSP, PRPP and SPP Excess Contributions* can attract a late filing penalty too.

 Tax Moves

Careful planning is required to manage your RRSP contributions and deductions to your best tax advantage. A sound investment strategy also requires a plan for withdrawal from the RRSP account to avoid unusual spikes to marginal tax rates or a clawback of Old Age Security, EI or tax credits, or to split income in retirement with your spouse. In the meantime, don't miss out on claiming increased tax refunds and credits as a result of your RRSP contribution.

16 TIME OUT: Making the Most of Family TFSAs

YOU HAVE ALREADY LEARNED A LOT ABOUT planning to file a more timely and accurate tax return and how to structure your net and taxable income sources to be more tax efficient. From a planning point of view, there is one more thing you need to know about your tax filing "basics": a cornerstone of every tax plan is the inclusion of a *Tax-Free Savings Account* in the taxpayer's investment portfolio.

> **ESSENTIAL TAX FACT** ▶ If you contribute to your TFSA regularly and to the annual maximum throughout your lifetime, you will have a completely tax-free pension when you retire—putting you light years ahead of generations before you in the opportunity to secure peace of mind.

THERE IS NOTHING BUT GOOD NEWS. Resident taxpayers over the age of 17 may contribute up to $6,000 each year (indexed periodically to the nearest $500). Their relatives and supporting individuals may give them money as a gift to do so.

The income from the TFSA is exempt from the normal "Attribution Rules" which require higher earners to report earnings on their tax return, so long as the funds stay in the TFSA.

And, despite the fact that you might think it's almost too good to be true, indeed, investors may take the money out of their TFSA for whatever purpose they wish and *then put the money back into the TFSA to grow some more*. You do not lose your TFSA contribution room when the money comes out.

Audit Check Point

✔ **THERE ARE PENALTIES FOR "RE-CONTRIBUTING" TO YOUR TFSA AT THE WRONG TIME.** You have to wait until the required contribution room is re-created: January 1 of the next year.

There are three parts to this "Contribution Room," which must be considered:

- New Contribution Room created at January 1 of each new year.
- "Re-Contribution" Room based on prior year withdrawals. This "re-contribution room" is created at *January* 1 each year.
- Carry forwards of the contribution and "re-contribution" room created above if left unfunded.

Neither withdrawals nor earnings can be included in income for any income-tested benefits, such as the Canada Child Benefit or Goods and Services Tax (GST) Credit. Investors at lower income levels can therefore save and earn on a tax-exempt basis while continuing to benefit from income redistribution provisions.

TOP TEN TFSA TAX FACTS. Following are some additional facts about TFSAs you may find helpful as you consider adding this investment to the portfolio of each adult in the family:

1. *TFSA Eligible Investments.* The same eligible investments as allowed within an RRSP are allowed in the TFSA. A special rule prohibits a TFSA from making an investment in any entity with which the account holder does not deal at arm's length. For example, the TFSA cannot hold shares in the owner's small business corporation. A penalty tax on the income earned on such investments will apply.

2. *TFSA Excluded Investments.* Prescribed excluded property includes any obligation secured by mortgage so that individuals cannot hold their own mortgage loan as an investment in their TFSA unless that mortgage is insured and active business activities carried on in a TFSA.

3. *Interest Deductibility - TFSA.* Interest paid on money borrowed to invest in the TFSA is not deductible. It should be noted that rules are in place so that if the loan is not an arm's length arrangement or was made to allow another person (or partnership) to benefit from the tax-free status of the TFSA, the TFSA will be deemed to no longer be a TFSA.

4. *Stop Loss Rules - TFSA.* A capital loss is denied when assets are transferred into a TFSA. This means you can't claim a loss if you transfer your losing shares into your TFSA.

5. *Using TFSA as Security.* A TFSA may be used as security for a loan or other indebtedness.

6. *Excess Contributions.* When taxpayers make contributions over the allowed maximum, they are subject to a 1% per month penalty until the amounts are removed. However, if taxpayers are willing to pay the penalty tax in order to keep the money in the plan, hoping to reap an even higher tax-free return on the excess contribution, 100% of the gains will be subject to tax when deliberate overcontributions occur.

7. *Swapping for Tax-Free Gains.* When taxpayers swap investments from non-registered accounts for cash in the TFSA, and then swap them back out for a revised, higher price point, thereby leaving gains in the TFSA to be tax-free, 100% of the gains are subject to tax.

8. *Departure Tax.* The TFSA is not caught by the departure tax rules. In fact, a beneficiary under a TFSA who immigrates to or emigrates from Canada will not be treated as having disposed of their rights under a TFSA. No TSFA contribution room is earned for those years where a person is non-resident and any withdrawals while non-resident cannot be replaced. However, it will make sense to remove capital properties from the TFSA on a tax-free basis immediately prior to emigrating and then trigger the deemed disposition on departure to avoid taxation in the destination country. *Do not make TFSA deposits as a non-resident.*

9. *Marriage Breakdown.* Upon breakdown of a marriage or common-law partnership, the funds from one party's TFSA may be transferred tax-free to the other party's TFSA. This will have no effect on the contribution room of either of the parties.

10. *Death of a TFSA Holder.* Upon the death of the TFSA holder, the funds within the account may be rolled over into their spouse's TFSA or they may be withdrawn tax-free so long as the surviving spouse has been designated as the successor holder of the TFSA. Any amounts earned within a TSFA after the death of the taxpayer are taxable to the estate.

ESSENTIAL TAX FACT ▶ **Plan CPP Premiums with the TFSA in Mind.** The TFSA may be a much better choice than investing more money into the Canada Pension Plan, if you are still working after age 64. You have the option to discontinue those premiums at age 65 by starting your retirement benefits.

TFSA, RRSP, RESP OR RDSP? What comes first, a *Tax-Free Savings Account* (TFSA) or an RRSP? That's a hotly debated question these days. If you have children for whom you need to save education funds or a disabled dependant there are further choices for scarce savings dollars: should you consider an RESP (*Registered Education Savings Plan*) or a RDSP (*Registered Disability Savings Plan*)?

From an income perspective, it's tough to beat the advantages of the *Tax-Free Savings Account* (TFSA), because all your earnings will remain tax-free, while the money is in the account and after when you withdraw your earnings, too. However, the savings you invest in that plan is money upon which someone in the family has likely already paid taxes; and no tax deduction is created when you invest. Also, your annual investment is limited to a maximum of $6,000 (indexed, depending on future inflation rates.) This topic will be raised again as we discuss investments later in this book.

The RESP and the RDSP are also important tax shelters. In both cases, the government adds grants and bonds to sweeten the investment. Free money is always a good thing and so that's an important advantage to be considered, too. Again, funding for these plans comes from tax-paid savings, and there are lifetime contribution maximums to consider.

However, neither the TFSA, RESP or RDSP will help you decrease your family's tax burden today, nor will they help you maximize social benefits, or reduce your marginal tax rate. That's where the RRSP can really pull rank. If you want to grow your savings exponentially, and maximize all the family tax filing benefits available to you, it pays to invest in an RRSP, because it reduces both net and taxable income.

Bottom line: if you can, maximize each of these investments.

 Tax Moves

It's worth mentioning again—especially to young adults—that the TFSA is an absolute gift to your future financial freedom. *It will help you create a tax-free pension.*

Given its full accumulation period (age 18 to date of death), every adult resident of Canada has the opportunity to become a millionaire, by simply investing up to your maximum annual contribution limit (currently $6,000) each year. Ask your financial advisor to do a projection for you.

Why would you give up this great tax move?

17 THINKING AHEAD: Education Planning with RESPs

A REGISTERED EDUCATION SAVINGS PLAN (RESP) is a tax-assisted savings plan set up for the purposes of funding a beneficiary's future education costs. It also serves as a way to split income earned in the plan with the beneficiary, who will be taxed at a lower rate than the contributor, as a general rule, when earnings are withdrawn.

ESSENTIAL TAX FACT ▶ **The Government Incents Your Savings.** What gives the RESP weight as an important family investment, is that the federal government encourages family educational savings by contributing to your efforts with the *Canada Education Savings Grants* and *Canada Learning Bonds*.

A contributor can invest up to $50,000 per beneficiary as a lifetime maximum. But, government contributions are maximized if contributions are spread over time rather than in one lump sum. You should also know:

- The plan must terminate after 35 years (unless the beneficiary is disabled).
- Minor siblings can substitute as plan beneficiaries if the intended beneficiary does not become a qualifying recipient.

Transfers may be made between RESPs with no income tax consequences. In fact, tax-free transfers between individual Registered Education Savings Plans (RESPs) for the benefit of siblings will be allowed without triggering the repayment of Canada Education Savings Grants (CESGs) so long as the beneficiary of the recipient plan is less than 21 years old at the time of the transfer.

There are several tax advantages to an RESP investment. The subscriber, who contributes money into the plan, does not receive a tax deduction at the time of investment. However, income earned within the plan on the contributions is tax-deferred until the beneficiary student qualifies to receive education assistance from the plan by starting to attend post-secondary school, either on a part-time or on a full-time basis.

ESSENTIAL TAX FACT ▶ **Be Sure to Tap Into the CESG.** The sweetener to RESP savings is the *Canada Education Savings Grant (CESG)* which provides additional funds for education. It's free money given to anyone who contributes to the RESP; there is no income testing.

The grant is 20% of the first $2,500 contributed to an RESP for children under the age of 18. The lifetime maximum CESG is $7,200. To receive the money, the beneficiary of the RESP must have a Social Insurance Number. The CESG room of up to $500 a year (20% of $2,500) can be maximized each year including the year the child turns 17.

Unused CESG contribution room can be carried forward until the child turns 18, however, the grant may not exceed $1,000 in any one year. This means that the catch-up of the grants is limited to two years at a time so it's better to make contributions each year rather than in a lump sum.

An additional CESG is available if the family net income is low enough. For families with net income in the lowest tax bracket (below $47,630 in 2019, $46,605 in 2018), an additional grant is 20% of the first $500 deposited (maximum $100 additional grant).

For families with net incomes in the second tax bracket (between $47,631 and $95,259 in 2019), the additional grant is 10% of the first $500 deposited (maximum $50 additional grant).

ESSENTIAL TAX FACT ▶ **Low Earners—Don't Miss Out on the Canada Learning Bond (CLB).** There's more good news. The first time a child qualifies, an initial Canada Learning Bond entitlement of $500 is available.

This will generally happen under one of two circumstances:

- the year of birth or
- a subsequent year if the family net income is too high in the year of birth.

The entitlement is $100 in each subsequent year that the family is eligible until the year the child turns 15. Once 16, the CLB is no longer allocated to the child.

Qualification for the Canada Learning Bond. This entitlement is based on family net income and the number of children in the family. For families of three or fewer children, the maximum family net income is $47,630 in 2019. For larger families, the maximum family income level increases by just under $6,000 per child.

In order to turn these amounts into real money, the Canada Learning Bond must be transferred into a Registered Education Saving Plan (RESP) for the benefit of the child. This can be done at any time before the child turns 21. If the CLB is not transferred to an RESP by the time the child turns 21, the entitlement will be lost.

No interest is paid on unclaimed Canada Learning Bonds, so it is important that the CLB be transferred to an RESP as quickly as possible so that the amount can begin to earn income within the plan. The CLB transfers to an RESP do not otherwise affect the limits of contributions to the RESP and the CLB deposits are not eligible for the Canada Education Savings Grant.

In the year the child is born, if the family net income is below the upper limit of the lowest tax bracket, the parents should:

- obtain a social insurance number for the child (required for an RESP)
- open an RESP account with the new child as beneficiary*
- apply to have the Canada Learning Bond amount transferred to the new RESP.

*An extra $25 will be paid with the first $500 bond to help cover the cost of opening an RESP.

USING THE EDUCATION ASSISTANCE PAYMENTS (EAPS). When a student is ready to go to post-secondary school full time, payments can be made out of an RESP. These are called Education Assistance Payments (EAPs). The amounts represent earnings in the plan as well as government contributions and are taxable to the student.

TAX FORM FACT. Each RESP provider will have their own form to request an Education Assistance Payment.

The actual contributions may be either returned to the subscriber or paid to the student with no income tax consequences. The CESG will form part of the EAPs.

ESSENTIAL TAX FACT ▶ **Stay in School to Access All Your RESP.** For full-time studies, the maximum EAP is $5,000 until the student has completed 13 consecutive weeks in a qualifying education program at a post-secondary educational institution.

After 13 weeks, any amount up to the maximum annual EAP limit ($23,976 in 2019) may be withdrawn without verification.

For part-time students, who spend a minimum of 12 hours a month on coursework, the maximum EAP is $2,500 per 13-week semester.

Starts and stops. Beneficiaries under an RESP are allowed to receive EAPs for up to six months after ceasing enrolment in a qualifying educational program. But, if for a period of 12 months, the student does not enroll in a qualifying education program, the 13-week period and the $5,000 limitation will be imposed again.

Studying Abroad? The 13-week period for full-time students is reduced to 3 weeks for students studying outside Canada.

Audit Check Point

✔ **USE THE MONEY AS INTENDED.** If amounts are withdrawn from the RESP for purposes other than EAP payments, the lesser of the undistributed CESG amounts and 20% of the amount withdrawn will be returned to the government by the RESP. Should the beneficiary be required to repay any CESG amounts received as Educational Assistance Payments, a deduction for the amount repaid may be taken on the tax return.

ACCUMULATED INCOME PAYMENTS (AIPS). If the student does not attend post-secondary school by the time s/he reaches the age of 31, and there are no qualifying substitute beneficiaries, the contributions can go back to the original subscriber. If this happens, the income earned in the plan over the years will become taxable to the subscriber, but it is also subject to a special penalty tax of 20% in addition to the regular taxes payable. Such income inclusions are called "Accumulated Income Payments" or AIPs. Form T1172 *Additional Tax on Accumulated Income Payments from RESPs* must be completed to compute this tax.

As an alternative, if the subscriber has unused RRSP contribution room, AIPs can be contributed into the subscriber's RRSP, up to a lifetime maximum of $50,000.

TAX FORM FACT. If amounts are transferred to an RRSP, Form T1171 *Tax Withholding Waiver on Accumulated Income Payments from RESPs* may be used to reduce or eliminate tax withheld on the AIP.

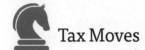 ## Tax Moves

It's hard to beat the free money offered to RESP contributors by the CESG or CLB. But, you may want to consider using a Tax-Free Savings Account as an adjunct to an RESP for accumulating funds for your child's education. It does offer flexibility that is not available in the RESP, with no fear of penalty if the kids don't go to school.

Remember, there are no time limits on the TFSA contributions, no age limits on the beneficiaries, and no limits to the amount that can be withdrawn in any given year, and the withdrawals will never be reported in income—whether the beneficiary becomes a student or not. However, you can't set up a TFSA in the name of your child 'til they turn 18 so you'll have to use your own plan (or your spouse's) if your child is under 18.

18 RDSPs: Support for the Disabled

MANY FAMILIES WHO CARE FOR VULNERABLE PEOPLE are only too familiar with the difficulties of dealing with too few resources—time, money and people both in the public health care system and at home. Fortunately, it is possible to save in a tax-assisted way to create the funds to privately supplement support gaps when they occur, and in particular, to provide for a private pension benefit for the disabled.

In 2008 a new type of registered saving plan was introduced in Canada, designed to accumulate funds for the benefit of a disabled person in the family. The *Registered Disability Savings Plans (RDSPs)* are structured very much the same way as RESPs are, which allows for tax-assisted grants and bonds that can significantly enhance your savings.

> **ESSENTIAL TAX FACT** ▶ Any person eligible to claim the *Disability Tax Credit (DTC) Amount* can be the beneficiary of an RDSP.

TAX TREATMENT. While contributions are not deductible, income accumulates in an RDSP tax free. Contributions withdrawn from an RDSP are not taxable either, but all other amounts—accumulated investment income, and the lucrative government grants and bonds (discussed below)—are taxable in the hands of the beneficiary as withdrawn. When RDSP income is withdrawn, it is reported to the taxpayer in Box 131 of a T4A slip. These amounts must be included in income.

> **ESSENTIAL TAX FACT** ▶ **The RDSP is a Great Place for an Inheritance.** There is no annual limit on contributions to an RDSP but lifetime contributions cannot exceed $200,000. Contributions are permitted until the end of the year in which the disabled beneficiary turns 59.

But, it may not be a good idea to contribute a lump sum, because you'll want to plan the contributions to maximize the *Canada Disability Grants* and *Canada Disability Bonds*.

ADDITIONAL GOVERNMENT SUPPORT FOR THE DISABLED. The Federal government will provide direct financial assistance to help you plan additional private pension funding through the RDSPs in two ways: with a *Canada Disability Savings Grant (CDSG)* and *Canada Disability Savings Bond (CDSB)*.

The Canada Disability Saving Grant. There is a lifetime maximum of $70,000 that will be funded under the CDSG; an RDSP will not qualify to receive a CDSG after the year in which the beneficiary turns **49**.

FAMILY NET INCOME (2019) AND CDSG ENTITLEMENTS

Up to $95,259	Over $95,259
First $500—300% (maximum $1,500)	First $1,000—100% (maximum $1,000)
Next $1,000—200% (maximum $2,000)	
Therefore: $1,500 contributed to RDSP generates $3,500 CDSG	Therefore: $1,000 contributed to RDSP generates $1,000 CDSG

Family income is calculated in the same manner as it is for Canada Education Savings Grant purposes except that in years *after the beneficiary turns 18* family income is the income of the beneficiary and their spouse or common-law partner.

Canada Disability Savings Bond. Unlike the CDSG, there is no requirement that a contribution be made to a RDSP before a savings bond contribution is available. The maximum annual CDSB contribution is $1,000 and is earned where family income does not exceed $31,120 (2019). The CDSB amount is phased out completely when family income is $47,630 (2019).

> **ESSENTIAL TAX FACT** ▶ **Tap Into $20,000 More with the CDSB.** There is a lifetime maximum of $20,000 available for CDSBs. Like the CDSG, CDSBs will not be paid after the beneficiary of the RDSP turns **49**.

CATCH-UP OF RDSP GRANTS AND BONDS. When an RDSP is opened, CDSG and CDSB entitlements will be calculated for the 10 years prior to the opening date (but after 2008) based on the beneficiary's family income in those years. CDSB entitlements from the catch-up period will be paid into the plan in the year the plan is opened. When contributions are made to the plan, the CDSG rate earned by those contributions will be paid as if the contributions were made in the year that the entitlements were earned.

WITHDRAWING AN RDSP PENSION. Only the beneficiary and/or the beneficiary's legal representatives can withdraw amounts from an RDSP. That beneficiary must start to withdraw funds from the RDSP in the year he or she turns 60. Maximum annual withdrawal amounts are to be established based on life expectancies but the beneficiary may encroach on the capital sooner, although a portion of the grants and bonds may have to be repaid (see below).

The maximum *Lifetime Disability Assistance Payment* (LDAP) is no less than 10% of the fair market value of the assets in the plan at the beginning of the year. Where the maximum amount under the existing LDAP formula exceeds 10% of the asset value, a different formula is used.

RESP investments, after CESG and CLBs have been repaid (AIPs), may be rolled over to an RDSP so long as the plan holder has sufficient RDSP contribution room. These contributions will not generate CDSB or CDSGs. Withdrawals of rolled-over AIPs will be taxable.

SPECIFIED DISABILITY SAVINGS PLANS. Where a beneficiary has a shortened life expectancy, a repayment of grants and bonds will not be required if a DAP, up to a specified limit, is made to the beneficiary.

In this case, the plan holder must file the prescribed form along with a letter from a medical doctor certifying that the beneficiary is not likely to survive more than five years, with the RDSP issuer, who must notify the government. Once the election has been made, the RDSP will be considered a Specified Disability Savings Plan (SDSP) and assistance payments can begin to a maximum of $10,000 per year.

REPAYMENT OF GRANTS AND BONDS. For withdrawals from RDSPs, a portion of the CDSGs and CDSBs received will have to be repaid. The amount of that repayment is the lesser of

- the amount removed x 3 and
- the amount of the CDSG and CDSB amounts received in the past ten years.

DEATH OR CESSATION OF QUALIFICATION. When an RDSP beneficiary ceases to qualify for the Disability Amount, the beneficiary may make an election to continue the plan for up to four calendar years after the end of the calendar year in which the beneficiary ceases to be eligible for the Disability Amount. During the election period, no contributions will be permitted, no new CDSB or CDSGs will be paid into the plan and withdrawals will be permitted subject to the proportional repayment rule.

IMPACT OF RDSP INCOME ON INCOME-TESTED SUPPORTS. RDSP withdrawals will not affect any other means-tested support delivered through the income tax system including, in particular, the clawback of OAS or Employment Insurance benefits.

WHO CAN ESTABLISH THE PLAN? The plan can be established by the disabled person or by an authorized representative, and anyone can contribute to an RDSP—they need not be a family member. But contributors can never receive a refund of their contributions.

Where it is not clear whether the disabled individual is contractually competent and they do not have a legal representative, certain family members (spouse or common-law partner or parent) will be allowed to become the plan holder for the disabled adult. If it is determined that the disabled individual is able to enter into a contract, they will replace the family member as the plan holder.

Where the disabled individual is found not to be contractually competent, a legal representative of the disabled individual may replace the family member as the plan holder. This measure will be in effect until December 31, 2023.

A family member who becomes an RDSP holder under these temporary rules will continue to be the holder after 2023. After 2023, a qualifying family member will only be allowed to open an RDSP if they are transferring an existing plan for which they are the holder.

 Tax Moves

It takes a village to raise a family. When that village can collaborate to build a private pension for the disabled, it's a wonderful thing. If you support a disabled adult, look into funding their future, with the help of the generous matching program by the federal government.

Tax Moves & Audit-Busters

TAX GAME DAY STRATEGIES

LEAVING SINGLE LIFE? The goal of tax filing changes when you live together in a family household. To achieve best tax filing results, individual filers need to shift focus. The opportunity is to file your family returns to the *household's overall best benefit*.

PROGRESSIVE TAX RATES WORK IN A FAMILY'S FAVOR. File family tax returns together to get the best out of them. Maximize the Basic Personal Amount each person is entitled to—almost $1000 a month.

MAKE YOUR FAMILY A TAX-EFFICIENT ECONOMIC UNIT. Families that plan for the creation of both income and capital as a household get great after-tax results. Invest to plug "tax efficiency gaps" by taking a close look at each person's RRSP and TFSA contribution room.

MAXIMIZE REFUNDABLE CREDITS. There are three important refundable tax credits to claim by filing a tax return, even if you are a parent or supporting individual with no income: The *Canada Child Benefit (CCB)*, the *GST/HST Credit* and the *Canada Workers Benefit*. Provincial governments can offer more. Keep your family net income below income testing thresholds to take full advantage. An RRSP can help if you are eligible.

THE RRSP: A TOP DEFENCE PLAYER. Every family member with "earned income" can create RRSP contribution room, with a tax deduction resulting from any contributions. Used at your option this year, or in the future, the deduction reduces income taxes payable, increases tax credits and earnings are not taxed while the funds remain in the plan. These plans offer income splitting opportunities later in life, too.

PLAN FOR TAX-FREE RRSP WITHDRAWALS. All amounts removed from an RRSP are taxable as ordinary income unless they are withdrawn under the *Home Buyers' Plan* or the *Lifelong Learning Plan*. For those purposes they are tax-free, as long as a specified repayment schedule is later met.

TWO RRSPS ARE BETTER THAN ONE. Spousal RRSPs provide a means of transferring assets from one spouse to another so long as the funds are not removed from the plan until at least three calendar years after the last spousal contribution. In the meantime, the contributor gets the tax deduction. It's a great way to plan low-taxed withdrawals before age 65, when pension income splitting rules come into play.

WORK AROUND THE ATTRIBUTION RULES. They make income splitting and joint asset accumulation more difficult with spouses and minor children, but opportunities exist if you follow proper procedures. You've seen the opportunities with RRSPs. Transferring other sources of income and capital within the framework of the law will save you money, too.

THE TFSA IS YOUR TICKET TO TAX FREEDOM. Make sure you contribute the maximum annual dollar amount for each resident adult in the family every year. Earnings are not taxed either in the plan or when they are removed. It provides an excellent parking place for transferred assets from the higher-income taxpayer to lower-income taxpayers in the family.

BUILD EDUCATION FUNDING WITH SWEETENERS. The RESP is a registered plan designed to fund post-secondary education costs. Contributions are not tax deductible, but government assistance is made through Canada Education Savings Grants and Bonds, and that sweetens the opportunity to save more money in an investment which will result, statistically, in higher individual earnings and wealth accumulation.

WITHDRAW STUDENT INCOME WISELY. Amounts contributed to RESPs may be returned tax-free to the contributor but grants, bonds and earnings are taxable to the beneficiary if they become a student or, if not, grants and bonds must be returned and the remaining earnings in the plan are taxable to the contributor and subject to a 20% penalty tax. To avoid this, contribute these amounts to an RRSP. Seek professional advice if study plans get put on hold or stop completely.

PLAN PRIVATE PENSIONS FOR THE DISABLED. Health care and home care is expensive to governments and can leave gaps in services that you may find unacceptable for your loved one. An alternative is private funding for additional care. The RDSP can help. It is a registered plan set up for a disabled individual. Contributions are not deductible but generous government assistance is available in the form of Canada Disability Savings Grants and Bonds. It's a good way to ensure dignity in disability.

WITHDRAW RDSPS WITH CAUTION. Amounts withdrawn from RDSPs are taxable to the beneficiary as Disability Assistance Payments. If withdrawals are within ten years of receiving grants or bonds, some portion may need to be repaid, except in the case of a specified disability savings plan (where the beneficiary has a life expectancy of not more than five years).

Tax Tools of the Trade

- **TAX ON SPLIT INCOME** *File a form T1206 to compute the amount for kiddies and adults*

- **ELIGIBLE FOR THE DISABILITY AMOUNT?** *Have a medical professional complete form T2201 Disability Tax Credit Certificate. Then claim the credit on Schedule 1.*

- **WANT TO SPLIT ELIGIBLE PENSION INCOME WITH YOUR SPOUSE?** *Both you and your spouse need to file form T1032 to request the transfer.*

- **CONTRIBUTED MORE TO YOUR RRSP THAN ALLOWED?** *File a form T1-OVP to determine the penalty tax—and withdraw the money as soon as you can!*

- **CLOSING AN RESP?** *File form T1172 to determine your additional tax on accumulated income payments—or save the tax by transferring the amount to your RRSP and file Form T1171 to eliminate that tax.*

- **REDUCE TAX WITHHOLDING WHEN YOU MAKE AN RRSP CONTRIBUTION.** *File a form T1213 to request CRA to authorize your employer to reduce the taxes withheld from your paycheque.*

- **ERRORS ON YOUR RETURNS? USE FORM T1ADJ** *Adjustment Request* to request adjustments to errors or omissions in your filings and be ready to show documentation to justify your request if you paper filed. If you used NETFILE, you will be able to use a feature called ReFILE to request an electronic adjustment. Or, simple use *MyAccount* to change your return.

Your Audit-Buster Checklist

- ✓ **MODERN FAMILY LIFE IS SUBJECT TO A UNIQUE AUDIT RISK.** Because CRA distributes generous income-tested tax credits to households based on the combined net incomes of supporting individuals, it wants to be sure that your family net income is right, and that you are not claiming more kids than you actually support.

- ✓ **ALWAYS AUDIT-PROOF YOUR TAX CREDIT CLAIMS.** To claim non-refundable credits for your spouse or equivalent, use the dependant's individual net income. However, you will have to combine net income levels for the purposes of claiming refundable tax credits like the *Canada Child Benefit.*

- ✓ **BEWARE OF OVERCONTRIBUTIONS.** Taxpayers who are at least 18 may over-contribute to their RRSP above their contribution room, but only by $2000. Above this, excess contributions are subject to a 1% per month overcontribution penalty and failure to file Form T1-OVP *Individual Tax Return for RRSP, PRPP and SPP Excess Contributions* to report this can attract a late filing penalty too.

✔ **STUDENTS: USE RESP MONEY AS INTENDED.** If amounts are withdrawn from the RESP for purposes other than EAP payments, the lesser of the undistributed CESG amounts and 20% of the amount withdrawn will be returned to the government by the RESP. Should the beneficiary be required to repay any CESG amounts received as Educational Assistance Payments, a deduction for the amount repaid may be taken on the tax return.

PART IV

THE ASSETS
Honing Your Tax Moves

19 HUMAN CAPITAL: Securing Exponential Returns

YOUR HUMAN CAPITAL REFERS TO THE PACKAGE of knowledge, skills, personality and health you bring to the workplace, that determines your earning potential; the definitive economic value for your productivity—what you add to the bottom line of the enterprise you work in[5].

The role of human capital in building family wealth and peace of mind usually precedes the acquisition of financial capital. The more you earn, the more you are paid, and technically, the more you should be able to save. But there are opposing forces to either plough through or work around. It's easier to do the latter, especially if the obstacle to be removed is tax.

When you think about it, the greatest potential for earning the income you need may not rest with you. Sure, investing in yourself, your ongoing education, and in improving your role within your workplace will determine how much earning power you will have. But determinedly investing your money has better long term prospects. Quite simply that's because human capital eventually diminishes with age, disability, retirement or death.

So it is the productive capacity of both, your human and financial capital, that you must keep your eye on. Making the right tax moves along the way, will enable you to exponentially increase both.

Most people begin their work life at a young age as an employee, although it is possible to earn taxable income as a self-employed teenage babysitter or snow clearer. We will discuss ways to invest your hard earned money to increase your financial potential later in this section.

But for now, what's important is to know how to plan your compensation

---

5 This term and definition by American economist and professor Gary Stanley Becker.

structures at your workplace to pay the least amount of taxes possible, and as a result, turbo-charge your personal productivity to take more money *to the bank*.

ESSENTIAL TAX FACT ▶ **Put a Focus on Your Pre-tax Earnings.** The sooner you put a whole dollar to work for you, the sooner your capital—human and financial—will increase its productivity.

Understand Your Employer-Employee Relationships. When you work for someone else as an employee, you are in an "employer-employee relationship." CRA defines this as a verbal or written agreement in which an employee agrees to work on a full-time or part-time basis for a specified or indeterminate period of time, in return for salary or wages.

Under this type of arrangement, the employer has the right to decide where, when and how the work will be done, and takes all the risk for collecting money from clients and pays for the assets required to generate the company's revenues. When your efforts add exponentially to your employer's bottom line, there is more money to pay higher salaries *or other benefits* to employees.

ESSENTIAL TAX FACT ▶ **Use Corporate Dollars to Fund Your Lifestyle if Possible.** Your employer will likely pay a lower tax rate corporately than you will pay personally. The availability of both taxable and tax free benefits as part of your compensation package can add significant value for expenditures you would need to work longer for.

MAXIMIZING YOUR INCOME FROM EMPLOYMENT. When low taxed corporate dollars pay for important costs for you—your retirement savings, health and dental care plan, continuing education, health club membership, vacation and sick leave, severance package, investment and mortgage loans, insurance coverage, etc., the economic value of being employed is significantly increased.

When you negotiate for perks that can increase your standard of living at a fraction of the cost you would pay yourself with after-tax dollars, you will have more money for investment purposes.

In other words, it's those job perks—especially the tax-free ones—that can be exponentially more valuable in helping you accumulate personal wealth, than another raise.

In fact, you may be able to negotiate a compensation package that is extremely diverse: an employer-provided car, vacations, education, uniforms, meals, memberships to fitness clubs, and so on, may be taxable, but others will, to your delight, be tax free. Following is a run-down of both taxable and tax free benefits that will increase your personal productivity:

TAX FORM FACT. Take the Time to Read Your T4 Slip Carefully. You need to know that taxable benefits will be included in Box 14 of your T4 *Statement of Remuneration Paid (slip)*. That means you will not need to add them into income again when you file your return. Some of them qualify for certain deductions and so you may see reference to them in Boxes 30 to 88 at the bottom of the slip:

Taxable Benefits Checklist

☐ *Housing, Board and Lodging:* which can include a cleric's housing allowance, rent-free or low-rent apartments provided to caretakers, or subsidized meals or travel in a prescribed zone or for medical travel. Offsetting deductions may be included for clerics or those who qualify for the northern residents deduction.

☐ *Employer-provided Vehicle.* Amounts for employee's personal use of employer's auto. It is possible that the employee may offset this benefit with a claim for Employment Expenses using Form T777 *Statement of Employment Expenses.* See detailed explanation under Employment Expenses, later.

☐ *Interest-Free Loans and Low Interest Loans:* A deduction for carrying charges may be possible if the loan is used for investment purposes.

☐ *Employee home relocation deduction:* this deduction is discontinued for new home relocation loans used in 2018 and subsequent years.

☐ *Security Options:* a deduction may be possible, but subject to certain limits to employees of large firms starting in 2019.

☐ *Other taxable benefits,* including amounts included for health or educational benefits may qualify for non-refundable credits like medical expenses or Tuition Amounts.

Bring on the Tax Free Perks. Consider the following valuable list of options you may wish to discuss with your employer, when planning your compensation. Some of these items which your employer can pay for, may be tax free. However, there is a caveat:

Audit Buster Checkpoint

- ✔ **BE AWARE OF CRA AUDITS OF BENEFITS.** Be sure you understand your rights to the perks you receive and their tax status, to be confident in your ability to challenge the CRA, if your return is chosen for audit. CRA has backed down from some of their more aggressive audit practices recently, relating to the taxation of employee discounts, for example.

In the last several federal budgets, CRA has been given the authority to look more closely at the books of private corporations and the way that compensation payable to family members who work in the business is taxed. In auditing for income sprinkling, a review of all forms of remuneration for all employees is therefore possible.

SUMMARY OF TAXABLE AND TAX FREE BENEFITS OF EMPLOYMENT

Perk	Taxable	Non-Taxable
Employer-Paid Educational Costs	Taxable when the training is primarily for your personal benefit. Amounts included in your income for tuition will be eligible for the tuition tax credit if they would have been eligible had they been paid by you personally.	Non-taxable when training is paid for by your employer for courses taken primarily for the benefit of the employer.
Financial Counselling and Tax Return Preparation	Yes	Financial counselling services in respect of your re-employment or retirement not taxable.
Frequent Flyer Points	Taxable if: • the points are converted to cash, • the plan or arrangement is indicative of an alternate form of remuneration, and • the plan or arrangement is for tax avoidance purposes. • the employer controls the points (e.g. using a company credit card).	Yes
Non-Cash Gifts Under $500	Only taxable on amount over $500. Additional long service/anniversary gifts over $500 taxable on amount over $500.	First $500 is not taxable. A separate non-cash long service/anniversary award may also qualify for non-taxable status to the extent its total value is $500 or less.
Items of nominal value	Not taxable	

Perk	Taxable	Non-Taxable
Overtime Meals, Allowances	Not taxable if: • the value of the meal or meal allowance is reasonable ($17 or less) • the employee works two or more hours of overtime right before or right after his or her scheduled hours of work, and • the overtime is infrequent and occasional in nature.	Taxable if: • Cost exceeds $17 per meal • Employee regularly works longer shifts • Employee does not work 2 hours overtime when meal provided.
Trips	Not taxable if: • Employee's presence is required for business purposes • Expenses are reasonable.	Taxable if: • No business activity related to trip • Trip is extended to provide personal time (cost of extension taxable) • Trip includes family members not participating in business activities (additional costs are taxable).
Loss on home due to relocation	Reimbursement of one half of amount of loss over $15,000 is taxable.	Not taxable if both loss and reimbursement are less than $15,000.
Parking	Generally taxable.	Not taxable if parking available to general public or parking is limited and on a first-come, first-served basis. Not taxable if employee is required to use their own vehicle for business and parking is provided for business reasons.

Employer-Paid Health Care Premiums. The tax status of premiums paid, and benefits received from employer-sponsored group and non-group health plans can be confusing but is very important in the overall scheme of compensation to the employee. These plans can provide important peace of mind when expensive health care costs arise. Premiums will be taxable in two instances:

• where the employer pays or reimburses you for the employee portion of premiums to a provincial health care plan; or

• where the employer pays some or all of the premium under a non-group plan that is a wage loss replacement, sickness or accident insurance plan, a disability insurance plan, or an income maintenance insurance plan. However, payroll source deductions made for the payment of the premiums are considered to be payments made by you, not the employer.

If the wage loss replacement plan is a group plan, or if the health care plan is private, then the employer's portion of the premiums paid is not considered to be a taxable benefit.

If the plan was funded, in whole or in part, by the employer, then the benefits received are taxable, but you are entitled to a deduction for the lesser of the amount received from the plan and all premiums that you have paid since 1968 and not previously deducted.

Low Interest Loans. Employees should always strive to build capital—assets that can produce other sources of income or grow in value to supplement their human capital. One way to do so is to use your employer's money—at preferred low or no-interest rates, to invest in the company your work for, or elsewhere in the marketplace. This differential between market rates and the interest rate extended by your employer, will give rise to a taxable benefit.

For example, the employer may loan funds for investment purposes to you or your spouse. In either case, a taxable benefit would accrue to you, unless your spouse is also an employee of the same employer, in which the benefit will accrue to him or her. The same rules will apply when you receive a loan from a third party, if the employer is involved in securing the loan for you.

TAX FORM FACT. If the employer-provided loan was used to acquire income-producing investments, the amount of the interest benefit shown on the T4 will be deductible as a carrying charge.

On a no-interest loan, the amount of the benefit is equal to:

- the interest on the loan at CRA's currently prescribed rate (rising to 2% at the time of writing), plus
- any payments made by the employer, less
- amounts of interest paid back by you to the employer either during the year or within 30 days after the end of the year.

This benefit is included in your income and will be reported on your T4.

If the loan bears interest, there is no taxable benefit where the interest rate on the loan is equal to or greater than a commercial rate so long as you actually pay the interest. Special rules apply to housing loans and home relocation loans.

ESSENTIAL TAX FACTS ▶ **Shareholders Can Earn Benefits, Too.** The rules above apply to shareholders as well as to employees. The difference between a shareholder loan and an employee loan is that the benefit accrues to the employee, even if the loan is to someone else. However, the benefit accrues to the debtor if the loan is a shareholder loan.

This is because of a special anti-avoidance rule that prevents a shareholder from indefinitely postponing the recognition of income from a corporation by taking continuous shareholder loans. Professional help should be sought to report these transactions.

ESSENTIAL TAX FACT. ▶ **Loan Forgiveness Has Tax Consequences.** Where the employer-provided loan is forgiven or settled for an amount less than the amount outstanding, the forgiven amount must be included in your income.

Where the shareholder is also an employee, certain loans will be allowed the treatment given to any employee if it can be established that bona fide loan arrangements are made, the loan is repaid over a reasonable period of time and the loan is a direct result of the employer-employee relationship. This means that the company must make similar loans available to all employees.

Stock Option Plans. Employees may be presented with an opportunity to purchase shares in the employer's corporation at some future date, but at a price set at the time the option was granted. This is known as the exercise price.

There are no tax consequences when an employee stock option is granted. But when you exercise these stock or security options a taxable benefit arises, equal to the difference between the market value of the shares purchased and the exercise price. When is this taxable? It depends on the type of corporation.

ESSENTIAL TAX FACT. ▶ **Exercising Stock Options Has Tax Consequences.** If the employer is a Canadian Controlled Private Corporation (CCPC), a taxable benefit is deemed to arise when you *dispose* of the shares. In the case of a public corporation, the taxable benefit arises when you exercise the option.

When the security options taxable benefit is included in income, you will also be eligible for the *Security Options Deduction* which is equal to one-half of the taxable benefit. New rules start in 2019. See Appendices.

It is wise to get some professional help before stock options are exercised or the shares disposed of, as complicated technical provisions must be observed. For example, if the shares acquired under such a stock option are donated to a registered charity or to a private foundation, you may claim a deduction equal to the taxable benefit. In addition, be sure to get professional help if you previously deferred your stock option benefits; a provision no longer available for stock options exercised after March 4, 2010.

Personal Use of Employer's Motor Vehicle. The value of the benefit derived by an employee from the personal use and availability of an automobile supplied by an employer is required to be included in calculating the employee's income. This is also known as a stand-by charge.

For most employees, the automobile standby charge is set at 2 per cent per month of the original cost of the vehicle where the employer owns the vehicle, or two-thirds of the lease payment for leased vehicles. However, for car sales persons, the benefit is 1 1/2%.

Reduction of Stand-by Charge. The reduced standby charge applies to the extent annual personal driving does not exceed 20,004 kilometres, and the automobile is used primarily—that is, more than 50 per cent—for business purposes.

For example, where a vehicle is driven 25,000 kilometres a year for business and 15,000 kilometres a year for commuting and other personal driving, the reduced standby charge will be 75 per cent (15,000 divided by 20,004) of the regular standby charge.

Auto Operating Expense Benefit. Amounts paid for the operation of the employer's vehicle and not reimbursed by the employee within 45 days after the end of the tax year, will be considered to be a taxable benefit. The benefit is determined as a flat per kilometre rate, regardless of how or how much the employer paid for the expenses. It may therefore make sense that if the employer paid only a minimal portion of the expenses, that these be reimbursed by the employee by February 14 (45 days after the year end) to avoid an unnecessarily large taxable benefit inclusion in income.

For tax year 2019, this flat rate is 26 cents per kilometre for regular employees and 23 cents for auto salespeople. This value includes GST, PST or HST.

TAX FORM FACT. Use Form RC18 *Calculating Automobile Benefits* to reduce the standby charge your employer calculates for your auto benefits if you use the employer-provided vehicle more than 50% of the time for business purposes and your personal use driving is not more than 1667 kilometers per 30 day period, or a total of 20,004 kilometres per year. Operating expenses can also be calculated as one half the normal stand-by charge.

Employer-Provided Vehicle Required to be Taken Home at Night. Normally, when a vehicle is provided to an employee, the employee is deemed to have received a taxable benefit at the currently prescribed rate. However, in June 2009, CRA announced that it will accept (no date specified) the use of the operating benefit rate (about half the prescribed rate) if the following circumstances are met:

- The motor vehicle is not defined as an automobile under subsection 248(1) of the Act.

- The terms under which the motor vehicle is provided to the employee prohibit any personal use of the motor vehicle other than commuting between home and work and the vehicle has in fact not been used for any other personal use.

- The employer has bona fide business reasons for requiring the employee to take the motor vehicle home at night, for example, there are security issues with leaving the vehicle at the place of employment or the employee is on call and would require the vehicle to perform the on-call duties.

- The motor vehicle is specifically designed, or suited for, the employer's business or trade and is essential in a fundamental way for the performance of the employment duties (other than transportation of the employee)

DEDUCTIBLE EMPLOYMENT EXPENSES. Most employees are not allowed to claim out-of-pocket expenses for the costs of going to work. That's right, items such as the cost of driving to and from work, eating out at lunch or dry cleaning are not deductible.

A non-refundable tax credit is provided for these purposes. It's called the *Canada Employment Amount (CEC)* and it is claimed on Schedule 1 of the tax return. In addition, for low income earners, the Canada Worker's Benefit will supplement some of these out-of-pocket costs. See *Essential Tax Facts Appendices* for numeric details.

However, an important tax move will supplement your personal productivity at work if you have other unreimbursed employment expenses and earn salary or commissions or a combination of both. You may be able to claim an Employment Expenses Deduction, provided you complete two tax forms, and verify with your employer that these expenses were a necessary condition of employment and that you have receipts for them, in case of audit.

TAX FORM FACT. Employment Expense Claims Attract Auditors. The *Income Tax Act* is very specific about the expenses that may be claimed by employees, and their perks. Report expenses on Form

T777 *Statement of Employment Expenses* and keep on hand Form T2200 *Declaration of Conditions of Employment* signed by the employer to ace a tax audit. Keep receipts and an auto distance log.

Commissioned sales people can claim more expense categories—sales and promotion expenses, for example—because they are expected to foster relationships with clients in their negotiation of contracts for their employers. Let's discover the difference between the claims for salaried employees who don't earn commissions and others who do.

Employees Who Earn Salary Only. Claim these out-of- pocket expenses:

- accounting, but not including income tax preparation, except if you are a commissioned sales person
- legal fees may be claimed if incurred to establish a right to collect salary, wages or a retiring allowance or pension benefits, but these costs may not exceed the amount of those sources that you report in income. Any non-deductible components may then be carried forward and deducted in any of the seven subsequent tax years in which further income from these sources is reported. When pensions or retiring allowances are transferred to an RRSP, the deductible legal expenses must be reduced by the amount of the transfer.
- motor vehicle expenses (including Capital Cost Allowance (CCA)— the tax equivalent of depreciation, interest or leasing costs, as well as operating costs), but only if the employee is not in receipt of a non-taxable allowance for the use of the motor vehicle.
- travel expenses, including rail, air, bus or other travel costs, meals, tips and hotel costs, providing the excursion is for at least 12 hours and away from the taxpayer's metropolitan area. Meals and tips are subject to a 50% restriction.
- parking costs (but generally not at the place of employment).
- supplies used up directly in the work (stationery, maps, etc.).
- salaries paid to an assistant (including spouses or children if a salary equivalent to fair market value is paid for work actually performed).
- office rent or certain home office expenses (discussed later).

Note: the cost of tools acquired by employed mechanics are generally not deductible, however a special rule exists for new tool costs incurred by apprentice vehicle mechanics and tools acquired by tradespersons.

Employees Who Earn Salary and Commission. Employees who earn their living negotiating contracts for their employers or selling on commission may claim for the expenses itemized above, as well as income tax preparation costs, legal fees incurred to defend charges incurred in the normal course of business, and auto and travel expenses.

This is allowed only if they are required to pay their own expenses and regularly perform their duties away from their employer's place of business.

ESSENTIAL TAX FACT ▶ **Sales Persons Must Earn Enough to Claim All Expenses.** Expenses claimable by commissioned employees are categorized into two groups: deductible *travel* and deductible *sales* expenses. This is because you cannot claim sales expenses that exceed commissions earned in the year.

1. *Deductible travel expenses* allowed include:

- *Auto operating expenses* like gas, oil, repairs and fixed costs like licenses, insurance, interest, leasing and capital cost allowance. The latter three expenses are limited to annual maximums if a passenger vehicle is used.

- *Travelling expenses* such as the cost of air, bus, rail, taxi or other transportation, which takes the employee outside the employer's metropolitan area. However, travel expenses are claimable only if the employee does not receive a tax-free travel allowance.

Note that when these two types of expenses only are claimed, the amounts *may exceed commissions* earned (as reported in Box 42 of the T4 slip) and excess expenses may be used to offset other income of the year.

2. *Deductible sales expenses* allowed include the expenses above plus:

- promotional expenses;

- entertainment expenses (subject to a 50% restriction for the personal component of the expense);

- home office expenses.

When you are claiming expenses under category 2 above, your claim *may not* exceed commissions earned in the calendar year *except* for interest and capital cost allowance on a motor vehicle.

Special Rules for Assets Purchased by Employees. Employees are not allowed to make a claim for capital expenditures, like a computer or cell phone at all. However, leasing costs are deductible. In the case of the cell phone, air time is deductible.

The reason is this: the employer is expected to provide those assets for the employee.

There are three exceptions: the purchase of vehicles, musical instruments or aircraft used in performing the duties of employment. Therefore, it is wise tax planning to lease computers, cell phones or other equipment.

Special Rules for Artists and Musicians. Artists and musicians may claim expenses for items specific to their profession, including capital cost allowance on musical instruments. These claims are limited to the lesser of $1,000 and 20% of the employee's income from related employment. Claims may be for such items as ballet shoes, body suits, art supplies, computer supplies, home office costs as well as rental, maintenance, insurance and capital cost allowance on musical instruments.

Special Rules for Forestry Workers. Employees working in the forestry industry may claim the actual costs of operating a power saw, including gas, oil, parts and repairs providing an itemized statement is prepared and saved in case of audit requests. The power saws may be written off in full but, in the case of a new saw, the claim must be reduced by trade-in value or sales proceeds received from the disposal of the old saw during the year.

Special Rules for Apprentice Vehicle Mechanics. Apprentice vehicle mechanics may claim expenses incurred in purchasing tools in excess of $1,500. If the taxpayer does not take the maximum deduction in the tax year, the unused portion may be carried forward to apply against income earned in a future year. Apprentice vehicle mechanics may also claim the Tradesperson's Tools deduction.

Special Rules for Tradespersons. Tradespersons are also able to claim a deduction (to a maximum of $500) for the cost of tools in excess of the *Canada Employment Amount* (CEA) for the year. If the cost of tools is less than the CEA, then no deduction is allowed.

Electronic communication devices and electronic data processing equipment do not qualify as tools for the purposes of this deduction (i.e., a cell phone, PDA, tablet, or laptop is not a "tool").

GST/HST Rebates. Employees who claim deductible employment expenses may be able to receive a rebate of the GST/HST paid using Form GST370 *Employee and Partner GST/HST Rebate Application*. Rebates received are added to income in the year received, unless they apply to capital assets, in which case the cost base of the asset will require adjusting. These claims are often missed and can be complicated! Be sure to file an adjustment to prior-filed returns if you have missed it, with the help of a tax pro if necessary.

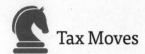 Tax Moves

While employment income is usually taxable as received, a few special tax preferences exist to help the employee defer some compensation into the future. Tap into these wherever you can. But start with a good, long-term contract, a substantial perk package, and a "golden parachute" in case things don't work out—valuable benefits your employer can deduct, in order to help you pay for the costs of living.

Don't forget to claim employment expenses for out-of-pocket costs. Even employed teachers can benefit from a little tax vigilance: don't forget to claim the refundable Eligible Educator School Supply Tax Credit for out-of-pocket costs. There is some audit risk, but it's worth it, if you have the supporting documentation.

Remember that your greatest opportunity to secure income for your future after retirement, begins with saving more of your pre-tax earnings. For those reasons, always try to invest to your maximum RRSP contribution room.

20 NEW MANEUVERS: The Shift from Income to Capital

BY BETTER MANAGING THE TAX ADVANTAGES of earning employment income, you may find yourself positioned to more rapidly accumulate money in a variety of pension plans, public and private, as well as investment accounts, registered and non-registered. That's important because you will exponentially increase your personal productivity when you take control of your ability to save money.

Doing so with tax efficiency will increase the after-tax returns from your investments, thereby speeding up your journey to financial freedom. That's particularly critical as your personal productivity diminishes, either because you want to retire or because you can't work anymore for health-related reasons.

Tax efficiency is also important because you will need to plan for a longer retirement than ever before. That means you need to take control of the *purchasing power* of your savings in the future. Consider these statistics:

According to the *Update of Long Term Economic and Fiscal Projections published by Finance Canada on December 22, 2017*, the median age of your retirement will likely be 63.3 years. That makes the average length of retirement 24 years.

That's because the life expectancy at birth for females is projected to increase from 83.8 years in 2013 to 88.5 years in 2055. For males, the life expectancy at birth is projected to rise from 79.6 years in 2013 to 86.7 years in 2055.

But, depending on where you work, and how healthy you are, your average age of retirement may vary, according to Statistics Canada:

- Public Sector Employees; 90% of whom are enrolled in Defined Benefit pension plans (DB) retire at age 61.2.
- Private Sector Employees: 41.7% of whom are enrolled in private pension plans have DB plans, retire at age 64.1.
- The Self Employed: These folks must fund their retirements on their own and on average retire at age 66.9 (men retire at 68.3, women 64.6).

Capital Required to Fund Income in Retirement. Research provided to Finance Canada[6] has told us that retirement income adequacy "critically" depends on three things:

- the tax assistance for savings (TFSA, RRSP plus tax-efficient non–registered income sources),
- the timing of your investments and
- the type of investment you make.

ESSENTIAL TAX FACT ▶ **Tax-Efficient Investing Is A Critical Component of Retirement Income Adequacy.** Tax-efficient investing is the process of selecting investments with the most appropriate tax "preferences" for your age, family status and income, so you can exercise your rights to arrange your affairs within the framework of the law to pay the least amount of taxes on both income and capital.

In shifting your tax focus from your personal income earning capacity to that of your capital, the objective is to accumulate the right assets, in the right savings plans, in the right order, to get the best after-tax income results for retirement, in the fastest possible way.

If you were playing chess, you would want to first identify your key chess pieces, understand how they move, and how to protect them, all in order to beat your opponents and win the game.

Tax matches require a similar set up. Rather than a king, queen, rooks, bishops, knights and pawns, taxpayers move with several asset classes to produce a variety of income sources timed to defeat specific opponents: wealth eroders like taxes, inflation and the fees paid to financial intermediaries. Here's an example:

---

6 Investment Performance and Costs of Pension and Other Retirement Savings Funds in Canada: Implications on Wealth Accumulation and Retirement, Dr. Vijay Jog, December 2, 2009

Registered Accounts	Non-Registered Accounts	Other Assets
TFSA	Savings Accounts	Life Insurance
RRSP	GIC	Real Estate
RESP	Mutual Funds	Business Assets
RDSP	Segregated Funds	Personal Use Property
RPP	Securities	

Timing matters. At the start of your career, the key investments that give your active income the boost it needs to achieve the best after-tax results will be the RRSP, the TFSA, the RESP and, if there is a disabled person in the family, the RDSP.

These assets all feature tax deferred income growth, and come with a variety of restrictions and enhancements. Once you have fully funded these registered investment opportunities, it will be time to look beyond them, to non-registered financial assets and other non-financial asset categories, like real estate for example.

Using tax-assisted savings accounts, starting to contribute to them early and then choosing the right investment products to get the returns you need, all count in getting you over the finish line to financial freedom quickly. When you get that, and you get started, this three-pronged approach will allow more time to have fun with your savings, rather than worrying about whether they will last. That's the ultimate reward of tax-efficient investing.

FOCUS ON FOUR ELEMENTS TO MANAGE WEALTH. Over the years, in working with taxpayers and writing about and teaching taxes, I have met average people who became very wealthy—and thereby secured their financial future—by focusing consistently on four elements of wealth management throughout their lifetimes: the accumulation, growth, preservation and transitioning of their savings *with sustainability.*

Their capital, in other words, had "real" value, when they needed it; that is, it held its purchasing power—what was left after taxes, inflation and fees.

Those four elements in building wealth and their three wealth eroders are what we focus on in working with advisors and their clients at the Knowledge Bureau. We call this strategic process, *Real Wealth Management™.*

In fact, people who achieve "true" wealth—financial peace of mind—follow a consistent, purposeful process for deploying and leveraging both their earning and savings activities. And the wealthier they are, the more focused become on their biggest wealth eroder: taxation.

ESSENTIAL TAX FACT ▶ **Tax erosion never stops.** Much of the income you make personally will be reduced by taxes every two weeks throughout your lifetime; stunting the disposable income you have left to save for your future. Those savings will be subject to tax again when you use them for retirement and before a legacy is passed along to your heirs. A strategy focused on tax efficiency should therefore be a cornerstone of your financial planning activities.

The chart below, can help you visualize how to categorize your investment decision-making into those four important Real Wealth Management pillars and set specific goals for your order of investing and the *purpose* each asset class needs to achieve to build your wealth for you:

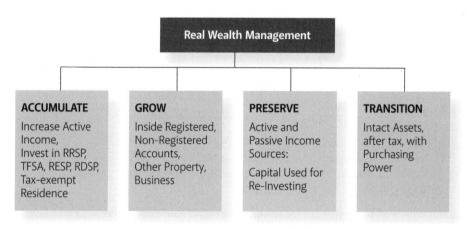

Real Wealth Management

ACCUMULATE
Increase Active Income, Invest in RRSP, TFSA, RESP, RDSP, Tax-exempt Residence

GROW
Inside Registered, Non-Registered Accounts, Other Property, Business

PRESERVE
Active and Passive Income Sources:
Capital Used for Re-Investing

TRANSITION
Intact Assets, after tax, with Purchasing Power

WORKING WITH QUALIFIED ADVISORS. Any strategic plan built to position you for a long retirement with worry-free financial solutions will be better served by a consistent, collaborative approach between you and the various advisors who help you with your money: accountants, lawyers, financial advisors, business valuators, etc. Consider these five steps in making better tax-efficient decisions both with your advisors and your family members:

1. **ESTABLISH BENCHMARKS** for your personal and family net worth according to your vision and your goals; then develop financial questions that require decision-making to discuss with your advisors.

TE more money by managing the tax attributes of your me sources; then analyze how to use what's left after tax ou will use it: in the present vs. in the future. Then plan your sources of capital to receive the variety of income ....ons that provide you with the best after-tax results.

3. **GROW** your capital and the investment income that results from it, for a long-term result that retains your purchasing power, preferably in a tax exempt, or tax-deferred investment vehicle.

4. **PRESERVE** both your personal productivity and that of your money, —by managing risks to their value: plan for the potential of critical illness and premature death with the right insurance products. Protect your financial assets by minimizing taxes on income and fees on capital accumulations.

5. **TRANSITION** assets intact—after taxes, fees and inflation—to your heirs and remember that wealth erosion from professional fees includes legal fees. Families without sound transition plans for financial management in cases of illness and death can often pay extensive legal fees to get things settled.

 Tax Moves

Your future retirement income security is dependent on the investment decisions you make when you are young. Retirement income planning begins with the first dollars you invest.

Your greatest opportunity to secure income quickly for your future after retirement, begins with saving more of your pre-tax earnings on a tax deferred basis. A TFSA, RRSP or an employer-sponsored RPP (Registered Pension Plan) are great investment vehicles. Choosing such a tax efficient route for those savings will help your money grow faster, so you will have more capital to last longer in retirement.

21 STRATEGIZING: Planning Tax-Efficient Investments

How WELL ARE YOU DOING, in your investment activities? For the answer, we look to the variation in your personal and family net worth year over year: total assets less total liabilities. The object of the trek to your financial freedom is to increase personal net worth every year along the way.

> **ESSENTIAL TAX FACT** ▶ **A Focus on Income, Assets and Debt Rounds Out Tax Efficiency Plans.** Making decisions that are tax-efficient enhances the performance of your money and increases net worth more quickly. It also makes sure your money has purchasing power when you need it because it hasn't been eroded by the cost of taxation, excessive professional fees or interest you have paid to your creditors.

To have a better focus on tax efficiency, you will want to address five key issues in making your strategic plans for investment product selections. Use this checklist to initiate a conversation about after-tax results with your financial advisor:

Investment Planning Checklist

1. **MANAGE DEBT.** Should I borrow to invest? When is interest tax-deductible?

2. **REDUCE MARGINAL TAX RATES.** What is the size of the next dollar I earn? Can I increase it in any way to secure more investment opportunities?

3. **AVOID, DEFER AND REDUCE TAX.** Are there any investment opportunities to avoid or postpone tax to the future when my income may be lower?

4. **CONTROL AND AVERAGE DOWN TAX:** How can I control the taxes I pay on income withdrawals? Can I plan to average down the tax I pay with a variety of investment income sources?

5. **PRESERVE INCOME AND CAPITAL:** How can I shift income to lower earners or alternate tax structures? When?

Managing Debt. Over half (52 per cent) of Canadians are only $200 away from insolvency according to a poll of 1,500 Canadians[7]. Canada's consumer-debt-to-financial-assets ratio is the highest among the G7 countries[8] and in the fall of 2017, Statistics Canada also confirmed that household debt to disposable income was at an unprecedented high: Canadians had 1.68 dollars in debt for each dollar of disposable income. That makes debt management a priority for most Canadians and an important factor in managing wealth management activities. Later in this part of the book you will learn more about how to make at least the interest on your debt tax deductible.

Audit Check Point

✔ The source of debt you must manage first is any outstanding balance with the CRA, which has recently received over $350 million to collect over $7 billion in tax debt [9].

CRA has enormous powers to collect tax debt. Consider these consequences:

- They will charge you interest, compounding daily at the prescribed rate plus 4%.
- Offset other tax refunds or refundable credits they owe you
- Garnishee wages and bank accounts by sending a requirement for your employer or bank to redirect funds to the CRA
- Certify your debt in the Federal Court of Canada, which puts it on the public record
- Seize and sell your assets, including your car, boat, cottage or personal residence as well as your business assets
- Hold others responsible for your debt, including your spouse, business partners or directors in your business.

Therefore it makes sense that to preserve your wealth, avoid tax debt and manage it first if you do. CRA will allow you to make arrangements to pay over

7 MNP Consumer debt sentiment survey Spring 2017

8 National Post January 2016

9 March 22, 2016 Federal Budget

time, with interest, so it's wise to make those arrangements before they take more drastic actions.

Marginal Tax Rates in Investment Planning. Your investment decision-making can be greatly improved when you know the marginal tax rates your investment income will be subject to—now and in the future. That can help you understand how big the dollar you get to keep is going to be.

Recall that the marginal tax rate (MTR) is the rate of tax paid on the next dollar earned. Income source and income level both factor into your MTR, as shown in the chart below. That means that you can arrange your affairs to diversify your income sources, to pay an overall lower average tax over the investment period.

TOP MARGINAL TAX RATES IN CANADA (2019)

Province	Ordinary Income	Capital Gains	Eligible Dividends	Ineligible Dividends
Alberta*	47/48%	23.5/24%	30.33/31.71%	41.41/42.56%
British Columbia	49.8%	24.9%	31.44%	44.63%
Ontario*	51.97/53.53%	25.98/26.76%	37.19/39.34%	45.60/47.40%

* Alberta and Ontario have a higher bracket than the highest federal bracket
Source: Knowledge Bureau, Inc.

You can see that the marginal tax rate will depend on the type of income you earn. You will end up with bigger after-tax dollars when you earn capital gains, which attract one-half of the marginal tax rate of ordinary income, which includes interest, for example.

Dividends are more attractive, too, but the MTR is not as easily calculated. Dividends reported on the tax return must be grossed-up. They are then offset by the dividend tax credit, which can vary with the type of dividend distributed. There are also variations in the dividend tax credits by province.

Recently there have been considerable changes to the taxation of dividends distributed from a private corporation starting in 2019. See *Essential Tax Facts Appendices.*

ESSENTIAL TAX FACT ▶ **Grossed-Up Dividends can Increase MTRs.** The effect the dividend gross-up has on clawbacks of tax credits and other government benefits must be taken into account in your planning activities, as it will increase net income on which these tax preferences are based.

Avoid, Defer and Reduce Tax. Whenever you can avoid or defer paying tax today, you should, to take maximum advantage of the time value of money.

The time value of money reflects the notion that a dollar invested today is worth more to you than waiting for a dollar to invest later. That's because that dollar in your pocket today has the potential to earn investment income.

The time value of money is an important concept in anticipating your savvy tax moves, because it underscores just how wrong it is to overpay your taxes and spend too much money on non-deductible debt; two significant wealth eroders. Time really is money, when you understand the power of compounding on the future value of your money, invested today:

VALUE OF $10,000 INVESTED AT A 3.5% RATE OF RETURN BEFORE TAXES

Years	Value	Increase in Principal
30	$28,000	181%
20	$19,900	99%
10	$14,100	41%
5	$11,900	19%

Investing longer, perhaps even over multiple generations, will result in exponential growth in your capital, if you have made all the right tax moves along the way: *always invest the first dollar you make, and a whole dollar if you can.*

ESSENTIAL TAX FACT ▶ **Tax Preferences Turbo-Charge the Time Value of Money.** Money grows faster when invested in a tax free or tax-deferred basis, sooner. A common way to do so is to invest in "registered" accounts.

Only the TFSA features tax free compounding and tax-free accumulation of value. No tax is paid on any earnings but note that the TFSA must be funded by tax-paid dollars... capital that has already been stripped by taxation.

The most common of the other registered investments, the Registered Retirement Savings Plan (RRSP), and for employees who belong to an employer-sponsored plan, or Registered Pension Plan (RPP), both provide for a tax deduction when principal is invested. In this way "whole dollars" are invested, pre-tax, and these bigger dollars will obviously grow more quickly.

But in addition, the tax on investment earnings that grow within the plan are deferred until withdrawal, causing even more exponential growth:

TRUE-TO-LIFE EXAMPLE ▶ REGISTERED VS. NON-REGISTERED INVESTMENT OVER 40 YEARS, 30% TAX BRACKET

If you had $5,000 to invest every year over a 40-year period, you would have deposited more than $200,000 into your savings.

If those funds were in a registered account (such as a TFSA or RRSP), the balance in the account at the end of the 40-year period would be **$494,133**, if you averaged a 4% return on your investment.

If you deposited the money into a non-registered account instead and paid the 30% taxes due on the earnings each year, the balance at the end of the 40-year period would only be **$370,454**. That's **$123,679 or 25%** less because the income is taxed as it is earned.

There's more to consider too. If you had deposited the money to an RRSP or RPP, you would have received a deduction. This deduction reduces net income on the T1 Return, which can increase social benefits and refundable tax credits, as previously described, as well as reducing your taxes for the year.

The combined savings—increased social benefits and credits and the tax savings themselves—can generate new capital for debt management or for other investments, like a TFSA. This is a great way to leverage one tax efficient investment into another to build even more wealth.

TRUE-TO-LIFE EXAMPLE ▶ YOUR AVERAGE TAX REFUND OF $1,765 IS REINVESTED IN A TFSA EVERY YEAR FOR 40 YEARS.

If you contributed your tax refund of $1,765 every year for 40 years into a TFSA which earned 4% interest, the balance in your TFSA one year after the last deposit would be $174,429.

You can see how a simple annual commitment to invest your tax refund into a TFSA can make you hundreds of thousands of dollars richer.

When you multiply these real wealth management initiatives within the family—each adult being tax savvy in this way—it can be worth millions of dollars to your family's combined net worth. This is a very effective way for your household to hedge your financial results against the wealth eroders you have no control over, like inflation.

Control and Average Down Taxes. To underscore: when you invest in a **registered savings account**, there is no taxable income inclusion on the investment earned along the way. However, except for the TFSA earnings, there will tax consequences when you withdraw the money from your other registered accounts.

In the case of the RRSP and RPP, withdrawals of both the principal and the earnings will result in a full income inclusion in the year of withdrawal. That's because when you contributed to these accounts, the principal was invested on a pre-tax basis (you got a deduction for the contribution).

ESSENTIAL TAX FACT ▶ **Plan Withdrawals from Registered Accounts as You Invest.** Your registered investment accounts can make you exponentially wealthier than those who don't use them. But, you'll get better after-tax results if you know how to arrange your income upon withdrawal to pay the least amount of tax over the retirement.

Astutely timed, your accumulated savings in these accounts will be withdrawn when you are in a lower tax bracket (for example, upon retirement or between jobs). It's also important to avoid lump sum withdrawals, which can spike your income into a higher tax bracket.

But what happens if you are now fabulously rich, because you did all the right things, and now find yourself—permanently—in a higher tax bracket than you ever imagined you would be?

ESSENTIAL TAX FACT. ▶ **Pension Income Splitting Reduces MTRs.** You can reduce taxes payable on with the power of income splitting with your spouse.

Up to 50% of eligible pension income can be split, by election, with a spouse, which can put the higher income earner into a lower tax bracket and reduce clawbacks of Old Age Security and other credits.

But if you are single, you will have to plan farther ahead to reduce your marginal tax rates on pension benefits: withdrawing smaller amounts annually over a long income averaging period will help.

In both cases, the key is to withdraw your taxable income in such a manner as to reach, but not exceed, the top of your current tax bracket.

This brings up another important question. Is there an optimal level of accumulations in a registered account? The correct answer is "it depends."

If you are married or live with a common-law spouse, the income splitting strategies that were discussed in the last section of this book, can be very effective in reducing the taxes on your registered accumulations. You will want to test for tax efficiency throughout your lifetime, and that of your spouse.

The Lifecycle of the Investment. With every dollar you invest, consider the net return you'll receive within the lifecycle of the investment. There are typically three tax milestones to consider:

- *Tax assistance for initial savings:* whether you invest with dollars that are smaller because they have already been taxed,
- *Taxation of investment income:* how your earnings are taxed in your investment account, and
- *Taxation of income and capital on withdrawal* in the future.

It is that final rate of return, at the end of an investing lifecycle that really counts.

If you were to think about this in an equation, you might call this *your tax efficiency quotient:*

$$\frac{\text{Total net earnings (after taxes)}}{\text{the net principal invested (after taxes)}}$$

EXAMPLE ▶ Net earnings: $1,000/Net Invested: $20,000; Tax efficiency quotient= 5%

EXAMPLE ▶ Consider the following "average" Canadian employees who are about to retire at age 65. Both George and Henry saved $5,000 faithfully every year starting at age 25 to age 65. George chose to save by making RRSP contributions and Henry chose to save in a non-registered account. Each made the same investments and over the 40-year accumulation period earned an average of 6% per year.

Each year, Henry reduced his savings in order to pay the income taxes on the earnings (20% in early years, 30% in later years). George enjoyed larger tax refunds of $1,000 in the early years and $1,500 in later years). The results of their savings are as follows after 40 years:

	George	Henry
Account Balance	$820,238	$565,505

Now, in retirement, both George and Henry have $15,000 in pension benefits annually from OAS and CPP and will add the maximum amount they can from their savings, assuming 4% annual return on capital, 2.7% inflation adjustment and a 20-year retirement.

The results are as follows:

	George	Henry
CPP and OAS	$15,000	$15,000
Starting Annual Pension	$48,000 (all taxable)	$33,000 (taxable $22,620)
Annual Income	$63,000	$48,000
Taxable Income	$63,000	$37,620
Average Tax Rate	17.7%	11.2%
Net After Tax	$51,830	$43,750

George has a higher taxable income and is paying tax at a higher rate because the full amount of his RRSP income is taxable whereas only the income portion of Henry's withdrawals are taxable.

However, in spite of the tax difference, George realizes $8040 more after-tax in the first year of retirement and even more in subsequent years due to indexing of their pensions.

The most compelling reason for the difference is that the taxes during the accumulation period in the non-registered account are higher (30% for the majority of the accumulation period) whereas taxes during retirement on the RRSP income are only 17.7%.

Should George and Henry have another source of income in retirement, such as an RPP—an employer-sponsored pension plan—the tax rate in retirement would be higher. If the rate in retirement exceeds the tax rate paid in the accumulation years, the situation could be reversed—Henry could end up with more after-tax income than George.

 Tax Moves

The strategic goal in planning your tax efficient investments is to keep your eye on four things: the most efficient way to accumulate, grow, preserve and transition the most sustainable wealth for the family over your lifetime.

The objective is to average down the taxes paid over the lifecycle of the investment by proactively planning to "realize" or withdraw income for tax purposes at the lowest possible marginal tax rates.

22 NON-REGISTERED INVESTMENTS: Scoring Higher

WE KNOW THAT GROWING MONEY IN A TAX-ASSISTED and tax-sheltered plan will make us richer over time, but there is a place for non-registered investment accounts, especially if we have taken advantage of all age- and income-eligible investing opportunities, or maximized deposit restricted opportunities, for example in the TFSA, RESP or RDSP.

> **ESSENTIAL TAX FACT** ▶ **Diversify Income Earned in Non-Registered Accounts to Get the Best Tax Results.** There are two broad classifications of taxable income these non-registered investment accounts will generate:
>
> - income from property: interest, dividends, rents, royalties, and
> - capital gains and losses, which occur on the sale or deemed disposition of several "categories" of assets.

EARNING INTEREST. Interest income is common to most investors. It can often accrue on a compounding basis (that is, interest is reinvested rather than paid out to the investor during the term of the contract). However, because it attracts the highest marginal taxes on income inclusion, it is the least efficient source of investment income.

The following are examples of "debt obligations" (investment contracts) that pay interest income:

- A *Guaranteed Investment Certificate (GIC)* which features a fixed interest rate for a term spanning generally one to five years.
- A *treasury bill* or *zero-coupon bond* which provides no stated interest but is sold at a discount to its maturity value.

- A *strip bond* or coupon bond.
- A Guaranteed Investment Certificate offering interest rates that rise as time goes on. These are also known as *deferred interest obligations.*
- An *income bond* or debenture where the interest paid is linked to a corporation's profit or cash flow.
- An *indexed debt obligation instrument* that is linked to inflation rates, such as Government of Canada Real Return Bonds.

Reporting interest income follows two basic tax compliance categories:

1. You must report the interest in the taxation year when it is actually received or receivable.
2. When compound interest is earned, it is paid out at the end of the contract term. However, you must report all interest income that accrues on an annual basis, in the year ending on the debt's anniversary date. An issue date in November of one year, for example, does not require interest reporting until the following year. In other words, the accrual of interest for the period November to December 31 is not required.

You can see why investments that produce interest are considered inefficient from a tax viewpoint: you must pay tax on income you have not yet actually received which means you must tap into other income sources to pay the tax on your interest-bearing investments.

Things get a little trickier when investment contracts have unique features:

- they may be non-interest bearing and sold at a discount to their maturity value
- the interest rates may be adjusted for inflation over time
- the rate of interest may increase as the term progresses
- interest payments may vary with the debtor's cash flows or profits
- where the instrument is transferred before the end of the term, a reconciliation of interest earnings must take place.

Here are some examples:

Coupon Bonds. Regular government or corporate bonds can also be called "coupon bonds" and pay a stated rate of interest. If the interest is from a Canadian source it will be reported on a T5 slip and entered on the tax return in the calendar year received in the normal manner. If from a foreign source, interest is reported annually in Canadian funds and may generate a foreign tax credit if taxes have been withheld at source in the foreign country.

Further complications arise when the bond or coupon is sold before maturity. In that case, the new investor receives interest on the next payment date, as usual, even though some of the interest may have accrued prior to the purchase. An adjustment must be made to ensure each bond owner reports the correct amount of interest up to the date of ownership change. In addition, a capital gain or loss might arise on the disposition.

Treasury Bills. These are short-term government debt obligations, generally available in three, six or twelve-month terms. If the T-Bill's term exceeds one year, the normal annual interest accrual rules would apply.

T-Bills are similar to strip bonds (discussed below) because they are acquired at a discount to their maturity value and have no stated interest rate. On maturity you will receive their face value, which will include the accrued interest amount. This is generally reported on a T5008 slip. If you sell the T-Bill before maturity, a capital gain or loss could result however because of the short term, T-Bill are seldom traded.

Strip Bonds. These are also known as zero-coupon bonds as they do not pay interest during the period of ownership. They are purchased at a discount and if held to term will yield a future value that is higher. The difference between the present and future value is considered to be the interest paid over the period to maturity. The resulting interest must be reported annually on the anniversary date of the bond's issue date each year.

If a strip bond is sold prior to its maturity date, a capital gain or loss may result. The Adjusted Cost Base (ACB) used in the calculation of the gain or loss will be the original amount paid for the strip bond plus the interest accrued from the date of purchase to the date of disposition.

Indexed Debt Obligations. These investments include, in addition to interest paid on the amount invested, a payment (or deduction) on maturity that represents the decrease (or increase) in the purchasing power of the investment during the term of the investment. This additional payment is reported according to the normal annual accrual rules. If in the year of disposition or maturity it is determined that interest has been over-accrued, the over-accrued amount can be deducted as a carrying charge.

Income Bonds and Income Debentures. A special type of bond or debenture may be issued with a term of up to five years by corporations that are in financial difficulty and under the control of a receiver or trustee in bankruptcy. A return on such an income bond is paid only if the issuing corporation earns a profit from its operations. Such amounts paid or received by the investor are then treated as a dividend for tax purposes.

Exchanges of Debentures for Securities. When a bond or debenture is exchanged for shares of a corporation, the exchange is not considered to be a disposition for tax purposes, providing that the share is received directly from the corporation which issued it. Therefore, there are no tax consequences. This is also true when one debenture is exchanged for another bond or debenture, providing that the principal amount is the same.

PLANNING WITH INTEREST INCOME. Recently, worried investors have flown out of the stock market to what they consider to be "safe" havens: Guaranteed Investment Certificates (GICs) and other interest-bearing debt obligations, like Guaranteed Income Certificates (GIC). The guaranteed return of principal is attractive to many, but with interest rates of half of one percent, the returns are dismal.

> **ESSENTIAL TAX FACT** ▶ **You Must Report Interest Income Earned Even if You Did Not Receive a T-Slip.** Due to recent low interest rates, many taxpayers have forgotten to report some of their interest earnings. An adjustment to prior filed returns can be made to avoid interest or penalties in those cases. Don't forget to include interest that CRA paid you on money it owed you.

Earn interest in registered accounts. Current rates on 6-year GICs were around 1.5% to 3%. Unfortunately, the tax efficiency rating on this investment choice is poor, and that's why we often try to earn interest within registered accounts, where the income is sheltered from tax until withdrawal, to boost its productivity.

When you take taxes and inflation into account, most investors will actually lose principal and purchasing power on an investment like GICs because it is neither tax efficient nor inflation-proof, as demonstrated below:

REAL AFTER-TAX RETURN OF $1,000 COMPOUNDING GIC*

Year	Interest Earned	Taxes	Inflation Adjustment	Principal and Earnings Left**	Real After-Tax Return
Principal	$1,000.00				
0	Plus:	Less:	Less:		
1	$15.00	$4.65	$20.00	$990.35	−0.97%
2	$15.23	$4.72	$20.10	$980.76	-1.92%
3	$15.45	$4.79	$20.20	$971.22	-2.88%
4	$15.69	$4.86	$20.30	$961.74	-3.83%
5	$15.92	$4.94	$20.40	$952.33	-4.77%
6	$16.16	$5.01	$20.51	$942.97	-5.70%
Total	$1093.45	$28.97	$121.51	$942.97	−5.70%

*Assumes 1.5% interest rate, inflation at 2% and a 6-year hold period. Taxpayer is in 31% tax bracket. **Amounts shown in current-year dollars.

Your return after taxes and inflation, after 6 years is actually a loss of 5.7% in real dollar terms.

Using a TFSA with Interest-bearing Investments. Another way to improve tax efficiency for interest-bearing investments is to hold them in a registered account such as a TFSA. Will the GIC fare better here? Consider the following:

REAL AFTER-TAX RETURN OF $1000 COMPOUNDING GIC IN A TFSA*

Year	Interest Earned	Taxes	Inflation Adjustment	Principal and Earnings Left**	Real After-Tax Return
Principal	$1,000.00				
0	Plus:	Less:	Less:		
1	$15.00	$0.00	$20.00	$995.00	-0.50%
2	$15.23	$0.00	$20.10	$990.13	-0.99%
3	$15.45	$0.00	$20.20	$985.38	-1.46%
4	$15.69	$0.00	$20.30	$980.77	-1.92%
5	$15.92	$0.00	$20.40	$976.29	-2.37%
6	$16.16	$0.00	$20.51	$971.94	-2.81%
Total	$1093.45	$0.00	$120.51	$971.94	-2.81%

*Assumes 1.5% interest rate, inflation at 2% and a 6-year hold period. Taxpayer is in 31% tax bracket. ** Amounts shown in current-year dollars

Because the 1.5% return does not exceed the inflation rate of 2%, your capital will be eroded, even in the TFSA, but because the income is earned tax-free, you save the $28.97 in taxes paid in the previous example. Your net after-tax return, therefore, is 2.89% more if the GIC is held within the TFSA.

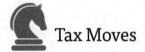 Tax Moves

Planning for the receipt of interest income could become more significant in the future if interest rates rise. Consider whether this income source should be earned inside a registered account to get the best tax efficiencies and hedge against inflation or a TFSA rather than in a non-registered account.

23 DIVIDENDs: Scoring Bigger Returns

A MORE TAX-EFFICIENT WAY TO INVEST is to look for an excellent quality stock that pays a dividend. This is the return of the after-tax profits of a corporation to its shareholders.

Dividends received by individuals from Canadian corporations are subject to special rules, to compensate for the taxes already paid by the corporation. To integrate the personal and corporate tax system, a "gross-up" of actual dividends paid to an individual is required to be reported as income; it is later offset by a "dividend tax credit" when calculating taxes payable.

> **ESSENTIAL TAX FACT** ▶ **Dividend Income is More Tax Efficient than Interest.** The "dividend tax credit," reduces federal and provincial taxes otherwise payable and could generate a "negative income tax", which offsets taxes on other income sources at certain tax brackets, making dividends a very tax-efficient form of investment income when compared to ordinary income or interest.

Eligible Dividends. If the dividend is paid from income that attracted a high rate of corporate tax, currently 15%, the dividend is called an "eligible dividend" and is grossed up by 38% for 2012 and later years. The dividend tax credit is 15.02% of the grossed-up amount.

Note that starting in 2019, more small business corporations will be reporting eligible dividends on distribution, if their passive investment earnings within the corporation exceed $50,000, resulting in a reduction of their Small Business Deduction. See *Essential Tax Facts Appendices* for details.

Non-eligible Dividends. If the dividend is paid from income that attracted a low rate of tax (generally within a private, Canadian-controlled small business corporation which has passive investment earnings of less than $50,000), the dividend is grossed up by 15% starting in 2019, and the dividend tax credit is 9.03% of the grossed-up amount.

Historical Data. For 2018, the gross-up was 16% with a dividend tax credit rate of 10.03% and for 2017 the gross-up was 17% with a dividend tax credit rate of 10.5% of the grossed-up amount. These dividends are sometimes called "ineligible dividends" or "other than eligible dividends."

Earning Tax-Free Dividend Income. A taxpayer can earn a significant amount of eligible dividends on a tax-free basis, depending on the province of residence. Some business owners, especially those in their 60's who may not wish to make further Canada Pension Plan or RRSP contributions, might be tempted to forgo receiving employment income sources in favor of dividends from the investment in their business.

> **TRUE-TO-LIFE EXAMPLE** ▶ Maggie operates a small business in BC. She could pay herself up to $22,300 dividends from her corporation and still not pay any income tax.
>
> Trevor operates a small business in Ontario. He could pay himself over $26,300 without paying any income taxes.

At first glance, astute retirees might plan a move to BC for more than the mild weather; that is, to earn out dividends in a more advantageous provincial tax regime.

> **ESSENTIAL TAX FACT** ▶ **Be Aware that the Dividend Gross-Up Calculation Might Have Negative Effects.** Be sure to consider social benefit clawbacks, provincial health care, nursing home and the cost of gas and pharmaceuticals in developing retirement plans.

Retirement Planning. Business owners in their pre-retirement years will also want to be careful to create some "earned income" for the purposes of creating pensions from the CPP and RRSP, as part of their retirement planning activities. Speak to your tax and financial advisor to discuss the latest tax changes for small business corporations and the increases that are coming to the Canada Pension Plan in 2019 to assist with these decisions.

Planning with Gross-up Dividends. You have learned that because the dividend "gross up" artificially increases net income, it may reduce your refundable or non- refundable tax credits, such as:

- The Canada Child Benefit
- The GST/HST Credit
- The Canada Workers Benefit
- The Age Amount
- Spousal Amount and Amount for Eligible Dependant
- Medical expenses
- Provincial refundable tax credits

An overweighting in dividend income may also negatively affect other financial transactions that are dependent upon the size of net income on the tax return:

- Old Age Security Clawbacks
- Employment Insurance Clawbacks
- Guaranteed Income Supplements
- Provincial per diem rates for nursing homes
- Certain provincial medical/prescription plans.

Therefore, income planning around investment options is important, especially for seniors, who should take into account all these obstacles in planning the optimal mix of investment and pension income within the lowest possible marginal tax rates.

TRUE-TO-LIFE EXAMPLE ▶ Roger is a senior Manitoba resident with taxable income of $80,000. If Roger earns an additional $1,000 of interest to his income, he will be subject to taxes at 37.90% plus a clawback of $150 (15% x $1,000) of his Old Age Security. The marginal tax rate on the interest income is therefore $379 + $150 = $529 or **52.9%**.

If that extra income was received as eligible dividends, instead, then $1,380 would be added to Roger's income and this would attract tax at 20.53% plus a clawback of $207 ($15% x $1,380). The marginal tax rate on the dividends income would then be $205.30 + $207 = $412.30 or **41.2%**.

There is a significant win for this taxpayer if the source of his retirement income has changed from interest to dividends **(11.7%)**.

OTHER TYPES OF DIVIDENDS. You should be aware of the tax consequences of the following types of dividend receipts you may be entitled to:

Capital Dividends. Sometimes a shareholder in a private corporation may receive a Capital Dividend. Such dividends are not taxable.

To qualify as a Capital Dividend, the dividend must be paid out of the Capital Dividend Account (CDA) of a private Canadian corporation. This account is set up to accumulate the non-taxable (50%) portion of any capital gains realized by the corporation, capital dividends received from other corporations, untaxed portions of gains realized on the disposition of eligible capital property, and life insurance proceeds received by the corporation.

Thankfully, the federal government backed down on proposals to cancel the CDA as part of its tax reforms for private corporations.

Capital Gains Dividends. These are dividends received from a mutual fund company. They are reported on a T5 Slip and Schedule 3. Capital gains dividends are actually capital gains and not dividends (that is, 50% of gains are included in income; they are not grossed up and there is no dividend tax credit).

Note: The March 2019 Federal Budget proposed changes to the calculation of mutual fund and ETF redemptions which may result in previously allowed capital gains treatment to be considered fully taxable income. Check with your financial advisor to see how this will affect your retirement income and plans for gifting through a transfer of funds with accrued gains to your favorite charity.

Stock Dividends. This type of dividend arises when a corporation decides to issue additional shares to its existing shareholders, instead of paying a cash dividend. Like regular dividends, stock dividends must be included in income, and are subject to gross-up, and the dividend tax credit. The amount of the dividend is the amount that the corporation adds to its various capital accounts on issuing the share. See *Essential Tax Facts Appendices* for more information.

Where the stock dividend is paid by a public company, this is usually the fair market value of the shares issued.

 Tax Moves

Earning dividends can be an effective way to reduce marginal tax rates, however some unintended results may occur when the grossed-up dividend reduces either social benefits or refundable and non-refundable tax credits on the tax return. For these reasons, ask your financial advisors to prepare an estimate of tax in advance of making investment decisions, particularly if planning the distribution of dividends from a corporation you own is part of your tax-efficient investment income planning process.

---

24 RENTAL INCOME: Embellishing on Your Tax Moves

MANY INVESTORS RECENTLY HAVE INCREASED their personal net worth by investing in real property. If that investment is in a principal residence, a tax-exempt gain on the sale of your home is possible. This is so even if you earn income from that tax-exempt residence—by renting out a room or rooms, for example, or by running a business from your home.

We'll dig deeper into the tax consequences of primary and secondary residences or rental properties later, but our mandate in this chapter is to discuss revenue properties held for investment purposes.

Audit Check Point

- ✔ Rental properties are often audited. In assessing whether revenue property ownership is right for you, consider the increased tax compliance issues you'll have when you become a real estate investor.

Those who collect rental income from a property rented to tenants will have tax consequences in acquiring and operating the property and usually upon the disposition of the property as well. In the first year, it is important to set up the tax reporting for a revenue property properly:

TAX FORM FACT. A *Statement of Real Estate Rentals* (Form T776) must be completed to report income and expenses; this is done on a calendar year basis—January to December.

Technically, a landlord is supposed to use accrual accounting in reporting revenues and expenses. However, as there are generally few major differences between cash and accrual accounting for individual landlords; the CRA will accept cash accounting so long as the cash income does not differ significantly from accrual income. Other tax reporting facts include:

Checklist for Rental Property Owners.

INCOME:

- [ ] *Income reporting.* Gross rental income must be reported. It is best to open a separate bank account to keep this in. If you rent to someone you are related to, you must report fair market value rents if you rent for less.
- [ ] *Advance rent payments.* This is included in income according to the years they relate to.
- [ ] *Lease cancellation payments* received are included in rental income.

EXPENSES:

- [ ] *Profit motive required.* In order to deduct operating expenses from rental income, there must be a profit motive (i.e. revenues should exceed expenses).
- [ ] *Fully deductible* operating expenses include maintenance, repairs, supplies, interest, taxes.
- [ ] *Partially deductible* expenses could include the business portion of auto expenses and meal and entertainment expenses incurred (but generally only if you have a number of rental properties).
- [ ] *Expenditures for asset acquisition or improvement* cannot be deducted in full. Rather Capital Cost Allowance (CCA) schedules must be set up to account for depreciation expense. If an expenditure extends the useful life of the property or improves upon the original condition of the property, then the expenditure is capital in nature and not 100% deductible. See Appendices for new rules.
- [ ] *Land is not a depreciable asset.* It is necessary to separate the cost of land and buildings on the CCA schedule. A rental loss cannot be created or increased with a CCA claim.
- [ ] *Not deductible* are any expenses that relate to personal living expenses of the owner, or any expenses that relate to the cost of the land or principal portions of loans taken to acquire or maintain the property.

Rentals to Family Members. Rentals to family members can be tricky and often fail audit tests when taxpayers attempt to claim rental losses against other income sources.

No Tax Reporting is Required if There is No Profit Motive. When you rent a portion of your home to a family member for a nominal rent you may not claim a rental loss, as there is no profit motive. But on the good news side, when there is no profit potential, you need not include the rent in income.

TRUE-TO-LIFE EXAMPLE ▶ Will and Emily rent out their basement (30% of the living space in their home) to Emily's brother who recently lost his job. They charge him $300 per month. Similar accommodations in town normally rent for $500 to $600 per month.

After property taxes, mortgage interest and utilities for the home the rental statement shows a loss of $2,700. Because there is no profit motive in this arrangement and the rent is below market value, the $2,700 loss cannot be claimed. However, since the expenses exceed the income, it is not necessary to include the rent collected in income.

Deductible expenses. Expenses are usually deducted on a cash basis as paid, so long as this does not result in a material difference from accrual basis accounting, as mentioned. If you report on an accrual basis, expenses are to be matched with the revenue to which they relate, so that expenses prepaid in one year are not deducted then but in the later year to which they relate.

Checklist of Common Deductible Operating Expenses—Rental Property

☐ *Advertising*—Amounts paid to advertise the availability of the rental property.

☐ *Condominium fees*—Amounts applicable to the period when the rental condo was available for rent may be deducted.

☐ *Insurance*—If the insurance is prepaid for future years, claim only the portion that applies to the rental year, unless you are using cash basis accounting.

☐ *Landscaping costs* may be deducted in the year paid.

☐ *Legal, accounting and other professional fees*—There are unique rules to consider in deducting fees paid to professionals:

　– Legal fees to prepare leases or to collect rent are deductible.

　– Legal fees to acquire the property form part of the cost of the property.

　– Legal fees on the sale of the property are outlays and expenses which will reduce any capital gain on the sale.

　– Accounting fees to prepare statements, keep books, or prepare the tax return are deductible.

- ☐ *Maintenance and repairs*—Costs of regular maintenance and minor repairs are deductible. For major repairs, it must be determined if the cost is a current expense or capital in nature.

- ☐ *Management and administration fees*—If you pay a third party to manage or otherwise look after some aspect of the property, the amount paid is deductible. Note that if a caretaker is given a suite in an apartment block as compensation for caretaking, a T4 Slip must be issued to report the fair market value of the rent as employment income.

- ☐ *Mortgage interest*—Interest on a mortgage to purchase the property plus any interest on additional loans to improve the rental property may be deducted.

- ☐ *Motor vehicle expenses*—Travelling expenses are generally considered to be personal living expenses of the landlord. And, if you own only one rental property, then motor vehicle expenses to collect rent are not deductible. However, if you personally travel to make repairs to the property, then the cost of transporting tools and materials to the property may be deducted.

- ☐ *Office and office supplies*—Office and other supplies used up in earning rental income are deductible as are home office expenses in situations where you use the office to keep books or serve tenants.

- ☐ *Property taxes*—These are deductible.

- ☐ *Renovations for the disabled*—Costs incurred to make the rental property accessible to individuals with a mobility impairment may be fully deducted.

- ☐ *Utilities*—If costs are paid by the landlord and not reimbursed by the tenant, they will be deductible. Costs charged to tenants are deductible if amounts collected are included in rental income.

Multiple rental property owners. When two or more taxpayers jointly own a revenue property, it is necessary to determine whether they own the property as co-owners or as partners in a partnership. If a partnership exists, CCA is claimed before the partnership income is allocated to the partners. In effect, all the partners are subject to the same CCA claim. If a co-ownership exists, each owner can claim CCA individually on their share of the capital costs. The next chapter covers the consequences of revenue property dispositions.

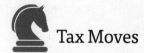 Tax Moves

The acquisition of a revenue property can significantly improve net worth. For tax purposes, rental income is considered to be "income from property." This investment will be subject to ongoing tax audit exposure to ensure expenses—in particular—maintenance and repairs are properly reported.

Taxpayers are most often caught when improvements to the property are fully expensed, rather than depreciated on the Capital Cost Allowance schedule. Losses on rentals to family members can also be disallowed when there is no reasonable expectation of profit.

25 WINNING: With Capital Gains

PEOPLE WHO BECOME WEALTHY HAVE TYPICALLY worked hard to invest their money on a tax-exempt, pre-tax or tax-deferred basis, and with a view to paying tax at the lowest marginal rates. They will seek to do that on the increases in values of their assets, too, when the time comes to sell them. Fortunately, there are some attractive tax preferences for investors in income-producing assets.

ESSENTIAL TAX FACT ▶ **There is No Tax Payable as Value Appreciates on Your Capital Assets.** This includes the value of real property, business properties and financial assets held in non-registered accounts.

However, when an income-producing asset is disposed of for an amount greater than its cost base on acquisition, plus certain adjustments, a capital gain will arise. Fifty per cent (50%) of that gain is taxable.

Capital Losses Matter. On the flip side, if an asset is disposed of for less than its adjusted cost base (ACB), a capital loss is the result. That loss will first offset capital gains of the year, and if unabsorbed, can be used again in "carry over" periods, which we will explain below.

So Do Personal Use Properties. Although it is usually income-producing assets like stocks, bonds and real estate that fall within the capital gains provisions, certain personal items may also be subject to capital gains tax. This can include second homes, coins, and rare jewelry.

ESSENTIAL TAX FACT ▶ **There are Restrictions on Claiming Personal Losses.** Although gains on personal-use property are taxable, losses on personal use property are not (except for a few specific property types).

To calculate the amount of a capital gain (or loss), take the difference between the proceeds received from disposing of the asset and the adjusted cost base (ACB) of that asset and reduce this number by any outlays and expenses incurred in disposing of the asset.

These terms are foreign to most, but are important, so that you can understand other elements of planning; for example, how to transfer assets back and forth between family members and maximize your tax advantages, too.

Use this equation to compute your capital gains or losses:

CALCULATION OF CAPITAL GAINS OR LOSSES

Proceeds of Disposition	−	Adjusted Cost Base	−	Outlays and Expenses	=	Capital Gain or Loss

Proceeds of Disposition. The proceeds of disposition will normally be the actual sales price received. But proceeds can also be a "deemed" amount (usually the fair market value) in cases where there is a taxable disposition but no money changes hands—on death, gifting or emigration, for example.

Those deemed events can be involuntary (death) or voluntary (transfer of assets to children). In each circumstance they required planning in advance.

Adjusted Cost Base. The adjusted cost base starts with the cost of an income-producing asset when acquired. This could be the cash outlay, or in the case of acquisition by way of a transfer by gift, inheritance, etc., the fair market value (FMV) at the time of transfer.

The ACB may also be increased or decreased by certain adjustments: the cost of improvements to the asset, for example, or in the case of land, non-deductible interest or property taxes.

> **TRUE-TO-LIFE EXAMPLE** ▶ Jonas buys shares for $10,000 plus $10 commission and sells them six months later for $20,000 less $20 commission.
> - The "Adjusted Cost Base" of the shares is $10,010 (price paid, including commissions).
> - The "Proceeds of Disposition" are $20,000.
> - The $20 commission on sale is an "outlay and expense" of sale.
> - The "Capital Gain" is $20,000 − $10,010 − $20 = $9,970.

Capital Gains Inclusion Rate. The amount of capital gain that is included in income is called the "taxable gain" and this is determined by the capital gains inclusion rate. This has changed a number of times since the introduction of capital gains taxes in 1972, but currently it is 50% of the net gain, after capital losses are accounted for, that are reported as income on the T1 Return.

Working with Losses. Capital losses may only be used to reduce capital gains in the current year. If losses exceed gains in the current year they may be carried back to reduce capital gains in any of the previous three years or in any future tax year.

> **TAX FORM FACT.** File *Form T1A Request for Loss Carry Back* to offset capital gains of prior or future years.

Losses at Death. When the taxpayer dies, unused capital losses can no longer be carried forward so the unused capital losses (reduced by any capital gains deduction previously claimed) may be used to offset other types of income in the year of death or the immediately preceding year.

Capital loss deductibility can be a very important part of estate preservation, so be sure to keep records of these important transactions.

Limited Partnership Losses. A special rule applies when investors lose money on disposition of units in a limited partnership. Limited partnership losses up to the partner's "at-risk amount" may be deducted against other income. However, when losses exceed the at-risk amount, they cannot be used to offset other income or be carried back. Instead, they must be carried forward until the taxpayer reports income from that limited partnership. In that year, limited partnership losses of other years are deducted on the tax return.

Limited partnership losses not claimed at death *will expire*; again, something important to keep in mind as you plan your investments for the four elements of Real Wealth Management: accumulation, growth, preservation and transition of your wealth at death, on an after-tax basis.

Trading Identical Securities. Shares in public companies or units in a mutual fund that have identical rights, and which cannot be distinguished one from the other. Therefore, they must be grouped together for tax purposes to properly calculate gains and losses.

The cost of all identical shares in the group must be determined and then divide the sum by the number of shares held to determine the *average cost per share*.

> **TRUE-TO-LIFE EXAMPLE** ▶ Derek is a fairly active trader. Last year he purchased shares of XYZ Corporation and traded them as follows:
>
> • June 28: Purchased 1,000 shares at $8.00 per share
> • July 5: Sold 1,000 shares at $8.30 per share

- Aug 2: Purchased 3,000 shares at $7.00 per share
- Oct 1: Purchased 4,000 shares at $8.00 per share
- Oct 23: Sold 5,000 shares at $7.50 per share

The brokerage fee on each transaction was $25

The July 5 sale showed a gain of ($8.30 x 1,000) – ($8.00 x 1,000 + $25) – $25 = $8,300 – $8,025 – $25 = $250.

The October 23 sale resulted in a capital loss (negative gain) of ($7.50 x 5,000) – [($7.00 x 3,000 + $25) + ($8.00 x 4,000 + $25)] x 5,000/7,000 – $25 = $37,500 – $37,892.86 – $25 = –$417.86.

The net result of these transactions on his tax return is a net capital loss of $167.86 which can be used to offset any other gains in the year.

Audit Check Point

✔ Post-tax season can be difficult for disorganized taxpayers who cannot find the right documentation to report the disposition of identical properties.

Without adequate records of the dates of acquisition and disposition plus costs/proceeds, and the fees charged, it would be impossible to determine the correct amount of income to report. Be sure to save these details in a permanent file you can pull out when a disposition occurs.

Superficial losses. There is a special rule to take note of when capital properties are acquired after a loss transaction. If such assets are purchased within 30 days prior to the disposition, or within 30 days after the disposition, this "superficial loss" will be disallowed and is generally added to the Adjusted Cost Base of the replacement property.

TRUE-TO-LIFE EXAMPLE ▶ Katherine owned shares of XYZ Corp which had an ACB of $12.00 per share. When they fell to $10.00 per share, she sold them. Since they recovered quickly, she repurchased the shares the following week for $11.00 per share. The $2.00 per share loss is deemed to be a superficial loss and cannot be claimed. The ACB of the repurchased shares is $11.00 + $2.00 = $13.00 per share.

Transfers to Registered Accounts. A similar result can also occur when assets held in a non-registered account are transferred into a registered account. The loss on such a transfer is deemed to be nil and it is therefore recommended that shares that have decreased in value not be transferred to a registered account but rather sold and the proceeds contributed to the account.

TRUE-TO-LIFE EXAMPLE ▶ Jason wants to make an RRSP contribution, but he does not have the cash to make the contribution. He has $10,000 worth of shares but these shares have an ACB of $12,000.

If Jason transfers the shares to his RRSP, he will receive an RRSP contribution receipt for the fair market value of the shares ($10,000) but his loss on the deemed disposition will be nil.

Jason should instead sell the shares for $10,000, claim the $2,000 capital loss and then make his RRSP contribution with the $10,000 cash proceeds.

Donating Publicly Traded Shares. In certain cases, when you dispose of capital assets, you may not have to include the capital gain in your income at all. For example, when you donate publicly traded shares to a registered charity or private foundation, your capital gains inclusion rate is deemed to be zero and—you get a donation credit for the value of the shares. *But you don't have to pay any tax on the gain!*

TRUE-TO-LIFE EXAMPLE ▶ Diana purchased shares for $5,000 several years ago. The shares have done well and are now worth $15,000. If she donates the shares to a registered charity, she will receive a donation receipt for $15,000 and will not have to pay taxes on the $10,000 capital gain.

If she were to sell the shares and donate the proceeds, she would still receive a donation receipt for $15,000 but she would also have to report and pay tax on a $5,000 taxable capital gain.

Replacement Properties. In cases where you dispose of a capital asset that is being used in a business and replace the asset with another, you may be able to defer any capital gains on the original asset until the replacement is disposed of. *This rule does not apply to investment or rental properties.*

TRUE-TO-LIFE EXAMPLE ▶ Peter's company owned a storage lot which has become too small for the company's needs. The lot was purchased for $75,000 and is currently worth $200,000. The company sold the lot and purchased another nearby for $300,000.

Rather than pay the taxes on the $125,000 capital gain on the sale, the company may elect to adjust the ACB of the replacement lot by the amount of the capital gain. If this election is made, no capital gain is reported and the ACB of the replacement lot is reduced by $125,000 to $175,000. This has the effect of postponing the capital gain on the disposition of the old lot until the replacement property is sold.

MUTUAL FUNDS. Mutual funds are common investments but can often cause some tax confusion, particularly because investors don't understand their real returns from these investments, after fees and taxes.

This is because mutual fund companies are required to distribute all interest, dividends, other income and net capital gains to their unit holders at least once every year. With the exception of any return of capital, these distributions are taxable.

> **ESSENTIAL TAX FACT** ▶ **Time Mutual Fund Acquisitions Carefully.** In the year you acquire a mutual fund, you will usually receive a full annual distribution, even if you invested late in the year. You may wish to hold over your purchase, therefore, to the new year to better manage quarterly instalment payments and clawbacks of tax credits and benefits.

In addition, rarely is this income received in cash, so your earnings will not help with the tax bill or your quarterly instalments. Rather, the income is used to buy more units in the fund and those reinvested amounts are added to the Adjusted Cost Base.

This makes the reporting of sales or deemed dispositions of mutual funds a more difficult undertaking at tax time, because you will need to have kept track of your ACB. Most mutual fund companies can help you with this.

Switches and Exchanges. When you exchange an investment in one fund for another (e.g. from an equity fund to a balanced fund), a taxable disposition is considered to have occurred, with normal tax consequences.

Tax Consequences Upon Disposition of the Units. Mutual fund units or shares are classified as "identical properties" for tax purposes. As you have learned previously, the average cost of the shares/units must be calculated each time there is a purchase by dividing total units owned into the adjusted cost of the units/shares including all reinvested earnings. This provides you with the cost per unit required to calculate the capital gains or losses properly. Note that dispositions do not affect the adjusted cost base of the remaining units.

> **TRUE-TO-LIFE EXAMPLE** ▶ Scott purchased 1,000 units in an equity fund last year. The cost of the units was $12.40 per unit. He received a T3 slip showing that income of $254 was allocated to him. Rather than receiving the $245 in cash, he received 20.32 additional units in the fund.
>
> This year, he decided to move his investment into a bond fund with the same company. The 1,020.32 units of the equity fund were exchanged

for 539.96 units in a bond fund with an ACB of $12,662.17.

The ACB of the bond fund units at the time of the transaction will be the deemed proceeds of disposition of the equity fund units.

The ACB of the equity fund units is $12,400 (original cost) + $254 (income allocated to Scott last year). Scott will report a capital gain of $12,662.17—($12,400 + $254) = $8.17.

New Tax Changes. Mutual fund trusts which convert ordinary income to capital gains may be more expensive in 2019 based on new calculations on redemption, which will raise over $350 million over the next five fiscal years (2019 – 2024). A new rule may deny the trust certain deductions if the allocation of capital gains to a unitholder who redeems assets from an ETF or mutual fund is imprecise. Specifically, mutual funds will be prevented from allocating capital gains to their redeeming unitholders if fully taxable ordinary income has been re-characterized as a capital gain or tax has been inappropriately deferred. See Appendices.

SEGREGATED FUNDS. A segregated fund is similar to a mutual fund in that it is a pooled investment, but it tends to have more advantageous tax attributes. It is established by an insurance company and the funds invested are segregated from the rest of the capital of the company.

> **ESSENTIAL TAX FACT** ▶ **Segregated funds have tax advantages.** The main difference between a segregated and a mutual fund is that most segregated funds include a guarantee—that a minimum amount will always be returned to the investor regardless of the performance of the fund over time.

In addition, however, a segregated fund can allocate a loss to the unitholder (while a mutual fund may not). This can be used to offset other capital gains of the year, or the carry-over years.

Segregated funds may also offer maturity and death guarantees on the capital invested and, specifically, reset guarantees—which is the ability to lock in market gains. This can be a very attractive feature of this asset, although the fees paid for these features can be more expensive.

The tax consequences are as follows:

- *Guarantee at Maturity.* If at maturity the value of the fund has dropped, the insurer must top up the fund by contributing additional assets to bring the value up to the guaranteed amount. There are no tax implications at the time of top up. However, there will be when the taxpayer disposes of the fund. This will be the difference between the ACB (which includes allocations of income over time) and the proceeds received.

- *Guarantee at Death.* The unitholder is deemed to have disposed of the contract at its fair market value at time of a deemed disposition—death or emigration for example. If the value of the assets in the fund increases, the gain will be taxable to the unitholder when the policy matures or to his estate if the policy owner dies.

- *Decreases in Value.* If the value of the assets in the fund decreases, and a guarantee is in place the taxpayer is deemed to have acquired additional notional units in the fund so that their proceeds are not less than the guaranteed amount. A capital loss may occur if the guaranteed value is less than 100% of the investment.

Investors may own other capital assets that have special tax consequences on disposition. The tax consequences of assets like your principal residence—a personal-use property—will be discussed in this section.

Other properties, like listed personal properties and the disposition of small business shares are discussed in the professional certificate tax courses offered online by *Knowledge Bureau*. Laypeople are invited to start the program with a course entitled *Introduction to Personal Tax Preparation*.

 Tax Moves

Adding capital assets to your investments will help you to accrue value on a tax deferred basis until there is an actual or deemed disposition of the property.

When the assets produce income—dividends, rents, royalties or interest, for example—those income sources may have special tax attributes that help you to average down the taxes you pay throughout your lifetime.

On disposition, only 50% of the taxable gain is added to income. Capital losses, too, can be lucrative as they can offset current year gains or if there are none, be carried back three years or carried forward indefinitely to offset future capital gains.

Experienced tax help is important before you buy, sell or transfer your assets, but despite the complexity, adding capital assets to your wealth management plan is a smart tax move.

26 ACCOUNTING: For Investment Expenses

THE DIFFERENCE BETWEEN GOOD AND BAD DEBT often lies in its tax deductibility. Those who leverage their assets as part of their strategic plan to build wealth, will often do so more successfully by earning more income and increasing their net worth. However, should you borrow to invest, claiming tax deductible interest is often the only consolation for the eroding effect that the costs of debt can have on personal wealth.

> **ESSENTIAL TAX FACT** ▶ **Carrying Charges, Such as Interest Expenses May be Deducted when there is a Potential for Earning Income from Property.** In the case of investments, that means income from property: interest, dividends, rents and royalties. Capital gains are specifically excluded from this list. Interest is not deductible unless you acquire an asset with the potential to earn income from property.

Borrowing to Invest in Registered Accounts. When you incur expenses to invest your money, a tax deduction is only allowed if the potential to earn income is in a non-registered environment. That means interest on loans used for the purposes of investing in an RRSP, TFSA, RESP or RDSP is not deductible. Nor is interest paid on a tax-exempt property, like your principal residence, unless there is an expectation rental income will be earned.

> **TAX FORM FACT.** Eligible carrying charges are all claimed on the T1 Return—See *Statement of Investment Income, carrying charges.*

The total carrying charges are then deducted on Line 221 and serve to offset all other income of the year, so they can be an important way to reduce overall tax burdens and increase eligibility for social benefits and credits. But for this reason, these expenses are often audited.

Audit Check Point

- ✔ You must be prepared to trace all interest you have claimed back to a non-registered investment that has the potential to earn income.

Consider the following list of deductible amounts carefully to be sure you haven't missed any. If you have, consider filing Form T1ADJ Adjustment Request to recover these errors or omissions up to 10 years back.

Checklist of Deductible Carrying Charges

- ☐ *Accounting fees* relating to the preparation of tax schedules for investment income reporting.

- ☐ *Investment counsel fees.* These do not include commissions paid on buying or selling investments. These commissions form part of the adjusted cost base of the investment or reduce proceeds of disposition from the investment.

- ☐ *Taxable benefits reported on the T4 Slip for employer-provided loans* that were used for investment purposes. (Again, often missed: ask your tax specialist about this if you have been fortunate enough to receive this perk of employment)

- ☐ *Life insurance policy interest costs* if an investment loan was taken against cash values. Complete form *T2210 Verification of Policy Loan Interest by Insurer* to justify the claim.

- ☐ *Management or safe custody fees* (but not a bank safety deposit box, which is no longer tax deductible after 2013).

- ☐ *Interest paid on investment loans* if there is a reasonable expectation of income from the investment, even if the value of the investment has diminished.

Leveraging to Invest. Now that you know what can be deducted, know this: many investors wonder if they should leverage existing capital assets in order to invest more into the marketplace. Often, they are approached to consider different leveraged loan arrangements, particularly if they believe they have not saved enough for retirement.

Be sure to crunch the numbers over the life of the loan. The potential for investment income must be present, not just from a tax point of view, but also in order for you to pay off your interest (before tax). You will need cash flow to do this. The investment must be able to pay real dollars on a guaranteed basis before your risk can be properly assessed. Otherwise you will have to dip into other funds to pay your loans. You need to assess those possibilities with your financial advisor, so that you can sleep at night.

Diminished Value in Assets. Have your assets diminished in value since you acquired them with a loan? Will your interest still be deductible in that case? The answer is yes. You can continue to deduct the interest until the loan is fully repaid, even if you sell the assets. If you did not use the proceeds to pay down the loan, then you can deduct only the portion of interest that would have been paid had you done so.

 Tax Moves

Borrowing to invest, particularly in a low interest rate environment, will help you to build wealth. However, it's important not to let the tax tail wag the dog. You must be able to pay back the loan, even if your assets diminish in value.

In addition, borrowing costs to invest in a registered account, like an RRSP or a TFSA will not be deductible. Remember that one of the ways to increase the returns on your investment is to be vigilant about interest costs and management fees. If you must pay them, be sure they are tax deductible.

27 MANAGING CORNERSTONES: Your Principal Residences

THE OWNERSHIP OF A PRINCIPAL RESIDENCE is a very important part of building your net worth and there are significant tax advantages for doing so, too. Under current rules, each household (that is, an adult taxpayer and spouse if they have one) can designate one principal residence to be tax exempt on sale.

But, a principal residence is classified to be "personal-use property," which means that any losses on disposition are deemed to be nil (that's right—not claimable on the tax return).

> **ESSENTIAL TAX FACT.** ▶ **A Tax Exempt Principal Residence is a Solid Cornerstone of Wealth for Canadian Households.** A principal residence can include a house, cottage, condo, duplex, apartment, or trailer that is ordinarily inhabited by you or some family member *at some time during the year*. There is no minimum number of days for this purpose, either.

Principal Residences on Large Land Holdings. There is more good news. Except where the principal residence is a share in a co-operative housing corporation, the principal residence also includes the land immediately subjacent to the housing unit and *up to one-half hectare* of subjacent property that contributes to the use of the housing unit as a residence. If the lot size exceeds one-half hectare, it may be included in the principal residence if it can be shown to be necessary for the use of the housing unit.

For tax compliance purposes, if you have had only one principal residence, used solely for personal use in the entire period you have owned it, all you have to do at the time of disposition, is to report the disposition of the property on Schedule 3 and provide the address, proceeds and year you acquired the property.

TAX FORM FACT. ▶ Report the disposition of your principal residence on *Form T2091—Designation of a Property as a Principal Residence by an Individual.*

Do so even if there are no taxes to be paid. As discussed, it is possible that gain on your eligible property is tax exempt.

Audit Check Point

✔ Starting in tax year 2017, it is a requirement to file Form T2091, with big penalties for failure to do so, even if your disposition is fully tax exempt.

Penalties for Failure to File T2091. It's expensive not to comply fully with these new rules: penalties for late reporting of a principal residence sale will be $100 per day, to a maximum of $8,000.

Also, the CRA can look back to the 2016 tax year for any audit activity in the future, it's important to keep good notes on the reasons for the disposition. CRA has recently cracked down on real estate transactions in which the intention was to make a profit by flipping the property quickly. That has serious income tax consequences—your property can be considered to be inventory with resulting gains considered to be fully taxable.

But these transactions could have GST/HST consequences too. If the intention is the flip the property, or if the residence is outside of Canada, the home will not qualify for the new housing rebate on GST/HST paid.

It pays to see a tax professional to check out your obligations to report a sale, transfer or deemed disposition of a personal residence anytime after 2015. There are additional rules for non-residents or trusts which hold a principal residence.

More Than One Residence. Where more than one property is owned, and the family uses both residences at some time during the year, the calculation of the principal residence exemption becomes slightly more difficult when one property is disposed of.

If you owned your properties for a long period of time, as is the case with many family cottages, for example, know that for periods including 1971 to 1981, each spouse could declare one of the properties as their principal residence. This allowed for the sheltering of any capital gain that accrued in this period provided that each property was owned by a different spouse.

But starting in 1982, only one property per year can be designated as a principal residence for the family.

As you can imagine, these rules can be quite confusing to most taxpayers. Fortunately, it is all sorted out on *Form T2091—Designation of a Property as a Principal Residence by an Individual*. This form helps you to calculate the exempt portion of any capital gain when you sell one of two or more principal residences in the family.

$100,000 Capital Gains Election. It's also very important for anyone who made a capital gains election on capital assets in 1994 to keep a copy of *Form T664 Capital Gains Election* with their will so that executors can take that 1994 valuation into account on the disposition of assets on the final return. It bumped up the cost base of eligible properties to $100,000.

This is especially important for executors of estates to know. Do get some professional help with this form.

Mixed Use of Principal Residence. When you start using your principal residence for income-producing purposes, for example as a rental or home office, "change of use" rules must be observed for tax purposes. The fair market value of the property must be assessed in this case, because you are deemed to have disposed of the property and immediately reacquired it at the same fair market value, changing its classification from a personal-use property to an income-producing property.

> **ESSENTIAL TAX FACT** ▶ **Gains on Change of Use of Principal Residence Can be Deferred.** An election can be made not to recognize the change in use of the property until the time of sale of the property or when you rescind the election. Any capital gain will then be accounted for. But the capital gain is exempt if the home is designated in each year as your principal residence and you are a resident of Canada.

In the meantime, so long as the personal use of your property remains more than the rental use; simply report rental income as usual. If you use it as a home workspace, claim the expenses in the appropriate manner. However, it's very important that, while your property is used for income-producing purposes of any kind, no Capital Cost Allowance (CCA) is used as a deduction, even for a small portion or in one particular year. This will compromise the principal residence exemption on that portion of the property and the change of use rules.

If, at some time in the future, there is a change in use again, for example, if the property is used solely as a principal residence, the same FMV assessment must be made, as you are deemed to have disposed of and reacquired the property for this new use. Again, an election is made so that the tax consequences are accounted for on actual disposition of the property in the future.

Flipping Principal Residences. During a real estate boom, the disposition of real property can be very lucrative, especially if you can earn one tax-exempt gain after another with your principal residence. But, how often can you do that before it raises eyebrows at the CRA?

If you buy and sell real estate too often, CRA may disallow your claim for the principal residence exemption. Even worse, they could disallow the capital gains treatment that comes with a 50% inclusion rate and require reporting of 100% of the gain as a gross profit if they think you are in the business of buying and selling homes.

The more closely your business or occupation is related to commercial real estate transactions, for example, if you are a real estate broker or builder, the more likely it is that any gain realized from such a transaction will not qualify for the principal residence exemption at all and be considered business income rather than a capital gain.

The courts have considered some of the following criteria on a case-by-case basis to guide us in assessing the right tax filing requirements:

Checklist for Determining Tax Attributes of Real Estate Dispositions

- ☐ the taxpayer's intention with respect to the real estate at the time of its purchase,
- ☐ feasibility of the taxpayer's intention,
- ☐ geographical location and zoned use of the real estate acquired,
- ☐ extent to which these intentions were carried out by the taxpayer,
- ☐ evidence that the taxpayer's intention changed after purchase of the real estate,
- ☐ the nature of the business, profession, calling or trade of the taxpayer and associates,
- ☐ the extent to which borrowed money was used to finance the real estate acquisition and the terms of the financing, if any, arranged,
- ☐ the length of time throughout which the real estate was held by the taxpayer,
- ☐ factors which motivated the sale of the real estate, and
- ☐ evidence that the taxpayer and/or associates had dealt extensively in real estate.

Employer-Required Moves. When your employer requires you to move at least 40 kilometers closer to your place of employment and you keep your principal residence but rent out your home while you are gone, it is possible to elect no change in use and designate that property as your principal residence while you are gone. This election is valid for up to four years but may be extended if you move back into the home before the end of the year in which your employment terminates.

Claiming Moving Expenses. Where the move is required by the employer and you sell your home at a loss, it is possible to receive a tax-free reimbursement of those losses, in amounts up to $15,000, should your employer choose to assist you. After this one half of the reimbursement over $15,000 is tax free. See the discussion of perks in this section.

In other cases, you may have to move and leave a vacant residence behind while you try to sell it. You may claim up to a maximum of $5,000 as a moving expense on your tax return for the costs incurred in the meantime, including mortgage interest, property taxes, insurance and utilities.

Audit Check Point

✔ When it comes to moving expenses, be sure to keep those receipts and speak to your tax advisor about eligibility requirements before filing your return. Complete form T1M. These claims are often subject to audit.

To qualify to claim moving expenses, the taxpayer must move at least 40 kilometres closer to the location where they earn income from employment or self employment. Students can often claim moving expenses to be in full time attendance at a post-secondary program at a university, college or other educational institution.

In addition, the taxpayer must stop working or operating a business at the old location, and establish a new home where the taxpayer and family will reside. The following income sources earned at the new location *will not be considered qualifying income* for the purposes of claiming moving expenses:

• investment income

• employment insurance benefits

• other income sources, except student awards (see below).

Checklist of Allowable Moving Expenses

- ☐ cost of selling the former residence, including real estate commissions, penalties for paying off a mortgage, legal fees, and advertising costs

- ☐ costs of keeping a vacant old residence (to a maximum of $5,000) while actively attempting to sell it, including mortgage interest, property taxes, insurance premiums and heat and power

- ☐ expenses of purchasing the new home (as long as the old home was owned), including transfer taxes and legal fees

- ☐ temporary living expenses (meals and lodging) for up to 15 days

- ☐ removal and storage costs including insurance for household effects, costs of moving a boat, trailer, or mobile home (to the extent the costs of moving the mobile do not exceed the costs of moving the contents alone)

- ☐ transportation costs

- ☐ costs of meals en route (100%—no 50% restriction)

- ☐ cost of cancelling an unexpired lease

- ☐ cost of revising legal documents to show the new address, replacing driver's licenses and auto permits, cost of utility connections and disconnections

INELIGIBLE EXPENSES—The following expenses are not deductible:

- expenses to make the former property more saleable

- losses on the sale of the former property and expenses incurred before the move (such as house hunting or job hunting)

- value of items that could not be moved (plants, frozen foods, paint, cleaning products, ammunition, etc.)

- expenses to clean a rented residence

- replacement costs for items not moved such as tool sheds, firewood, drapes, etc.

- mail forwarding costs and cost of transformers or adaptors for household appliances

- GST/HST on new residence and expenses that are reimbursed

Note: students claiming moving expenses may be affected by the rules which exempt scholarship, bursary and fellowship income after 2006 when they are full-time students. Since moving expenses are limited to taxable income from employment, self-employment, or scholarships, it is possible that students with non-taxable scholarships will be unable to claim moving expenses.

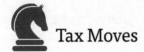 Tax Moves

Your principal residence can be a great investment if you can use the principal residence exemption to pocket your accrued gains in the future. But, your principal residence exemption may be at risk if you don't follow proper tax filing procedures.

You must file Form T2019 even for a tax exempt gain. And if you flip your principal residences often enough, the gains may be fully or partially included in income. Therefore, guard your access to this lucrative exemption well—it can significantly increase your net worth—but you will need to pay attention to the tax rules on changing the use of your home to earn rental income as well as CRA's power to dispute and reclassify your income reporting on disposition.

28 MIXED USE: Home Office & Auto Expenses

AUTO AND HOME OFFICE EXPENSES are common claims made by employees, self-employed people and rental property owners. For these reasons, we are discussing them at the end of this section.

Audit Check Point

✔ Auto expenses and home office claims are amongst the most commonly audited by the CRA, and the tax rules for claiming them can be complicated. For these reasons, keep the required distance logs and receipts used to make these claims.

Employees are subject to further requirements:

- A completed Form T2200 *Declaration of Conditions of Employment*, on which the employer certifies that the employee is required to maintain the home office or use the car for employment purposes, and pay the expenses out-of-pocket is required. This form must be signed by the employer.

- Employees' claims for home workspace and auto expenses are made on Form T777 *Statement of Employment Expenses*.

We'll start with the simpler of the two: the expenses of the home workspace, and then take you through a case study in claiming auto expenses, too.

HOME WORKSPACE EXPENSES. For an employee to qualify to make home workspace expense claims, the space must be

- the place where the individual principally (more than 50% of the time) performs the office or employment duties, or

- used exclusively in the period to earn income from the office or employment and, on a regular and continuous basis, for meeting customers or other persons in the ordinary course of performing the office or employment duties.

The home workspace must be separated from other living areas in the home, but does not need to be a separate room. The home may either be owned by the taxpayer or rented.

To determine the amount of deductible home office expenses, total expenses for the costs of maintaining the home are pro-rated by the following formula:

$$\frac{\text{Square footage of the home workspace}}{\text{Square footage of the entire living space}} \quad X \quad \text{Total Eligible Expenses} = \text{Deductible Expenses}$$

ESSENTIAL TAX FACT ▶ **The Rules for Claiming Home Offices Differ by Taxfiler.** Can employed and self-employed people claim the same expenses? The answer is no.

Whether you are employed or self-employed matters, when claiming home office expenses, as described below. Rental property owners also face different rules.

- *Employees who do not earn commission.* These taxpayers may claim utilities, maintenance and repairs, including light bulbs and cleaning supplies, and rent.

- *Commissioned sales employees* may claim utilities; maintenance and repairs, including light bulbs and cleaning supplies, rent, insurance, and property taxes.

- *Self-employed people* can claim: utilities, maintenance and repairs, including light bulbs and cleaning supplies, rent, insurance, property taxes, interest; and capital cost allowance (although this is not a good idea if the home is your principal residence, as you have learned. CCA claims will compromise the principal residence exemption.)

Claims are Limited to Income. An employee may not claim home office expenses that exceed income from the employer. A self-employed person may not create or increase a business loss with a claim of home office expenses. But the good news is that non-deductible home office expenses may be carried forward (indefinitely) to reduce income in future years.

Rental Property Owners. Office in the home expenses can be claimed when the taxpayer is earning income from a business or property. Rental income is classified as income from property. But to be deductible, the expense must be made for the purpose of gaining or producing that income, it must not be on account of capital or to produce exempt income, it must not be a personal or living expense and it must be reasonable. When these criteria are met, the home workspace expenses should be allowed. Office expenses such as pens, pencils, paper clips, stationery, and stamps are also allowed.

AUTO EXPENSES. The rules of claiming these costs are similar for both employed and self-employed people, but for rental property owners, there are special rules.

Employees. Automotive expenses can only be deducted if they are not reimbursed by the employer. An employee who receives a reasonable allowance for the use of the vehicle may not claim the related expenses. Otherwise, employees can deduct auto expenses when they pay their own auto expenses and are required to use their vehicle in carrying out their duties of employment.

For any expenses of employment to be allowed, the employer must sign Form T2200 *Declaration of Conditions of Employment*, stating the employee must use the auto for employment and is responsible for paying auto expenses, does not receive a reasonable allowance for auto expenses, and will not be reimbursed for them (if there is a partial reimbursement this must be accounted for).

Rental Property Owners. For those who own *one property*, reasonable motor vehicle expenses can be deducted if all the following criteria are met: income is received from only one property in the general vicinity of where you live, you personally do some or all of the necessary repairs and maintenance on that property and you use your vehicle to transport tools and materials to the property. In this case you can't claim auto expenses for rent collection.

Audit Check Point

- ✔ Know the difference in audit requirements when you rent one property as opposed to two or more.

If you own two or more properties, you can claim auto expenses incurred to collect rent, supervise repairs and manage the properties in addition to the expenses listed above. The properties don't have to be in your neighborhood, but they must be in at least two different sites away from your residence.

Business vs. Personal Driving. For those who use their vehicle for both personal and business/employment purposes, it is necessary to keep an auto log that records distance driven for both purposes, for at least one year (the base year).

After this you can keep the records for as few as three consecutive months. So long as your driving patterns do not vary on either side by more than 10%, you will be able to claim the ratio determined by the formula:

$$\frac{\text{Current Year Km for Log Period}}{\text{Base Year Km for Same Period}} \quad \text{X} \quad \text{Base Year Full-Year Ratio}$$

Personal use includes vehicle use by other family members, friends, etc. In other words, total personal use of the vehicle is assessed, not just the use by the person using the auto for business or employment.

Mixed Use of Auto. When there is a "mixed use" of the car, the expenses are first totalled. This is based on your actual receipts and a log of cash expenditures, like car washes or parking. Then the total costs are multiplied by the allowable business use ratio.

What auto expenses can be claimed? There are two types of auto expenses that can be claimed: fixed and operating, and this can have an important effect on the type of car you buy or lease and how much money you spend.

- *Fixed Expenses include:* Capital Cost Allowance (subject to a maximum cost of $30,000, plus taxes—see below), leasing costs (subject to a maximum of $800 a month, plus taxes—see below), interest costs (subject to a maximum of $300 a month—see below)

- *Operating expenses include:* gas and oil, tires, maintenance and repairs, car washes (keep track of coin operated washes), insurance, license fees, auto club memberships, parking (generally parking expenses while on business travel trips are fully deductible and not subject to a proration for personal component)

In addition, you should know that in general, "cents-per-kilometer" claims are disallowed except in specific instances where a "simplified method" is allowed. These include claims for medical travel or moving expenses, but not employment or business expenses.

Fixed Cost Restrictions for Passenger Vehicles. How much you can claim for fixed expenses is restricted, as you can see, and this depends on the cost of the car you drive and for what purposes. Unfortunately, there is more complexity here: there are two types of vehicles for tax purposes, which depends on their design and use:

- *Passenger Vehicles* are designed to carry no more than nine passengers and are not on the "specifically excluded" list below.
- *Motor Vehicles* are vehicles that are not passenger vehicles. There are no restrictions on the deductible amount for depreciation, leasing or interest expenses.

Vehicles are passenger vehicles if they are designed to carry nine or fewer passengers unless they fall into a specifically excluded list:

- ambulances, taxis, busses used in the business of transporting passengers;
- hearses and other vehicles used in the transport of passengers in the course of a funeral;
- any clearly marked emergency medical vehicle which is used to transport paramedics and their emergency medical equipment;
- motor vehicles acquired to be immediately sold, rented or leased;
- pick-up trucks that are used more than 50% of the time to transport goods;
- vans that are used more than 90% of the time to transport goods; and
- extended cab pick-up trucks used primarily for the transportation of goods,
- equipment or passengers in the course of earning or producing income at a work site at least 30 kilometres from any community having a population of at least 40,000.

ESSENTIAL TAX FACT ▶ **Think Tax Before Buying Your Car.** The first rule to remember when buying a car "for tax purposes" is that you may not be able to write off the full cost if it is a passenger vehicle.

Claiming Capital Cost Allowance. For tax purposes you will claim a deduction for depreciation or wear and tear on your vehicle or other income-producing assets on a Capital Cost Allowance (CCA) Schedule, which applies a specific rate to specific classes of assets. If you're claiming the cost as part of your employment expenses, this CCA schedule will likely be associated with the T777 form. New rules increased the available deductions for assets acquired after November 20, 2018.

Class 10. Motor Vehicles and Passenger Vehicles that Cost Less Than $30,000 Belong to Class 10. CCA is used at your option, so if your income is not high enough, you can save your *"Undepreciated Capital Cost"* (UCC) balance to make a larger claim next year. Note, in the year that the vehicle is purchased, the claim is limited to 50% of the normal CCA allowed. This is known as the "half-year" rule.

Things get complicated when you dispose of these assets. If, for example, it was the last asset in the Class 10 pool of assets, the remaining balance must be deducted as a *Terminal Loss*. If other assets exist in the Class 10 pool, then the reduced CCA balance is used to calculate the CCA claim for the year.

If after removing the amount from the Class 10 pool, the balance in negative, this negative amount is taken into income as *Recapture*. This means you have taken too much for your CCA deduction over the years and must include the over-deducted amounts in income.

Class 10.1 Passenger Vehicles Belong in Class 10.1 if They Cost More Than $30,000. These cars are subject to restriction. If the cost of your car was $50,000 claim only $30,000 plus taxes. There is a "half-year rule" on acquisition: only 50% of the normal CCA is claimed in the year you acquire the luxury car.

Again, it gets more complicated: when you dispose of a Class 10.1 asset, there is another half-year CCA calculation. There is no terminal loss or recapture of capital cost allowance on the disposition of a Class 10.1 vehicle. This restriction reflects the fact that the class never included the full capital cost of the vehicle to begin with.

Change of Use Rules for Your Automobile. If the use of a vehicle changes from business to personal use, the CCA pool must be adjusted. The estimated Fair Market Value of the vehicle at the time of the change must be removed from the CCA pool as a deemed disposition and this could cause some of the tax consequences described above (recapture or terminal loss for a motor vehicle or the half-year limitation for a passenger vehicle).

Interest Costs. Remember that your claim for interest costs will be restricted to $300 a month if you own a passenger vehicle. In a low-interest rate environment, this shouldn't be a big problem, but your software will be calculating the restriction, and you need to know why.

Leasing Costs. These costs will be restricted to $800 a month plus taxes, if you lease a passenger vehicle, something to think about before you choose the Bentley.

Is it better to own or lease a car for tax purposes? Use your tax software to project forward your after-tax results for at least three years to work out any CCA restrictions, including the "half-year rules." That will give you a good understanding of the tax results. Or, ask your tax or financial professional to do this for you.

BE CAREFUL WITH RESTRICTED USE CLAIMS. Home office and auto expenses are amongst the most common discretionary claims made by Canadians but they are fraught with tax audit risk. Be sure to understand the rules and how to defend your claims before making them.

Tax Moves & Audit-Busters

TAX EROSION NEVER STOPS. Much of the income you make personally will be reduced by taxes every two weeks throughout your lifetime; stunting the disposable income you have left to save for your future. Those savings will be subject to tax again when you use them for retirement and before a legacy is passed along to your heirs. Hone your tax moves for all your earnings—active and passive—to come out ahead.

PUT YOUR FOCUS ON YOUR PRE-TAX EARNINGS. The sooner you put a whole dollar to work for you, the sooner your capital—human and financial—will increase its productivity.

USE CORPORATE DOLLARS TO FUND YOUR LIFESTYLE. You can exponentially increase the value of your compensation package by negotiating for tax free or taxable benefits. Your employer will likely pay a lower tax rate corporately than you will pay personally. Those bigger, after-tax dollars can fund certain costs, like a car, education or athletic club membership, at a fraction of what it would cost you. That leaves you with more money for investment purposes.

MANAGE THE TIME VALUE OF MONEY, AND YOUR DEBT. Use the *time value of money* to your advantage—never to that of your creditors. When you pay expensive, non-deductible interest costs to your creditors, the time value of money works in their favor, not yours. If you are serious about honing your tax moves to win in your financial life, reduce non-deductible debt and increase tax-assisted savings as a priority. Start by creating "new money pools" from low lying fruit: tax refunds, tax-exempt social benefits and the return of tax-paid capital. Then, start making progress in paying off your debt and redirecting funds towards your future.

TAX PREFERENCES TURBO-CHARGE THE TIME VALUE OF MONEY. Money grows faster when invested in a tax free or tax-deferred basis, sooner. A common way to do so is to invest in "registered" accounts.

TAX-EFFICIENT INVESTING LEADS TO RETIREMENT INCOME ADEQUACY. Your greatest opportunity to secure future income, begins with saving more of your pre-tax earnings on a tax deferred basis. A TFSA, RRSP or an employer-sponsored RPP (Registered Pension Plan) are great investment vehicles. Choosing such a tax efficient route for your savings will help your money grow faster, so you will have more capital to last longer in retirement.

INVEST IN THE RIGHT ORDER. Because taxes can erode accumulated wealth at marginal tax rates of 50% and more over time, a focus on the right order of investing is important. To build purchasing power, returns must be higher than the rate of inflation annually, the rate of taxation, and professional financial fees.

IT'S IMPORTANT TO DIVERSIFY INCOME SOURCES IN NON-REGISTERED ACCOUNTS. You will want to earn income sources which attract the least amount of tax, and where possible, split investment income with other family members to pay the least taxes possible as an economic unit.

PLAN CAPITAL ENCROACHMENT WISELY. Time withdrawals of taxable income sources from registered and non-registered investments with a view to minimizing taxes. Keep your eye on four things when you make investment moves: how to accumulate, grow, preserve and transition the most sustainable wealth—after taxes—over your lifetime. The objective is to average down the taxes paid on over time by planning to "realize" income for tax purposes at the lowest possible marginal tax rates over the lifecycle of the investment.

Tax Tools of the Trade

INCREASE YOUR PRE-TAX EARNINGS. The sooner you put a whole dollar to work for you, the sooner your working capital will increase its productivity in your favor. Remember that employees can reduce tax erosion by completing the TD1 *Personal Tax Credit Return* and its sister, Form T1213 *Request to Reduce Tax Deductions at Source*, to reduce withholding taxes. The self employed should be sure to pay only the correct amount of quarterly tax instalments.

READ YOUR T4 SLIP CAREFULLY. You need to know that taxable benefits will be included in Box 14 of your T4 *Statement of Remuneration Paid (slip)*. That means you will not need to add them into income again when you file your return. Some of them qualify for certain deductions and so you may see reference to them in Boxes 30 to 88 at the bottom of the slip.

REDUCE THE COST OF YOUR AUTOMOBILE BENEFITS. The standby charge your employer calculates for your auto benefits can be reduced if you use the employer-provided vehicle more than 50% of the time for business purposes and your personal use driving is not more than 1667 kilometers per 30 day period, or a total of 20,004 kilometres per year. Operating expenses can also be calculated as one half the normal stand-by charge. Use Form RC18 *Calculating Automobile Benefits*.

EMPLOYMENT EXPENSE CLAIMS WILL ATTRACT AUDITORS. The *Income Tax Act* is very specific about the expenses that may be claimed by employees, and their perks. Report expenses on Form T777 *Statement of Employment Expenses* and complete Form T2200 *Declaration of Conditions of Employment* by the employer to ace a tax audit. Keep receipts and an auto distance log.

RECOVER TAXES PREVIOUSLY PAID ON CAPITAL GAINS. File *Form T1A Request for Loss Carry Back* to offset capital gains of prior or future years.

REPORT THE DISPOSITION OF YOUR PRINCIPAL RESIDENCE. Use *Form T2091—Designation of a Property as a Principal Residence by an Individual.* Do so even if there are no taxes to be paid. It is possible that gain on your eligible property is tax exempt.

CLAIM RENTAL PROPERTY INCOME AND EXPENSES. Use *Form T776 Statement of Real Estate Rentals* to report on a calendar year basis—January to December.

Your Audit-Buster Checklist

- ✔ **BE CONFIDENT IN YOUR TAXPAYER RIGHTS.** Be sure you understand your rights to perks and deductions and keep all documentation to mount a confident defense should your return be chosen for audit.

- ✔ **CRA HAS ENORMOUS POWERS TO COLLECT TAX DEBT.** This can include garnishing your wages or seizing your assets, including your principal residence. Therefore, the debt you must manage first is what you owe to CRA, which has recently received over $350 million to collect over $7 billion in tax debt.[10]

- ✔ **MOVING EXPENSES, AUTO EXPENSES, RENTAL PROPERTY EXPENSES AND HOME OFFICE CLAIMS ARE AMONGST THE MOST COMMONLY AUDITED.** For these reasons, keep the required distance logs and receipts. In the case of rental property owners, know the difference in claiming auto expenses in cases when you rent out one property as opposed to two or more.

---

10 March 22, 2016 Federal Budget

PART V

THE VICTORY LAP
Tax Savvy Retirements

29 MAXIMIZING: Your Tax-Efficient Retirement Income

ACCORDING TO THE CREDIT SUISSE GLOBAL WEALTH Report[11], wealth accumulates for three principal reasons:

1. *Precaution:* When people manage risks to their income and savings due to changing economic or life events,

2. *Readiness:* For the future, mainly for retirement income needs and

3. *Intergenerational Transfers:* People wish to pass on their wealth, and in doing so, dispose of debt and protect their financial assets from ongoing financial erosion.

Done well, the money you save and protect throughout your lifetime will help you do those three things: manage risks, prepare for retirement and help you pass along what's left for your heirs.

In between, are your tax moves: by making sure you use the tax preferences you have learned about end up in the right financial "buckets," in your retirement will enable you to maximize the purchasing power of your assets when your personal earning capacity stops.

As you move closer to retirement, your savings must be able to do three things:

(a) *Receive Adequate Pension and Investment Income* to sustain and increase your required cash flow to cover budgeted needs and cost increases due to the inflation, or unexpected issues: the increased cost of medical expenses, heating or gasoline costs, or tax hikes, for example.

---

11 2nd Global Wealth Report, 2011 in collaboration with the Credit Suisse Research Institute and Professors Anthony Shorrocks and Jim Davies, Oxford University Press.

(b) Continue to Grow Asset Pools, preferably on a tax exempt, tax reduced or tax-deferred basis, to meet new spending needs adequately, without too much interference by increasing taxation.

ESSENTIAL TAX FACT ▶ **You do have control over your tax costs.** Not so with new carbon taxes or increased medical deductibles. When it comes to your income taxes, always remember that it is your legal right to arrange your affairs within the framework of the law to pay the least tax possible as a family unit; one which you should optimize, with pension income splitting and retirement income layering techniques.

(c) Dodge Expensive Fees. Reducing the costs related to borrowing or investing will increase returns on your capital: debt servicing costs, financial management and investment fees, legal fees and accounting fees require annual review.

These three specific goals for the performance of your retirement income sources will help you to set ongoing investment priorities, when the time comes to live off your accumulated savings in retirement.

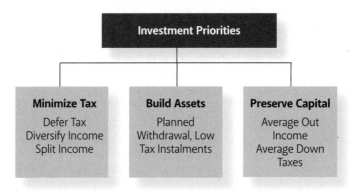

After-Tax Income Boosters for Retirees. It has recently become easier to benefit from tax preferences in retirement. The federal government has provided several tax breaks that help today's retirees increase their after-tax receipts from retirement savings.

Specifically, pension income splitting with your spouse, which was introduced in 2007, and the ability to save within a Tax-Free Savings Account (TFSA), introduced in 2008, provide retirees with the opportunities to develop winning strategies for their capital.

But there have been several additional changes, discussed in numerical detail in the *Essential Tax Facts Appendices.* For example:

- *Canada Pension Plan premiums* will be on the rise beginning in 2019 with a subsequent increase in benefits down the line, and, also in 2019, the CPP death benefit becomes a flat $2500 regardless of contribution level.

- A new *Canada Caregiver Amount* changes the way that infirm dependants are claimed.

- New *medical expenses* are added annually to embellish on tax assistance.

- *Indexing* has increased tax brackets, to reflect inflation erosion on purchasing power.

- *Taxation of Dividends from private corporations* will continue to change each year over the next few years, as a result of corporate tax reforms.

- The *Capital Gains Exemption* on shares of small business corporations has increased and is now indexed, while the *Capital Gains Exemption* on farm and fishing properties was increased to $1,000,000, where it remains without indexation.

- The *Clawbacks* or income levels at which the Age Amount and OAS is clawed back continues to benefit from indexing.

ESSENTIAL TAX FACT ▶ **Retirees Must be Concerned About Their After-Tax Incomes.** Because taxes arise on both income and capital pools; planning for a tax-efficient retirement requires the careful management of after-tax income through a process of income "layering", that limits the encroachment of capital to fund needs and wants and leaves the rest to grow with sound investment choices.

Retirement Income Planning. Most people will experience three retirement income planning stages, in which tax efficiency can add particular value:

- **PRE-RETIREMENT (PRE-AGE 60):** Certain employer-sponsored pension plans (Registered Pension Plans or RPPs) allow for a "phased-in" retirement at age 55 while continuing to accrue pension benefits, provided the employee is entitled to an unreduced pension by virtual of age or pensionable service. In other cases, taxpayers who have accumulated enough in their RRSPs may choose to make taxable withdrawals. In the first instance, income splitting with the spouse is allowed; not so for those who save within the RRSP. They must wait to age 65 to income split.

- **EARLY RETIREMENT (AGE 60 TO 70):** These are the years, in which both OAS and CPP benefits can be postponed. This will allow for a window of time in which other taxable income sources may be reported— RRSP accumulations, for example—in order to "average down" taxes on the capital accumulated here. Full retirement begins for the purposes of generating taxable income from the Old Age Security (age 65 to 70), Canada Pension Plan (it's mandatory to take it at age 70) and the Registered Retirement Savings Plan (you must withdraw funds to create a pension benefit in a Registered Retirement Income Fund (RRIF) or annuity, after age 71).

- **LATE RETIREMENT (AGE 71 AND BEYOND):** There are few tax deferral opportunities for pension income sources after age 71; with the exception of the Tax-Free Savings Account (TFSA). Money that is withdrawn from an RPP, RRSP or RRIF and subject to tax, can be reinvested in a TFSA to create a tax-free pension over time. Unfortunately the annual limits are low; nonetheless it is a great opportunity to save money on taxes in the future. Otherwise, a close eye on the orderly withdrawal of taxable pension benefits to the top of a tax bracket (but not the highest one) can provide tax relief. For high income earners, a diversification of investment income sources can help reduce overall marginal tax rates.

Choosing the right financial advisor is important in this period of transition. You may wish to look for an *MFA—Retirement Services Specialist* [TM12] for these skills. Following is a checklist of questions to consider in planning your retirement income withdrawal and investment strategies.

Pre-Retirement Planning Checklist:

☐ *Retirement Period.* What is your anticipated retirement period, based on your life expectancy?

☐ *Inter-Spousal Pension Income Plan.* Does your retirement vision match your spouse's? What will combined income levels be? How will capital preservation plans be impacted by each spouse's vision?

☐ *Required Pension and Investment Income level.* What is the required income level for your anticipated retirement period? (identify how to fund basic needs and lifestyle wants with a budget and tax estimation for income).

☐ *Income Risk Management Plan.* What expectations do you have for return on your investments in both the short and long term, and how much risk are you willing to take to achieve that?

---

12 The MFA designation is offered by Knowledge Bureau. For more information call 1-866-953-4769.

☐ *Anticipated Growth in Capital.* How much additional savings can you expect to create by taking a tax-efficient approach to the accumulation, growth, preservation and transition of your capital? Will preparing a new budget for anticipated needs and wants help? Can debt management help?

☐ *Capital Encroachment Strategy.* What is the precise amount of withdrawal you are prepared to make to fund needs or wants? This is important because withdrawing too much income, in the wrong hands, can put you into a quarterly tax remittance profile, which you will definitely want to avoid if you didn't need the money in the first place. Overpaying the government won't help preserve your capital pools.

STRATEGIES FOR ACHIEVING RESULTS. At Knowledge Bureau, we teach our students a "Real Wealth Management" strategy around which to think about family wealth management. It provides a consistent framework for strategic planning with your tax and financial advisors, focusing on the decisions required to continually accumulate, grow, preserve and transition wealth in the most tax and cost efficient way, *even in retirement.*

When we apply these elements to retirement income planning, the following process emerges to consistently make decisions about income requirements:

TAX-EFFICIENT RETIREMENT INCOME PLANNING GUIDE
©Knowledge Bureau, Inc.

1. Categorizing Your Concerns	What are the trigger questions that require financial decision-making?	Stage Your Solutions
☐ **Life Triggers**	• I want to retire in 3 to 5 years. What should I be thinking about? • What do I need to do to retire today? • I wish to retire gradually. What's the most tax savvy way to do this?	☐ Pre-Age 60 ☐ Age 60 to 70 ☐ Age 71 plus
☐ **Financial Triggers**	• When should I begin to encroach upon my investments to create pension income? • Should I take CPP early? Postpone my OAS? • How much can I receive in benefits from my employer-sponsored plan? • How much pension will my RRSP create? • I have lost my job and will not be going back to work. How can I protect my severance package from tax? • I have health issues and most leave my workplace. Should I tap into the CPP Disability Plan? Wage loss replacement? Medical insurance plans? • I have enough money, I have achieved my goals and I want to retire fully.	☐ Pre-Retirement ☐ Phased in Retirement ☐ Manage Unexpected Retirement ☐ Take Full Retirement

TAX-EFFICIENT RETIREMENT INCOME PLANNING GUIDE

©Knowledge Bureau, Inc.

2. Detail	Specific Questions to Discuss with Advisors	Document It

Family Financial Details	• Are you planning for one retirement or two?
	• Important data to obtain:
	    - Family member details—contact information, birthdates, income
	    - Cash flow details
	    - Net worth: assets, liabilities,
	    - Tax filing profile, history, returns
		☐ Budget
		☐ Cash Flow
		☐ Net Worth Statement
		☐ Tax Returns

Income Expectations	• What amount of monthly income, after tax, would provide you with peace of mind? • How much tax will you pay? When?	☐ Short term needs & wants: 1, 3 and 5 years from now. ☐ Long term: 10-20 years. ☐ Before, after tax

3. THE RETIREMENT INCOME PLANNING PROCESS

Sources	Data	Analysis

Analyze Income and Capital	• List sources of income today:
	    - Employment
	    - Employment Insurance
	    - Severance Package
	    - Wage Loss replacement
	    - Employment Insurance
	    - Self-Employment—Net Income
	    - Net Rental Income
	    - Public Pensions: CPP, OAS Benefits
	    - Private Pension Benefits
	    - Investment Income Sources—non-registered
	    - Capital Gains and Losses
	    - Tax-Free Savings Account balances
	    - Inheritances or other windfalls
	    - Spousal support
	• List sources of future income sources:
	    - RPPs, IPPs, RCAs
	    - TFSAs, RRSPs, RRIFs, RDSPs, DPSPs
	    - Non-Registered Pools of Money
	    - Non-financial Assets—business equity, real estate
		☐ Tax status of income source:
		  - Taxable
		  - Tax exempt
		  - Tax preferred
		  - Tax deferred
		☐ Debt analysis
		☐ Current year tax estimate
		☐ After tax income projections
		☐ Effective Tax Rate
		☐ Marginal Tax Rate

Income Management	• How much from each source? • When? • From which source first? • Which taxpayer?	☐ At what income level is next tax bracket? ☐ Can income be split? ☐ Clawbacks minimized?

3. THE RETIREMENT INCOME PLANNING PROCESS CONT'D

Sources	Data	Analysis
Portfolio Management - Today	• Accumulation of Capital: - Which bucket first? • Growth of Capital - Inside or outside a registered account - Risk management - Insurance options? • Preservation of Capital: Tax-efficient savings/withdrawal principles: - Pre-tax savings - Post-tax savings - Can we improve rates of return, yields? - Can we reduce risk exposure? - Should we insure against tax, health risk?	**Asset allocation:** ☐ Protect, grow or recreate capital? ☐ Is the portfolio in sync risk profile? **Product selection:** ☐ Tax exempt ☐ Tax preferred ☐ Tax deferred ☐ Taxable

4. DECISION-MAKING: RETIREMENT INCOME PLAN RECOMMENDATIONS

	The Action Plan	Benchmarks
Portfolio Management - Tomorrow	• Income Plan: Layer in the income sources: - Employment: full or part time - Self Employment - Rental income - Public Pensions: CPP and OAS - Private Pensions: RPP, RRSP, RRIF, foreign - Investments: ○ TFSA ○ Interest-bearing ○ Dividends—private corporations ○ Dividends—public corporations ○ Securities: Mutual funds Stocks, Bonds ○ Real Estate Business Interests Insurance ○ Return of Capital only ○ Blend: income/capital ○ Other	☐ How does the income plan affect portfolio construction? - Capital Encroachment - Redundant Income - Risk and Return - Asset Allocation - Taxes

 Tax Moves

When you have a strategic retirement income plan that complements your family wealth management plan, a more purposeful relationship with your tax and financial advisors can help you to accumulate, grow, preserve and eventually transition your wealth on a tax-efficient basis.

The earlier you start the retirement income planning process, the longer the retirement income period is and the more opportunities there are to "average down" taxes. This is done by planning what sources will be added to income every year to minimize marginal tax rates.

Another big opportunity is to use two retirements—that of both spouses—to split income and average down tax over both retirement periods.

30 TAKING POINTS BACK: The OAS and CPP

Tax efficient retirement income planning is about staging both your lifetime savings in such a way as to withdraw and keep the most benefits possible. Age 65 is a particularly significant milestone for three specific reasons:

1. Old Age Security (OAS) generally begins... although there is an option to postpone it.

2. New tax credits (like the Age Amount) and income splitting opportunities become available for those with RRSP investments.

3. Most Canadians start drawing pension benefits from the Canada Pension Plan (CPP), which is based on contributions from employment or self-employment.

Recent tax changes and their numerical values are discussed in the *Essential Tax Facts Appendices*. However, from a planning perspective, what follows are some suggestions to maximize your tax moves in retirement.

THE NEW OAS. Those who live in Canada qualify for the OAS if they are 65 or older, have lived in Canada for at least 10 years since adulthood and are a Canadian citizen or a legal resident at the time the pension is approved.

When people living outside Canada want to receive the OAS, they also must be 65 or older, must have lived in Canada for at least 20 years after reaching age 18 and finally, they must have been a Canadian citizen or legal resident of Canada on the day before leaving the country.

TAX FORM FACT ▶ Non-residents who receive OAS payments must submit an *Old Age Security Return of Income* (T1136) to determine whether a recovery tax for OAS clawback purposes is required on net world income.

Cumulatively speaking, the OAS is lucrative. It could represent almost $600 a month, $7,000 a year or, between spouses, or close to $350,000 of income in retirement, if each spouse lives 24 years. The OAS is also indexed to inflation. It's therefore very important for most people to minimize tax erosion to this income source and one other related provision on the tax return:

OAS Clawbacks. First, while it is a universal payment, which means it is initially paid to every Canadian senior, regardless of income, the OAS will be "clawed back" when an individual's net income is high; that is, approximately $77,500. However, OAS entitlements can be managed by planning income withdrawals from other sources.

Age Credit Clawbacks. While the Old Age Security is taxable each year, tax free zones are enhanced for people who turn 65.

TAX FORM FACT. A non-refundable tax credit known as the Age Amount is available to offset taxes payable, and this is in addition to the Basic Personal Amount, found on Schedule 1 of the T1 return.

A clawback of the Age Amount will occur for every dollar earned above a net income threshold; this time approximately $37,800. These clawback zones are indexed each year.

ESSENTIAL TAX FACT ▶ **Planning Income Levels to Avoid Clawbacks Reduces Marginal Tax Rates on Retirement Income.** Managing the clawback of the Old Age Security Benefit and the offsetting Age Amount is an important tax move in retirement income planning.

Deferring OAS. Since July 2013, taxpayers may elect to defer receiving their OAS pension for up to five years (to age 70). For those who elect to defer receiving their OAS pension, the amount they will receive will be increased by 0.6% for each month of deferral. The maximum increase in OAS (based on deferral to age 70) is 0.6% x 60 months or 36%.

Taxpayers who would be subject to full clawback of OAS in the year they turn 65 should elect this option. Calculations indicate that the cumulative OAS benefits received will be maximized for taxpayers who defer one year for each year that they will live beyond age 79 (to a maximum of five years). This means that if you live past age 84, your benefits from OAS are largest if you delay starting until you reach age 70.

Planning Income Levels. Planning with OAS hinges on what your current tax bracket is, and at what marginal tax rate your income will be taxed above this, taking into account the aforementioned clawbacks.

Therefore, when making decisions about how much money to withdraw from your various capital pools (public or private pension accumulations or your investments) consider your income thresholds carefully before you act:

- *Income levels <u>above</u> the OAS clawback zones:* Do you have anything to lose by postponing receiving the OAS and taking other income sources instead? Can you fill the extra income gap left by the postponed OAS with other taxable sources, like RRSP or RRIF withdrawals?

- *Income levels <u>up to the top</u> of the OAS Clawback Zone.* Should you compromise your Age Amount in order to bring income up to approximately $77,500 annually for a better long term, after-tax result?

- *Income levels up to the top of the <u>Age Credit</u> Clawback.* In this case, marginal tax rates on retirement income will be the lowest.

- *Income levels up to the top of your <u>current tax bracket</u>.* For most taxpayers with significant, untaxed accumulations in RRSPs, RRIFs or RPPs, income required to be reported on the terminal return at death can exceed top tax brackets. If your income falls below this during your lifetime, averaging in the reporting of other pensions can make sense, even if you are subject to clawbacks of the Age Amount and the OAS.

How to structure retirement income to avoid clawback zones and top tax brackets now and at death should be discussed with your tax and financial advisors.

Dividends and the OAS. Dividend income withdrawals from non-registered accounts may have an unanticipated negative effect on your OAS pension. Actual dividend income earned is "grossed up" in value on the tax return, thereby increasing net income, the figure used to determine the size of your OAS "clawback," plus the size of other refundable, or non-refundable tax credits, like the Age Amount.

> **TAX FORM FACT.** The taxes on these grossed-up dividends are offset by a corresponding dividend tax credit, which reduces taxes on income. Use *Schedule 1* of the T1 Return to do so.

Therefore, while dividend income is widely considered to be a very tax-efficient source of investment income, it can cause erosion of your OAS, thereby substantially increasing marginal tax rates on this income.

With this in mind, it is also important to acknowledge that there are three types of tax treatments for dividend income. The dividend income you receive from a public company is taxed in one manner, whereas the dividend income received from a privately-owned business is taxed at slightly higher levels, depending on which province you live in. Finally, the dividend income you receive from foreign (e.g. U.S.) public companies is fully taxed as income in Canada. There is no gross-up or offsetting credit for dividends received from non-Canadian companies.

Have your tax advisors work with your investment advisors to achieve the right dividend income mix in planning retirement income withdrawals.

THE NEW CANADA PENSION PLAN. The Canada Pension Plan is a mandatory, contributory pension plan to which employees and employers must contribute, in return for a variety of benefits including retirement, survivors, disability and death benefits. It features some indexing to inflation.

The Canada Pension Plan is governed by a separate Act (*Canada Pension Plan Act*) and is jointly administered by the Canada Revenue Agency and Service Canada.

TAX FORM FACT. Benefits received under the Canada Pension Plan are reported on the recipient's T4A(P) *Statement of Canada Pension Plan Benefits* slip and must be reported on the recipient's tax return.

On request, Service Canada will provide you with a *Canada Pension Plan Statement of Contributions* which shows how much your pension entitlement is. Your *Statement of Contributions* shows your pension entitlement as of age 65, the date most people elect to retire. You should review this annually as part of your retirement planning process.

The maximum retirement benefit receivable, in return for your lifetime contributions is based on 25% of the average maximum pensionable earnings over the prior five years. It's over $1,100 a month, as shown below.

CPP Benefit Category	2018	2019
Maximum monthly Retirement Pension (at age 65)	$1,134.17	**$1,154.58**
Maximum monthly Post-Retirement Benefit	$28.35	**$28.86**
Maximum monthly Disability Pension	$1,335.83	**$1,362.30**
Monthly Disabled Contributor Child Benefit	$244.64	**$250.27**
Monthly Survivor's Pension under age 65	$614.62	**$626.63**
Monthly Survivor's Pension over age 65	$680.50	**$692.75**
Monthly Orphan's Benefit	$244.64	**$250.27**
Monthly Combined Retirement (age 65) & Survivor	$1,134.17	**$1,154.78**
Monthly Combined disability & Survivor	$1,335.83	**$1,362.30**
Maximum Death Benefit	$2,500.00	**$2,500.00***

*as of January 1, 2019, the CPP death benefit is $2,500 regardless of CPP pension entitlement

Changes to CPP in 2019. Recently passed changes to CPP, which will begin in 2019, will boost the rate of benefits from 25% to 33% of pensionable earnings (although the full effect will not be felt until about the year 2040; current retirees will not see any of the benefits of the increase). To fund the increase CPP contribution rates will increase beginning in 2019. See *Essential Tax Facts Appendices* for details.

When calculating your CPP retirement benefits, the number of working years less a portion of nil or low-earnings years due to work interruptions such as job loss is taken into account. Under the Child Rearing Provision, the years in which the contributor left the work force to raise children, will also be removed.

Survivor Benefits. When one spouse dies, the surviving spouse may be eligible to receive a CPP survivor benefit, if the deceased spouse had made contributions to CPP. Recent changes have enhanced the eligibility for these benefits.

Note that once the surviving spouse begins to receive their CPP retirement benefit, the maximum benefit (retirement plus survivor benefits) is limited to the maximum monthly retirement benefit. For those who have earned the maximum pension through their own contributions, this effectively means that the survivor benefits may be lost entirely, and this is an unpleasant surprise to those who have contributed their maximums to the CPP throughout their careers.

WHAT'S NEW WITH CPP PLANNING? Effective since 2012:

- The requirement to stop working before you can start receiving CPP early (that is before age 65) was eliminated.
- All CPP benefit recipients are required to continue making CPP contributions if they go back to work in the "early retirement period" of 60-64 after starting to receive retirement benefits.
- An election not to continue to contribute to the CPP can be made if you are receiving your CPP retirement pension and you work between age 65 and 70. Continuing to contribute will increase your pension entitlements through a Post-Retirement Benefit (PRB).

Common questions pre-retirees have in relation to these changes include:

- When to begin to take benefits from the CPP—early or later?
- When to stop contributing to the CPP?
- What other income sources should I draw on if I delay benefits?

Expected longevity plays a role in assessing the cost-benefit ratio of contributing to the CPP, especially when deciding whether or not to draw your taxable retirement benefits early at age 60.

TRUE-TO-LIFE EXAMPLE ▶ Both Ivan's father and grandfather lived past age 90. Ivan who is 59 is trying to decide if he should take his CPP retirement pension at age 60, 65, or 70. His current Statement of Earnings indicates that he would be eligible to receive $900 per month at age 65.

Option 1: Early draw at age 60. Ivan will receive a reduced pension of $576 per month (64% x $900). If he lives to age 90, he will receive the pension for 30 years so, ignoring inflation adjustments, he will receive **$207,360** in pension benefits.

Option 2: Begin at age 65. Ivan will receive $900 per month (ignoring inflation adjustments). If he lives to age 90, he will receive the pension for 25 years so he will receive a total of **$270,000** in pension benefits.

Option 3: Late draw at age 70—Ivan will receive an enhanced pension of $1,278 per month (142% x $900). If he lives to age 90, he will receive the pension for 20 years so he will receive a total of **$306,720** from CPP, (again ignoring inflation adjustments).

Result: If Ivan is confident that he will live to age 90, he should wait until he reaches 70 to apply for benefits because he will receive more from the plan.

What are the CPP Tax Implications? CPP benefits are fully taxable. There are also other tax implications to consider, too.

For example, receiving a larger income from CPP may increase clawbacks of certain personal credits and/or Old Age Security benefits. Waiting to receive larger benefits from the CPP in the future, could also coincide with higher minimum payments from the Registered Retirement Income Fund (RRIF), causing a spike in marginal tax rates. However, do the math, because this may not be true in every case, as RRIF values may be lower due to withdrawals that began earlier.

Important CPP Milestones. How much you will receive on a monthly basis will depend on how much you contribute, how long you contribute and when you apply to receive benefits. A life events approach to managing your CPP is therefore important, as outlined below:

CPP PLANNING MILESTONES

Milestone	Pre- Retirement	Early Retirement	Late Retirement	Mandatory Retirement
Age	18-59	60-64	65-70	71
Contributions	Required	Required	Optional (if receiving CPP)	Not allowed
Regular Retirement Benefits	Maximum benefits available at 65; reduced at 60	Reduced; but PRB may increase	Increased	Benefits depend on when benefits began
Post- Retirement Benefits (PRB)	Regular be increased if working age 60-70	Mandatory Contribution creates PRB*	Optional Contribution creates PRB**	Contributions must cease

*Employer/Employee contributions mandatory **Employer must contribute if employee chooses to.

 Tax Moves

A tax-efficient approach to planning your entitlements to the CPP includes maximizing the benefits by paying the correct amount of premiums on employment earnings, self-employment in a proprietorship and on self-reported sources such as tips and gratuities.

When the time comes to take the CPP benefits into income, be careful to use tax opportunities to reduce tax: assign benefits to your spouse to split income, claim all your available deductions and non-refundable tax credits and if it otherwise makes sense, postpone receipt of the benefits to age 70.

31 PERFORMANCE REWARDS: Private Pension Benefits

IMAGINE: YOU HAVE SPENT MUCH OF YOUR LIFE accumulating money in your employer-sponsored pension plan (RPP) and your RRSP and now it is time to spend it! Believe it or not, that's a difficult concept for lifelong savers, who don't want to touch their precious accumulations.

However, the purpose of your RPP and RRSP is to create a retirement pension, and if you plan do so over a longer period of time, you'll quite likely be able to average down tax erosion. Let's discuss these in more depth now.

ESSENTIAL TAX FACT ▶ **The Pension Income Amount Can Help Reduce Taxes on Private Pension Withdrawals.** The withdrawals received from your registered savings accounts—RPPs, RRSPs, IPPs, DPSPs—are taxable in the year received. Structured as a periodic pension, the amounts may qualify for a $2,000 federal pension income amount and pension income splitting with your spouse. *PENSION INCOME CREDIT*

REGISTERED PENSION PLANS (RPPS). Commuting your employer-sponsored pension plans to provide a periodic pension plan requires planning, and, depending on the type of plan you have contributed to, may involve some withdrawal restrictions.

Particularly important however, is a feature that allows those age 55 or older, to begin a "phased-in retirement" under a defined benefit pension plan.

It's a triple win for some. Those living with a spouse or common-law spouse may split periodic income from an RPP by election when the tax return is filed. This can be done at any age; providing an advantage over those with RRSP accumulations only, who must wait to age 65 to take advantage of pension income splitting, as you will learn later in this section.

No conditions are imposed on whether the employee works part- or full- time. However, this ability to draw a pension while continuing to accrue benefits is not extended to designated plans (more commonly called "top-hat plans"), which are those that cover only one employee or a small group of highly-compensated individuals. Check with your employer and tax advisor about your eligibility for this option.

Tax-free/direct transfers. When an employee changes employers, arrangements to move the accumulated amounts in the employee's pension plan are often made. The Income Tax Act provides details of the allowable tax-free rollovers of funds from one RPP to another or to the taxpayer's Registered Retirement Savings Plan (RRSP) or RRIF or LIRAs. Such transfers must be made directly from one registered plan to the other without tax consequences.

> **ESSENTIAL TAX FACT** ▶ **Avoid Spiking Into Top Tax Brackets.** Amounts that are received in the hands of the taxpayer as a lump sum will be considered to be taxable income, so it's best to avoid that and plan for periodic withdrawals instead to minimize marginal tax rate spikes.

Given the income-splitting opportunities under the RPP, for taxpayers under age 65, it is likely more advantageous to structure periodic pension benefits from an RPP rather than through the transfer to an RRSP or RRIF or LIF where you must wait to age 65 to split income with your spouse. Discuss with your advisors in advance.

INDIVIDUAL PENSION PLANS (IPP). If you are running an incorporated business you may be in financial position to supplement your RRSP with an IPP, which is a defined benefit pension plan. The IPP offers both maximum tax relief and a maximum retirement pension. To qualify for an IPP, you must:

- Have employment income reported on a T4;
- Be an employee of an incorporated company; and
- Own at least 10% of the shares of the company or be paid at least 2.5 times the maximum CPP pensionable earnings.
- Note – Starting in 2020 it is no longer possible to transfer funds from a defined benefit plan to a new IPP.

Checklist of IPP Features

☐ IPP contributions and expenses are fully tax-deductible to the business. If you borrow money or amortize the past service cost, you can deduct the interest charges.

☐ Employees may enjoy an annual maximum contribution that is higher than the maximum contribution for an RRSP.

☐ Pension benefits are protected from creditors under pension legislation.

☐ Extended contribution period: A company has 120 days after its year end to make an IPP contribution.

☐ Ownership of plan assets: At retirement, the IPP member owns any actuarial surplus. It may be used to upgrade pension benefits or the plan holder may pass it on to his or her spouse, heirs, or estate.

☐ Guaranteed lifetime income to IPP member and their spouses: This pension plan offers a predictable retirement income. An actuary determines the current annual cost of the future retirement income. Spouse pension benefits may be upgraded to 100% when the member retires or dies. The company is on the hook for this money.

☐ Full consumer price indexing, early retirement pension with no reduction, and bridge benefits can be structured to fill gaps left by the CPP or OAS.

☐ Annual minimum withdrawal amounts will be required from IPPs once a plan member is 72. These amounts will be based on current RRIF rules.

DEFERRED PROFIT SHARING PLANS (DPSPS). A deferred profit sharing plan (DPSP) provides for payments by an employer to a trustee, in trust, for the benefit of the employees or former employees, based on an employer's profits from the employer's business.

Employees may not contribute to a DPSP so there is no deduction available to the employee when contributions are made. Employer's contributions are deductible to the employer however. Members of a DPSP will be subject to a pension adjustment which means that contributions to an RRSP will be limited as a result of membership in the DPSP.

> TAX FORM FACT. *Direct transfers to another DPSP, RPP or RRSP.* When the employee leaves the employer, vested DPSP funds may be transferred to another DPSP, RPP or RRSP or RRIF. The transfer must be a direct transfer, using form T2151 *Direct Transfer of a Single Amount Under Subsection 147(19) or Section 147.3* to recognize the transfer. On death of the DPSP plan member, the funds in the DPSP may be transferred tax-free to the surviving spouse or common-law partner's RPP, RRSP, DPSP or RRIF. Use Form T2151 *Direct Transfer of a Single Amount Under Subsection 147(19) or Section 147.3* to recognize the transfer.

Amounts received by the taxpayer out of a DPSP are taxable and are eligible for the Pension Income Amount if received by a taxpayer who is over 64. The DPSP must pay all amounts vested in the plan to the beneficiary no later than the end of the year in which the beneficiary turns 71. But, the DPSP may provide for the conversion of the plan funds to an annuity.

THE RRSP. Making a contribution to a tax deductible registered plan, like your RRSP, is a good thing if you want to reduce the taxes you pay along the way and claim more non-refundable credits like medical expenses. That's because net income, the figure upon which these amounts is calculated, is reduced by making an RRSP contribution.

> **ESSENTIAL TAX FACT** ▶ A lower net family income will also increase federal refundable tax credits like the *Canada Child Benefit*, the *Canada Worker's Benefit*, or the *GST/HST Credits*. It all means more cash for you throughout the year.

When it comes to tax advantages, investing within a registered account essentially enables some double-dipping: new dollars are created for investment purposes with your tax deduction, while tax on investment earnings in the registered account is deferred into the future.

But there is one catch: you will be restricted in the amounts you can sock away in your RRSP; for example only "earned income" sources qualify, and a maximum contribution rate and dollar limit exist. In addition you have to be under 72 to contribute (or have a spouse who is under 72).

Check your *Notice of Assessment* from the CRA for your *Unused RRSP Contribution Room*. If you have no available RRSP contribution room, be sure to contribute to a TFSA.

Understanding Contribution Room. The RRSP is an essential tool in building up your savings for retirement. So just how much can you contribute? RRSP contribution room is the lesser of:

- 18% of earned income from the prior tax year minus any net "Pension Adjustments" (PAs) for the current year, and
- the maximum RRSP "contribution limit" for the current year minus any net Pension Adjustments for the current year.

Let's define some of those terms. The "Pension Adjustment" is a measure of benefits accruing to you as a member of another tax-deferred plan at work; example, an RPP (Registered Pension Plan) or DPSP (Deferred Profit Sharing Plan).

The RRSP "contribution limit" is 18% of earned income to a dollar maximum of $26,500 in 2019. If you don't make the full allowable contribution to your

RRSP, the unused RRSP contribution room carries forward for use in the future.

ESSENTIAL TAX FACT ▶ To find out how much you can contribute begins with looking for your Unused Contribution Room on your *Notice of Assessment or Reassessment* from the CRA. But the number won't be accurate if you missed filing previous returns. Catch that up if you can to maximize your future earning power from the RRSP.

The RRSP deduction is recorded on Schedule 7 and from there on Line 208 of the tax return. This deduction can include:

- RRSP contributions made in prior years and not deducted or refunded
- RRSP contributions made in the tax year
- RRSP contributions made in the first 60 days after the end of the tax year.

Age Eligibility. Note that there is no lower age limit for contributing to an RRSP. As long as CRA has the unused RRSP contribution room recorded, even a young adult can make a contribution (although at low income levels, RRSP contributions are often not tax-efficient). On the other hand, RRSPs must be collapsed by the end of the year in which you turn 71.

Spousal RRSPs. You may contribute to your own RRSPs based on available RRSP contribution room and may also contribute some or all of the amounts to a spousal RRSP. This may provide for income splitting advantages on retirement and can help an age-ineligible taxpayer prolong the ability to use an RRSP deduction.

Spousal RRSPs are not subject to restrictive Attribution Rules; that is, you can contribute to a spousal RRSP and have the resulting income taxed in the spouse's hands... but there is a catch. Withdrawals from a spousal RRSP will be taxed in the contributor's hands if the money is withdrawn within three years of the last contribution to any spousal plan.

TRUE-TO-LIFE EXAMPLE ▶ John has been making contributions every year to equalize pension accumulations. If his wife Sofi withdraws money from a spousal RRSP within three years of the last contribution by John to any spousal plan, the amount of the withdrawal that represents John's contributions in the prior three years will be taxed in John's hands.

ESSENTIAL TAX FACT ▶ **Transfers of a Spousal RRSP to a RRIF are Granted an Exception.** In that case only the amounts in excess of the minimum amount you are required to withdraw will be taxed in the hands of the contributor to the spousal RRSP.

Note that if you are "age ineligible" for contributing to your own RRSP, that is, you are over age 71, you may still contribute to a spousal RRSP, based on your RRSP contribution room, if your spouse is under 72 years old.

If John in our example above, had turned 72 this year, he could no longer contribute to his own RRSP even though he still has unused RRSP contribution room. His wife Sofi is 65, though. John can choose to make a spousal RRSP contribution, thereby depositing the money into Sofi's RRSP. He can then take the deduction on his return.

Pension Income Splitting. The pension income splitting rules, which are discussed in detail in a subsequent chapter, may impact the amount of contributions some taxpayers may wish to make to the family's RRSPs. But remember, double-digit returns by way of tax savings will often result from an RRSP contribution; so even if you don't need to take all the deduction this year to get the after-tax results you need, take a moment to consider the benefits of a contribution.

> **ESSENTIAL TAX FACT** ▶ **It's a Smart Tax Move to Maximize RRSP Contribution Room.** Undeducted RRSP contributions may be carried forward indefinitely and used to offset income you declare in the future, even if you are otherwise age-ineligible for new RRSP contributions. Save the RRSP deduction in your back pocket to win new tax savings.

Any amounts contributed in the year and not deducted are considered to be "undeducted RRSP contributions." This will be noted on your Notice of Assessment or Reassessment from CRA.

The point of all of this is, of course, to increase your wealth for use in retirement income planning. An RRSP deduction creates new money for savings with an increased tax refund; defers tax on investment income, increases entitlements to refundable tax credits and reduce clawbacks of social benefits like the Old Age Security or Employment Insurance. Investing in it can be a great tax move!

> ***TRUE-TO-LIFE EXAMPLE*** ▶ Terry left his workplace last year on a disability claim. This year he took early retirement, investing much of his severance package in his RRSP. He finds his income is low this year and that he has some "undeducted RRSP contributions" left. That's good news, because he plans to sell his rental property and report a $100,000 taxable gain and use his undeducted RRSP contributions to offset the taxes payable.

As Terry found out, it can really pay off in a big way to claim your RRSP deduction when your marginal tax advantage is highest.

ESSENTIAL TAX FACT ▶ **Here's More Good News: RRSP Contributions May be Made in Cash or in Kind.** That is, you may transfer an eligible investment from your non-registered investments to your RRSP and claim a deduction for the fair market value of the asset at the time of the transfer.

If the fair market value at the time of the transfer is higher than the cost of the asset, you will have to report the capital gain in income for the year. Also, be aware that any income accrued prior to the transfer of assets, such as interest, must be reported on the tax return.

However, there's a trap here if the fair market value of the asset is less than its cost, at the time you wish to transfer it to your RRSP. The resulting capital loss incurred in your non-registered account before the money is invested in your RRSP will be deemed to be nil—not claimable.

Therefore, if you want to transfer an asset which has decreased in value to your RRSP in order to create a tax deduction, it's best to sell the asset, rather than transfer it, and then contribute the proceeds to the RRSP. You can then have the RRSP repurchase the asset. This method allows you to deduct the capital loss on your tax return.

Note, there are other "tax advantage" rules to ensure the taxpayer does not receive an advantage when assets are swapped from a non-registered account to a registered one, so check with your tax advisor before transferring assets back and forth. Non-compliance can result in expensive penalties.

Withdrawing RRSP Accumulations. Once you are ready to retire, your RRSP accumulations can be taken out in a lump sum; however this is not usually a good idea from a tax point of view, as the full amounts of principal and earnings will be taxed at that time; potentially at the highest tax rates. Refundable and non-refundable tax credits will be affected too.

Most people will choose to create a periodic pension benefit—monthly, quarterly, semi-annually, etc. and average out the tax on the benefits over their retirement period. This is also important if you wish to qualify for the $2000 *Pension Income Amount* and pension income splitting with your spouse, which is possible once you have reached age 65 (or are receiving the amounts as a result of the spouse's death).

TAX FORM FACT. Periodic RRSP withdrawals are reported on a T4RSP slip.

Withholding Taxes on RRSP Withdrawals. You will want to carefully plan withdrawals from your RRSP, as they will be subject to withholding taxes at the following rates:

Withdrawal Amount	Rate
Up to $5000	10%
$5001 to $15,000.	20%
Above $15,000	30%

Especially when you take a lump sum from your RRSP, it is important for you to take this withholding tax into consideration, to ensure you end up with the exact amount of funds you need for the purpose you have in mind. If it otherwise makes sense, keep withdrawals under $5,000. You may also wish to consider taking these withdrawals over two tax years—some in December and some in January—for a better after-tax result.

RRSP Over-Contributions and Excess Contributions. Over-contributions could happen, for example, when you instruct your employer to make RRSP contributions on your behalf through a payroll deduction plan, but forget to mention a change in your contribution room due to a tax reassessment. Other times, taxpayers have RRSP deposits at several financial institutions.

To cushion errors in contributions due to fluctuating RRSP room, or forgotten deposits, an over-contribution limit of $2,000 is allowed without penalty, provided you are at least 18 in the preceding taxation year.

Many taxpayers, in fact, use this rule for tax planning purposes. They purposely contribute the amount allowed under their contribution room plus $2,000 more. This is a great way to earn even more tax deferred income within your RRSP along the way.

> **TRUE-TO-LIFE EXAMPLE** ▶ Debbie has RRSP contribution room of $5,000, and she has maximized this room with a contribution this year. But she can contribute a total of $7,000 without penalty—a $2000 overcontribution. She decides to do so to earn tax-deferred investment income while the money is in the plan.

Avoid Making "Excess RRSP Contributions." Excess contributions to your RRSP are those which exceed your contribution room plus $2,000.

If you make an excess contribution, you need to create contribution room or pay a penalty tax and risk double taxation—the reporting of taxable withdrawals from your RRSP without the benefit of a tax deduction. Even worse, a very complicated tax form must be completed, so work with your tax and financial advisors to get this straightened out. Discuss the following opportunities in managing your RRSP withdrawals with your tax and financial advisor:

TAX FORM FACT. Amounts contributed to your RRSP and not yet deducted may be withdrawn tax-free and with no withholding taxes by filing Form T3012A, *Tax Deduction Waiver on the Refund of Your Undeducted RRSP Contributions*. The amount withdrawn will be included on a T4RSP slip and must be reported as income. You may, however, claim an offsetting deduction on your tax return by using Form T746 *Calculating Your Deduction for Refund of Unused RRSP Contributions*.

Excess RRSP contributions are subject to a penalty tax of 1% per month. Complete form T1-OVP *Individual Tax Return for RRSP Excess Contributions* by March 31 of the year following. Penalties will accrue until the excess contributions are withdrawn from the RRSP.

Tax-Free Transfers to an RRSP. You have learned that tax efficiency in retirement includes moving money into the right "buckets" so that layering of income sources is enabled with the goal to average down the overall taxes paid over the retirement lifecycle. The following capital sources may be transferred to your RRSP on a tax-free basis over and above the normal RRSP contribution limits plus the $2,000 allowable over-contribution:

- *Eligible Retiring Allowances.* Amounts received on job termination as a severance package may be rolled over into an RRSP on a tax-free basis depending on certain conditions. For service after 1995, no RRSP rollover is allowed. For service after 1988 and before 1996, a single limit of $2,000 per year of service can be rolled into an RRSP. And for service before 1989, it is possible to roll over $2,000 for each year of service plus another $1,500 for each year in which the employer's contributions to the company pension plan did not vest in you. The eligible amount will be shown on the T4A from the former employer. In applying these rules, a single day in a calendar year counts as a "year" of employment.

- *Funds from Another RRSP.* You may request a direct transfer of RRSP accumulations from one RRSP to another RRSP under which you are the annuitant. Form T2033 may be used to make the transfer.

- *Funds from a Spouse's RRSP.* On the breakdown of a marriage or common-law relationship, where the terms of a separation or divorce agreement require that the funds from one spouse's RRSP be transferred to the other, the funds may be transferred tax-free. Form T2220 must be used.

- *Registered Pension Plan (RPP) Amounts.* If you cease to belong to an employer-sponsored RPP, the funds from the RPP may be transferred to your RRSP. Form T2151 must be used.
- *Deferred Profit Sharing Plan (DPSP) Accumulations.* You may transfer funds from your DPSP to your RRSP. Form T2151 must be used.
- *Foreign Pension Receipts.* Lump sum amounts received from a foreign pension plan in respect of a period while you were a non-resident may be transferred to your RRSP. Amounts that are exempt from tax under a tax treaty with the foreign country may not be transferred.
- *Saskatchewan Pension Plan Amounts.* A lump sum payment out of the Saskatchewan pension plan may be transferred to your RRSP tax-free.

Tax-Free Transfers From an RRSP. Funds from your RRSP may also be transferred on a tax-free basis to the following accounts:

- *Another RRSP.*
- *A Registered Pension Plan* (only possible if the RPP terms allow this). Form T2033 may be used.
- The *RRSP of a spouse or former spouse on breakdown of marriage* or common-law relationship.
- *A RRIF.* You may transfer funds from your RRSP to a RRIF under which you are the annuitant. Form T2033 must be used.
- The *RRIF of a spouse or former spouse on breakdown of marriage* or common-law relationship. Form T2220 must be used.
- *An Annuity.* Amounts can be transferred from your RRSP to an annuity contract for your life or jointly for the life of you and your spouse or common-law partner with or without a guarantee period. If there is a guarantee period, it may not be for a period longer than until you (or spouse or common-law partner) are 90 years old.
- *RRSP of spouse or former spouse or dependant on death.*
- *RDSP of surviving child or grandchild.* Rollovers to an RDSP may be made on a tax-free basis if the surviving child or grandchild has sufficient RDSP contribution room.

Creating Your RRSP-Funded Pension. When it comes time to create your periodic pension withdrawals from an RRSP, the accumulations will generally be transferred into one of two investment vehicles that will enable a periodic taxable income that is properly blended for tax efficiency: a *Registered Retirement Income Fund (RRIF)*, which provides for gradually increasing payments over time or *an annuity* (which provides for equal monthly payments).

Under a RRIF, a minimum amount must be withdrawn according to a predetermined schedule based on your age. The payments are taxable in the year received. However you can withdraw more than this as required. As with RRSP payments, the amounts will qualify for the $2,000 pension income amount if you are over age 64 or receiving the amounts as the result of a spouse's death.

NEW ANNUITY OPTIONS. The March 2019 Federal Budget introduced two new options for annuitizing pension income. See Appendices.

Before you withdraw, speak to your tax advisor about the following:

Checklist of RRSP—RRIF Planning Questions

☐ Should RRSP accumulations be taken in a lump sum, transferred to an RRIF or taken as an annuity?

☐ Who should withdraw first or the most—the higher income earner or the lower earning spouse?

☐ What is the benefit of election to pension income split at age 65?

☐ Is each spouse claiming the $2000 pension income amount claimable by each spouse?

☐ How will the clawback of the Age Amount or Old Age Security be affected by your pension withdrawals?

☐ What effect do withdrawals have on quarterly tax instalment remittances?

☐ Can other income sources be split between spouses to reduce taxes— Canada Pension Plan benefits for example, if each spouse is at least age 60?

☐ Should all dividends earned in non-registered accounts be reported by the higher earner (a possibility only if a Spousal Amount is thereby created or increased)?

☐ Should one spouse be earning and reporting more or less interest, dividends or capital gains from non-registered sources to average down taxes for the household over the retirement period?

☐ Spouses can rollover untaxed RRSP/RRIF deposits to their spouse without incurring taxes in the year of death. However, if you expect the survivor to be in a higher marginal tax bracket at death, should you plan to withdraw more taxable income during both your lifetimes to bring overall taxes paid down?

♞ Tax Moves

Many people make the mistake of waiting too long to start drawing taxable income out of their registered pension plans and RRSPs. Your goal for couples is two equal incomes throughout retirement. Have you accomplished that in your accumulation plans?

Your goal for singles is to average down tax over a longer period of time and then save any "redundant" or unneeded income in a registered account. Are you thinking about your taxable reporting period with a long enough horizon?

Discuss retirement income layering with all your various income sources in an adequate pre-retirement period to maximize your tax moves.

32 ACCOLADES FROM AFAR: Foreign Pensions

CANADIAN RESIDENTS MAY BE SUBJECT TO TAX on foreign pension income sources, and tax treaties with foreign countries are put into place to help avoid double taxation. Even if your foreign pension income is deposited in an account offshore, know that because Canadian residents are taxed on world income in Canadian funds, all foreign pension income received—no matter where in the world—is taxable in Canada.

Further, CRA has received extensive funding to track down people who fail to report foreign income and governments have increased the sharing of tax information. That's why it is important for you to catch up on any unreported income from foreign sources as quickly as possible.

On the good news side, there are some tax provisions for you to take advantage of to avoid double taxation.

ESSENTIAL TAX FACT ▶ **A Foreign Tax Credit May be Claimed if the "Source Country" Withholds Taxes.** However, be prepared to translate supporting documents if the amount of taxes you paid to the foreign country can't be easily deciphered.

In addition to the foreign tax credits, certain tax exemptions are available to Canadian tax filers; of recent note:

Tax Exemption on U.S. Social Security. Recipients of U.S. Social Security will claim a 15% deduction on the Canadian tax return. U.S. Social Security benefits received after January 2010, will be eligible for a 50% deduction, if the social security pension began prior to 1996. This change should be reviewed with executors of estates receiving qualifying benefits as well.

German Social Security. German social security benefits became taxable in Canada in 2003. For pensions which began in 2005 or earlier, the portion of the pension that is non-taxable is 50%.

For pensions which begin after 2005, the percentage that is taxable in Canada is set in the year that the pension starts. The 50% rate for 2005 increases by 2% each year for the period 2006 to 2020, and then increases by 1% each year until the taxable percentage reaches 100%. See chart below.

This percentage is used in the year the pension begins and in the subsequent year. For each such subsequent year, the non-taxable portion is fixed at the amount (in Euros) that was non-taxable in the first full year that the pension is received. Yes, that's complicated, and warrants some expert help from a specialist in this area, because, tax departments on either side are well armed with expensive penalty provisions if you get this wrong.

Year Pension Starts	Taxable Portion	Year Pension Starts	Taxable Portion	Year Pension Starts	Taxable Portion
2005 or before	50%	2017	74%	2029	89%
2006	52%	2018	76%	2030	90%
2007	54%	**2019**	**78%**	2031	91%
2008	56%	2020	80%	2032	92%
2009	58%	2021	81%	2033	93%
2010	60%	2022	82%	2034	94%
2011	62%	2023	83%	2035	95%
2012	64%	2024	84%	2036	96%
2013	66%	2025	85%	2037	97%
2014	68%	2026	86%	2038	98%
2015	70%	2027	87%	2039	99%
2016	72%	2028	88%	2040 or later	100%

SNOWBIRDS. Canadians who live in the U.S. for the winter may have both Canadian and U.S. tax filing consequences. Follow the guide below to ensure you don't put yourself into an unintended tax filing position by overstaying your winter visit.

> **TAX FORM FACT.** A "closer connection" declaration must be made by June 15 on Form 8840. In this way the substantial presence test, and U.S. tax filing requirements can be avoided.

1. *What does it mean to be a U.S. resident or to have a U.S. resident alien status?* To avoid U.S. taxation on world-wide income, it is necessary for the snowbird to avoid U.S. resident alien status. This occurs when the "substantial presence test" is met.

2. *What is the "substantial presence test"?* This is a test to determine your U.S. filing status. In calculating the Substantial Presence Test, each day:

   - in current year counts as a full day;
   - in the prior year counts as one-third of a day; and
   - in the year before that counts as one-sixth of a day.

   Add up the total number of days you were present in the U.S. in the last three years, multiplied by these factors. If your total is at least 183 days, you are considered a resident alien for U.S. filing purposes in the year. If your total is less than 183 days, you are considered a non-resident alien. Even if you a resident alien because you meet the substantial presence test, you can be considered a non-resident alien if:

   - you were present in the U.S. for less than 183 days
   - your tax home is in Canada; and
   - you had a closer connection to Canada than to the U.S.

3. *Are there tax implications to renting our winter vacation home to others?* Rental income on a U.S. property owned by a Canadian will automatically have a 30%, non-refundable withholding tax applied on the income. To avoid this withholding tax the Canadian can file a U.S. tax return. However, don't forget that in Canada you must report offshore assets with a cost of $100,000 CAN or more on Form T1135 *Foreign Income Verification Statement* if they are used more than 50% of the time for rental use.

 Tax Moves

If you receive foreign pension income or travel and stay abroad extensively, it is essential to get tax help to comply with international rules and tax filing requirements.

Be sure to speak to a tax specialist about claiming foreign tax credits, foreign pension exemptions and also about any filing requirements for disposition of assets held at death in cases where assets are held offshore.

33 SHARING REWARDS: Pension Income Splitting

WITH OUR PROGRESSIVE TAX SYSTEM, the more evenly you can spread your household income amongst family members, the more likely it is that you'll pay the least amount of income tax as a family unit. During the active earning years, the opportunities for splitting earned income are limited, but several opportunities exist to split retirement income and thereby reduce your total tax bill. That's the subject of this chapter.

How is Pension Income Splitting Accomplished? There are a variety of methods; for example, you can plan to assign half your CPP benefits to your spouse who has arrived at age 60. You can accumulate your RRSP savings to ensure each spouse has equal amounts of money in their own RRSP; or you can use a spousal RRSP, which your spouse draws from, regardless of age, as required.

> **ESSENTIAL TAX FACT** ▶ **When You Reach Age 65, You Can Split Up to 50% of Your Accumulations in Your Matured RRSP or RRIF By Election with Your Spouse.** This is different from the rules for those who retire with a periodic pension from an employer-sponsored plan: these people can split that income with their spouse at any age. If income tax has been withheld on the pension income, the credit for the tax is split as well.

Pre-Age 65 Strategies. If you have not yet attained age 65, and therefore cannot yet make an election to split up to 50% of retirement income from a matured RRSP or RRIF with your spouse, you could have the lower earning spouse withdraw taxable funds from his/her own RRSP first; depleting that source if necessary while keeping the higher earner's RRSP intact. Alternatively (or in addition), withdrawals from a spousal RRSP can be made.

TRUE-TO-LIFE EXAMPLE ▶ Otto operated a small business for many years and his wife Johanna worked in the family business. Otto was not able to set up a pension plan for Johanna or for himself so instead he contributed half his RRSP contribution limit to his own RRSP and the other half to an RRSP for Johanna. Otto sold the business and retired at age 60.

In retirement, Otto can withdraw funds from his own RRSP to provide income. Any withdrawals that Johanna makes from her RRSP will be taxable to Otto to the extent that he made contributions in the year of withdrawal or the prior two years. Beyond that, any withdrawals that Johanna makes from her RRSP will be included in her income. The couple can each report retirement income even though all of the contributions were made by Otto.

Withdraw up to Bracket Strategy. Another important approach is to make additional RRSP withdrawals, in retirement, up to the next highest tax bracket or clawback zone. This income is going to be taxed at this same level at some point in time, so it may be prudent to withdraw the money now and reinvest it more tax-efficiently going forward, perhaps using a TFSA. Further, accumulations may be taxed at higher marginal tax rate when the second surviving spouse dies.

TRUE-TO-LIFE EXAMPLE ▶ Michelle is a widow. She is 78 and requires $60,000 to live on and withdraws just enough from her RRIF each year to meet those requirements. She currently has $300,000 in her RRIF.

Michelle's current marginal tax rate is just under 30%. When Michelle dies, her remaining RRIF balance will be included in her income and will take her into the highest income tax bracket (53.53%). To minimize taxes on her RRIF in her lifetime, she should withdraw as much as possible so that her rate remains at 30%. She could consider boosting her income to the lowest of $77,500 (start of OAS clawback zone) and the cap of the provincial and federal tax brackets she is in.

By withdrawing an additional amount each year, she will pay taxes on her remaining RRIF funds at 29.65% rather than 53.53% at death, saving 24% or well over $3,000 per year in taxes over her remaining lifetime. The additional withdrawal after tax should be deposited into a TFSA if Michelle has enough contribution room, otherwise it should be invested in another non-registered account.

SPLITTING ELIGIBLE PENSION INCOME. This lucrative tax provision became possible for retirees starting in 2007. Essentially, income that qualifies for the $2,000 pension income amount qualifies for pension income splitting. Up to one-half of such pension income received can be reported by the recipient's spouse by making an annual election to do so.

TAX FORM FACT. The election to split pension income is made by each spouse filing form T1032 *Joint Election to Split Pension Income* with their tax returns.

What is the Federal Pension Income Credit? The Pension Income Credit (or pension income amount) is a $2,000 tax credit that is claimed on Schedule 1 of the taxpayer's income tax return. This credit is multiplied by 15% on the federal tax return and therefore can reduce taxes payable by $300 each year for each spouse. A similar credit is available on the provincial return and its value varies by province. Don't forget to claim it.

To receive the pension income credit, you must first be receiving eligible pension income, described below. To maximize the benefit of this credit, it is extremely important and valuable to split at least $2,000 to a spouse's tax return so that this benefit could be doubled for the household.

Therefore, by first creating sources of income that would qualify for pension income splitting, and then by ensuring that at least $2,000 of the eligible pension income is shared each and every year between spouses, taxpayers can create significant tax savings in retirement.

TAX FORM FACT. "Eligible" pension income which can be split must qualify for the $2000 pension income credit, which can be found on Schedule 1 of the federal return.

The eligible income must be received periodically. It falls into two qualifying categories:

(a) *For those under 65:* periodic pension receipts of a life annuity from a registered pension fund or superannuation, or the amounts in (b) below if received as a result of a spouse's death.

(b) *For those age 65 or over:* periodic annuity payments from a matured RRSP, RRIF, LIF, LRIF, PRIF, spousal RRIF, registered annuity or non-registered annuity and/or GIC income from an insurance company investment.

Not Eligible. Specifically excluded from the definitions of pension and qualified pension income are the following sources, which don't qualify for the election using Form T1032 :

• Old Age Security,

• Canada or Quebec Pension Plan Benefits,

• a death benefit,

- foreign pension income which qualifies for a deduction or exemption (example: the exempt portion of U.S. Social Security),

- a payment received out of or under a salary deferral arrangement, a retirement compensation arrangement, an employee benefit plan, or an employee trust.

Optimizing the Pension Income Splitting Opportunity. Splitting of pension income between spouses can be beneficial but not for all taxpayers, so it's important to optimize the opportunity by doing the tax returns of each spouse a variety of different ways. The following should be taken into account:

Provision	Transfer From	
	Higher income spouse to	Lower income spouse
OAS Clawback	May reduce it	May increase it
Age Amount	May reduce it	May increase it
Spousal Amount	Will reduce claim	
Age Amount Transfer	Will reduce claim	
Pension Amount	No Effect	May increase it
Federal, Provincial Tax Rates	May be reduced	May be increased
Quarterly Instalments	May reduce them	May increase them

ESSENTIAL TAX FACT ▶ **Pension Income Splitting With Your Spouse Should Be Optimized.** You will want to manage specific deadlines, however.

- The deadline for filing the election is the due date for filing the return. However, late and amended elections will be accepted until three years after the due date for filing the return for the year.

- In a year of marital change, the maximum is prorated for the number of months the couple was married to the number of months in the taxpayer's year. Thus, in the date of death, there is no proration of amounts received by the deceased but there is for the survivor.

 Tax Moves

Pension income splitting with your spouse could save you thousands of dollars over your retirement years. It is a gift from government that can help you preserve and transition more wealth from all sources. Be sure to speak to your tax and financial advisors to optimize your opportunities.

34 RETAINING THE PRIZE: Retirement Income Layering

FROM OUR DISCUSSION SO FAR, YOU CAN SEE THAT drawdown strategies from various public and registered accumulations can be complicated and ineffective if not done well. Your goal is to reduce taxes on the timing of the income withdrawal, and to average down taxes over a period of years, while taking advantage of income splitting opportunities with your spouse.

To begin your planning, be sure to list all potential income sources available to each spouse and then develop a retirement income layering strategy over the course of your retirement period. This important exercise is the icing on the cake: it will preserve human and financial capital that has been expended throughout your lifetime to buy the most financial freedom in retirement.

ESSENTIAL TAX FACT ▸ **Both Income and Capital Can Be Preserved with the Right Tax Moves.** Income layering of all your income sources in retirement can not only help you get a better after-tax result, and help you preserve your capital for the future too.

RETIREMENT INCOME LAYERING SUMMARY

Source	Tax Status	Tax Reporting
Employment	Taxable	Report on T1.
Old Age Security	Taxable to recipient. Clawed back when individual's net income exceeds indexed income thresholds.	Call 1-800-277-9914 at Service Canada to apply. Report income from T4A(OAS) slip. Report income tax deducted.
Guaranteed Income Supplement & Allowance	Report as income for purposes of reducing tax credits—these sources increase individual net income.	Deduct so that income is not taxable under "Additional deductions".

RETIREMENT INCOME LAYERING SUMMARY CONT'D

Source	Tax Status	Tax Reporting
Canada Pension Plan	Taxable to recipient (except survivors benefits paid to minors, which are received by widow/widower but taxed to child).	Report from T4A(P) slip; split income with spouse who has turned age 60 with an assignment.
Retiring Allowances (Severance Pay)	Taxable but portions may qualify for tax free rollover to an RRSP or Registered Pension Plan (RPP).	Report amounts from T4 or T3 slips. Amounts in Box 66 of T4 can be transferred to an RRSP or RPP on a tax-free basis. Qualifying amounts on T3 slip are in Box 47.
Superannuation (Periodic Pension Benefits)	Taxable but up to 50% of income may be split with spouse.	Report amounts from T4A or T3; to split income complete form T1032 and follow reporting instructions.
Foreign Pension Income	Taxable in Canadian funds, however some are non-taxable due to a tax treaty.	Report gross amounts, but take treaty deductions. Most taxable periodic pensions qualify for the $2000 pension income amount (federal).
Annuity Payments	Amounts from general annuities, Deferred Profit Sharing Plans (DPSPs) are taxable.	Depending on age some of these amounts may qualify for the $2000 pension income amount and income splitting.
Retroactive Lump Sums	Taxable and may qualify for lump sum averaging. Includes employment income, certain damages, wage loss replacement, support from a spouse, RPP benefits, EI.	Attach form T1198 *Statement of Qualifying Retroactive Lump-Sum Payments.*
Interest Income	From bank accounts, term deposits, GICs, etc. are taxable on an annual accrual basis.	Note that in the case of bonds or T-Bills, a capital gain or loss may occur on disposition before maturity.
Capital Gains and Losses	Partially taxable. Income from the disposition of capital property is included at 50%.	Carry losses back 3 years or forward to offset capital gains in the future.

Source	Tax Status	Tax Reporting
Dividend Income	Taxable. Income can be received from "eligible" or "non-eligible" dividends; the latter coming from small business corps that qualify for the small business deduction.	The actual dividend is grossed up. Then an offsetting dividend tax credit is claimed.
RRSPs	Taxable. Both principal and earnings are taxable but qualify for pension income amount if taxpayer is at least age 65 or receiving the periodic amounts due to death of spouse.	Amounts that qualify for the pension income amount also qualify for pension income splitting.
Spousal RRSP	Taxable in hands of contributor if holding period of 3 years from last spousal RRSP contribution is not met.	As above. Pay attention to designation of benefits at death; tax free transfers on marriage breakdown.
RRIF	Taxable in hands of recipient.	As above. Note in case of spousal plan, transfers of RRSP accumulations to a RRIF results in minimum payments that are taxable to the annuitant. Amounts over this are taxed to spouse until holding period is over.
Self-Employment	Proprietors are taxed on net business income and must make CPP contributions at least to age 65. Optional between 65 and 70 if receiving benefits.	File a Form T2125 Statement of Business or Professional Activities. Incorporated taxpayers lose CPP pension building opportunity if drawing dividends only.
Retirement Compensation Arrangements (RCA)	When making a withdrawal from an RCA the income is fully taxable. The income comes from two parts: refundable tax from CRA and the RCA investment itself.	Income on a T4A-RCA slip Is "other income" not eligible for any off-setting deductions, credits. Unless RCA supplementary to an RPP, income is not eligible for pension income splitting.
Individual Pension Plans (IPP)	Taxable based on same rules followed for RRSP and RRIF.	See RRSP information regarding pension income splitting.

MANAGING RISK WITH INSURANCE. In the event you have one of more of the following insurance policies additional income may be available in times of need:

Disability Income	If premiums were paid by the employee, the income received is tax free. Any amount paid by the employer, renders the entire income taxable. Disability income plans, whether they are group or individual, pay to a maximum of age 65.	Report only taxable amounts as other employment income. Deduct premiums paid by employee if the amount is taxable.
Long Term Care Income	The income received is as a monthly tax-free benefit. The benefit is paid in the event the insured is unable to complete one or more "daily activities" as defined by the policy. Can be used for any purpose, based on home or facility care expenses.	Form T2201 Disability Tax Credit may assist with eligibility.
Critical Illness Insurance	These plans can be available up to the insured's age 75 or 80. A lump sum tax-free benefit would be received in the event the insured was diagnosed of having a critical illness.	The conditions covered under each plan vary, the three conditions found under all plans relate to heart attack, stroke or cancer.
Life Insurance Policies	Many life insurance plans accumulate cash on a tax- free basis, which can be withdrawn at any time. The tax implications at the time of the withdrawal will depend on the amount withdrawn and the "adjusted cost basis" of the contract.	As a general rule, the cost base will decline to zero, making the cash withdrawal 100% taxable. Report taxable amounts as Other Income. Amounts do not qualify for pension income splitting.
Line of Credit	A line of credit can often be secured for up to 75% of the cash value of a life insurance policy. This income is tax free; it is considered to be a loan.	No tax implications, but an important option in debt management for seniors.

A SIMPLE RETIREMENT INCOME PLAN. To illustrate the power of retirement income planning, consider a typical senior, Jonathan age 65 and his wife, Diana, age 55, who are retiring this year and planning their retirement income over the next five years. Shown below is a tax-efficient income layering plan given their income sources: OAS, CPP, superannuation, RRSP accumulations, TFSAs and Jonathan's dividends from his small business. Diana was a stay at home mom, then worked as a nurse and is now fully retired.

> *TRUE-TO-LIFE EXAMPLE.* ▶ Over the next five years, Jonathan and Diana will require $60,000 after-tax income (indexed) which will be composed of:
>
> • Jonathan's OAS, CPP, RPP (split with Diana for tax purposes), and small business dividends.
>
> • Diana's RRSP withdrawals to top up to the required income levels.
>
> TFSA balances should be preserved to ensure Diana has sufficient funds should Jonathan pass away unexpectedly, as his OAS pension, and potentially the CPP benefits, depending on the level of Diana's contributions, will cease on his death.

Consider the retirement income plan below: is the money taxed in the right taxpayer's hands to get the best after-tax results for this household unit now and after Diana turns 60? How could net after-tax results be improved?

	2019: Age:	Jonathan 65	Diana 55	2023:	Jonathan 70	Diana 60
OAS		$7,263			$8,020	
CPP		$9,800			$10,820	
RPP (split)		$15,700	$15,700		$17,334	$17,334
RRSP		$5,000			$5,000	
Dividends		$12,000			$13,249	
TFSA						
Total Income		$49,763	$15,700		$54,423	$17,334
– Income Tax		$5,376	$448		$5,067	$531

Some opportunities to bear in mind:

• **Split CPP Income**—Once both spouses have attained age 60, one half of CPP retirement benefits can be assigned to each spouse

• **Split RPP Income**—Jonathan's employer-sponsored Registered Pension Plan (RPP) qualifies for income splitting once he starts to draw benefits, regardless of the age of the spouse. This income can be split annually by election—up to 50% can be transferred to Diana's return. The amounts qualifies for the $2000 federal pension income amount.

- **Pay Dividends to Diana**—as long as Jonathan has reached age 65, Diana, the non-active spouse, can report 100% of dividends distributed to her under the new TOSI (Tax on Split income) rules.

- **Top up RRSP Withdrawals.** A lump sum withdrawal can be made from either spouse's RRSP to top income up to the top of each spouse's current tax bracket. But, this will be subject to withholding tax, tax on the current year's return, and increase quarterly instalment remittances.

- **Make a TFSA Withdrawal.** This is also a good way to get to the $60,000 after-tax income. But over the long run, the last surviving spouse wants to avoid paying high tax rates on taxable RRSP/RRIF or other income sources. Might be best to leave growth opportunities in the TFSA accumulations.

Remember that taxes payable will vary depending on province of residence; but across the board significant savings will occur over time, when income layering is properly managed. For these reasons, every retirement income plan is custom-designed and tweaked every year, preferably with the help of a tax and retirement income planning specialist.

 Tax Moves

A sound retirement income layering plan can provide significant tax saving that enhance the returns you get on your investments. Multiplied over an average retirement period of 20 years and more for each taxpayer, the savings can run into the tens of thousands of dollars. Those are important, and fantastic, tax moves you can't afford to miss out on.

35 GUARDING THE PRIZE: Minimizing Tax Instalments

SENIORS MUST OFTEN MAKE QUARTERLY TAX instalment remittances: due on the 15th of March, June, September and December. Farmers do so annually on December 31, based on their net income for the year. But, the fact is, that many taxpayers overpay their instalments every year. As vigilant as you must be to pay only the correct amount of tax while you are working, the same principle holds true in retirement.

Instalment Payment Threshold. The quarterly instalment payment threshold, used to determine whether instalments are payable, is set at the taxes owing in excess of $3,000 ($1,800 for Quebec filers) in the current and either of the two immediately preceding tax years.

Your opportunity is to monitor tax withholdings and income levels to stay out of the quarterly remittance requirement if possible, and keep your money working for you in your investment portfolio instead. Also, if you expect your income will drop this year over prior years, change your quarterly remittances.

ESSENTIAL TAX FACT ▶ **It is Not Mandatory to Follow the Instalment Notices Sent by CRA.** You can request to change your payments based on your prior year results or an estimation of current year income.

Most people aren't aware of these options. There are in fact, three methods by which CRA will accept those tax remittances from you. These are:

- *The current-year method:* You can pay your estimated taxes for the current year by paying 25% of that amount on each of the instalment due dates.

- *The prior-year method:* You can pay one-quarter of the taxes due in the prior year on each of the instalment dates.

- *The no-calculation option:* Use the instalment notices that CRA sends out and pay the amount specified. CRA calculates the amount due for the first two instalments as one-quarter of the taxes payable in the second prior year and the last two instalments as one-half of taxes payable in the prior year less the first two instalment payments.

TRUE-TO-LIFE EXAMPLE ▶ Gertrude's income consists of Old Age Security, CPP and investment income. Her taxes due in the past two tax years were $4,400 and $4,000 respectively. Per the CRA instalment notices her required instalment payments were:

- March and June: $1,100
- September and December: $900

Gertrude made her first three instalments as required (total $3,100). But as December rolled around, she found that her investment income for the year had dropped, so that her balance due for this year will only be $3,500. Since she has already paid $3,100, she can reduce her December instalment to $400.

 Tax Moves

Don't take money out of your investment portfolio to make quarterly tax instalment payments to CRA that you don't need to make.

Tax Moves & Audit Busters

SAVE WELL TO MAXIMIZE YOUR ECONOMIC POWER IN RETIREMENT. Tax-efficient retirement income planning begins with the first dollar you save. That makes retirement planning an important focus for everyone.

YOU DO HAVE SOME CONTROL OVER YOUR TAX COSTS. Not so with new carbon taxes or increased medical deductibles. When it comes to your income taxes payable in retirement, always remember that it is your legal right to arrange your affairs within the framework of the law to pay the least tax possible as a family unit; one which you should optimize with pension income splitting and retirement income layering techniques.

RETIREES MUST MANAGE THEIR AFTER-TAX INCOMES. Because taxes arise on both income and capital pools; planning for a tax-efficient retirement requires the careful management of after-tax income through a process of income "layering", that limits the encroachment of capital to fund needs and wants and leaves the rest to grow with sound investment choices.

PLAN YOUR CPP PENSIONS WISELY. CPP retirement benefits are not eligible for the $2,000 Pension Income Amount. However, spouses may "equalize" the taxable CPP retirement benefits with an assignment of half of them from a higher to lower earner. Also you may wish to continue to contribute to the CPP if you work after age 64, especially as benefits rise. However, remember you must "opt out" to stop contributing and you have to start to receive the taxable benefits, too.

HOW AND WHEN YOU WITHDRAW FUNDS MATTERS. The withdrawals you make from your registered savings accounts—RPPs, RRSPs, RRIFs, IPPs, DPSPs—are taxable in the year received. Structured as a periodic pension, the amounts may qualify for a $2,000 federal pension income amount and pension income splitting with your spouse, depending on your age. Be sure your level of withdrawals don't spike your income into the next tax bracket, if possible.

TAKE ADVANTAGE OF PENSION INCOME SPLITTING. When you have an employer-sponsored RPP, you may split income with your spouse no matter your age. Therefore, it's likely not a good idea to transfer these amounts to an RRSP or RRIF or LIF, as you must wait to age 65 to split income with your spouse under these plans. Discuss this with your tax advisor in advance before you commute your pension at work.

EMPLOYER-SPONSORED PLANS OFFER MORE BENEFITS. Members of some RPPs may choose to work on a part time basis, drawing up to 60% of the benefits accrued, while at the same time continuing to accrue more benefits. Speak to your HR department about the numbers to plan your early retirement to your maximum advantage.

PUT RRSP ACCUMULATIONS IN THE HANDS OF YOUR YOUNGER SPOUSE. Your unused RRSP contribution room carries forward for use in the future, but you must be under 72 to contribute. If you are "age ineligible" and have a younger spouse, contribute to a spousal RRSP, and get a tax deduction on your return. No need to stop accumulating wealth on a tax-advantaged basis!

AVOID MAKING "EXCESS CONTRIBUTIONS." These RRSP contributions exceed your contribution room plus the allowable $2,000. If you do have an excess, it can be expensive. You will need to create RRSP contribution room with eligible earnings or pay a penalty of 1% of the excess for each month that the funds remain in your RRSP. Withdraw them as soon as you discover the problem, and file the T1-OVP return by March 31 to pay the penalty. This form is so complex, it's an incentive never to have an excess!

SAVE YOUR RRSP DEDUCTION. Do you have "undeducted RRSP contributions"? These amounts may be carried forward (indefinitely actually) and deducted in future years. That could be a good thing if you anticipate an unusual uptick in income in the future.

DON'T FLIP LOSERS INTO YOUR RRSP. Cash poor? You can make RRSP contributions by transferring funds in non-registered accounts to the RRSP. Report accrued gains earned outside of the RRSP in the year of transfer. Investments that have declined in value should not be transferred, as the loss in value will not be deductible. Better to sell those, take the capital loss, and then contribute to the RRSP.

POSTPONE TAX WHEREVER POSSIBLE. If you need to take funds from your RRSP, consider withdrawing over two tax years to postpone paying tax to the next tax year. But, budget for the withholding taxes.

ALWAYS CONSIDER THE TIME VALUE OF MONEY. A dollar in your pocket today is more valuable than a dollar to be received in the future, especially if you can earn interest or other investment returns on it now. Don't over remit or overpay instalments in retirement. Try to keep your money working with top productivity for you in your investment accounts.

Tax Tools of The Trade

The following tax forms may be required to file for various provisions specific to retirees:

- T1032 *Joint Election to Split Pension Income.* Use this form to split eligible pension income with your spouse.
- T1198 *Statement of Qualifying Retroactive Lump-Sum Payments.* Taxpayers who receive a lump sum in the current year for payments that should have been made in a prior year, may reduce their incomes to the level it would have been taxed, if received in the years it was due. CRA will do the calculations for you.
- T2201 *Disability Tax Credit Certificate*—Taxpayers who have a marked restriction in the activities of daily living or who require a significant weekly time commitment for therapy to support vital functions may qualify for the Disability Amount. But Form T2201 must be signed by a medical professional and approved by CRA.
- *Old Age Security Return of Income* (T1136) must be filed to determine whether a recovery tax for OAS clawback purposes is required. Non residents must file it to report net world income. You can also

reduce your withholding for the Old Age Security Recovery Tax (your clawback) with a T1213 (OAS) *Request To Reduce Old Age Security Recovery Tax at Source.*

- *Tax-Free Transfers From an RRSP.* Funds from your RRSP may also be transferred on a tax-free basis to numerous registered accounts using form T2033 Direct Transfer Under Subsection 146.3(14.1), 147.5(21) or 146(21), or Paragraph 146(16)(a) or 146.3(2)(e)

- *Direct transfers from a DPSP to another DPSP, RPP or RRSP.* The transfer must be a direct transfer, using form T2151 *Direct Transfer of a Single Amount Under Subsection 147(19) or Section 147.3.* On death of the DPSP plan member, the funds in the DPSP may be transferred tax-free to the surviving spouse or common-law partner's RPP, RRSP, DPSP or RRIF. Use Form T2151 *Direct Transfer of a Single Amount Under Subsection 147(19) or Section 147.3* to recognize the transfer.

- Amounts contributed to your RRSP and not yet deducted may be withdrawn tax-free and with no withholding taxes by filing Form T3012A, *Tax Deduction Waiver on the Refund of Your Undeducted RRSP Contributions.* The amount withdrawn will be included on a T4RSP slip and must be reported as income. You may, however, claim an offsetting deduction on your tax return by using Form T746 *Calculating Your Deduction for Refund of Unused RRSP Contributions* to make an allowable deduction.

- Excess RRSP contributions are subject to a penalty tax of 1% per month. Complete form T1-OVP *Individual Tax Return for RRSP Excess Contributions* by March 31 of the year following. Penalties will accrue until the excess contributions are withdrawn from the RRSP.

- *Snowbirds:* A "closer connection" declaration must be made on June 15 on Form 8840. In this way the substantial presence test, and U.S. tax filing requirements can be avoided.

Audit Buster Checklist

✔ **MISSED TAX FORMS COST MONEY.** Failing to file some of the returns and forms above can cost you big money in terms of penalties and interest. You need to be mindful of time frames, especially for overpayments.

✔ **DECLARE FOREIGN INCOME AND ASSETS.** If you have income or assets offshore, pay attention to reporting of income and asset declarations on both sides of the border.

✔ **KEEP MEDICAL RECEIPTS AND FORM T2201 HANDY.** And, if you become ill, be aware that CRA aggressively audits claims for medical and disability amounts. Be sure to follow the rules for claiming these credits, but have a good professional advocate at your side if your return is chosen for audit.

PART VI

SPECIAL PROFILES

36 LEAVING WELL: Preparing For Change

FILING A TAX RETURN IS THE MOST IMPORTANT FINANCIAL event of the year for millions of Canadian families. In a time of great demographic and economic change, taxpayers often need help to ensure they are receiving all the benefits they can from their tax systems, because these times of change can also be financially challenging. The quality of relationships matter especially in stressful times, and this is true of your relationship with CRA as well.

In this chapter, we will discover interesting tax options for people with special taxfiling profiles. In each case, acquiring deeper tax knowledge can help ensure taxpayer rights. But in particularly stressful times, divorce or death for example, knowing more about your tax options can help you ask better questions of professional advisors at a difficult time.

NEWCOMERS TO CANADA: Did you know that in 2016, Canada had 1,212,075 new immigrants who had permanently settled in Canada from 2011 to 2016, representing 3.5% of Canada's total population? Special rules apply in the year of immigration, as these newcomers are here as part year residents for tax purposes. One million more will arrive in 2018–2020.

Immigrants may be required to report income, deductions and credits from two periods: the residency period, based on the actual number of days resident here during the year and the non-residency period on the same tax return, depending on their Canadian income sources generated before and after arriving here.

ESSENTIAL TAX FACT ▶ **Part-Year Residency Requires Special Filings.** Taxpayers who immigrate to or emigrate from Canada during the year are required to file a Canadian tax return to report their **world income** during the period in which they were **resident** in Canada.

Asset Valuation on Immigration. Those who immigrate to Canada must determine the Fair Market Value (FMV) of their assets at time of immigration. Canada is not able to tax any accrued capital gains before this; nor will Canada recognize accrued losses.

Income Reporting. For tax purposes, all income is reported in the normal manner, but only for the residency period. Here's what's unusual, though:

- Personal amounts are prorated according to the number of days the taxpayer was resident in Canada.
- Provincial taxes are due to the province of residence on the last day of residency for emigrants and the last day of the year for immigrants.
- Generally refundable tax credits (GSTC, CTC, and provincial credits) are not available to emigrants, but they are for immigrants.

Full Claims: Deduction. Allowable deductions taken to reduce income can include all deductions available but applicable to the residency period. This can include support payments made to an estranged spouse that are normally deductible, child care expenses, employment expenses and so on. However, it must be shown that these amounts are attributable to income earned in the period of Canadian residency.

Full Claims—Non-Refundable Tax Credits. The following non-refundable tax credits, which apply to the residency period can be claimed in full: CPP and EI premiums paid in the residency period, Provincial Parental Insurance Plan Contributions, Canada Employment Amount, Home Buyers' Amount, the Home Accessibility Tax Credit, Adoption Expenses, the Pension Income Amount, Interest on Student Loan Amount, Tuition Amounts, Medical Expenses, Charitable Donations, spousal transfers for income earned in the residency period, amounts transferred from child (tuition for residency period and a prorated disability amount)

Refundable Credits. Most refundable credits are allowed in full to immigrants and emigrants. The exception is the Canada Workers Benefit which is only available to taxpayers who are resident throughout the year.

ABORIGINAL PEOPLES. Canada has 1,673,785 aboriginal people, representing 4.9% of the population, which has grown 42.5% in the period 2006-2016, according to our Census. Approximately 75% have registered Indian status and 44% of these people live on reserves.

Investment income. Investment income earned on the reserve is tax exempt, if the following conditions are met:

- *Interest Income* from a savings or chequing account, a term deposit or guaranteed investment certificate (GIC) is earned at a financial institution located on the reserve will be tax exempt as long as the financial institution is required to pay the interest income to the taxpayer at a location of the financial institution on a reserve; and in the case of a term deposit or GIC, the interest rate is fixed or can be calculated at the time the investment is made.

- *Dividends,* too, will be tax exempt if the head office, management, and *principal income-generating activities* of the corporation are situated on a reserve. The same is true of *rental income* earned from property situated on the reserve. Moveable property rented to someone off the reserve is considered to be taxable. In the case of royalty income, if the underlying right is situated on-reserve, the royalty income will be tax exempt.

- *Capital gains* from the disposition of properties on the reserve are tax exempt.

- *RRSPs:* exempt income will not qualify for earned income purposes and so no RRSP deduction can be made. However, only income earned in these plans will later by taxable. If RRSPs are funded with taxable sources, regular rules apply.

Note: Old Age Security and Guaranteed Income Supplement payments are taxable. So are support payments made by an estranged spouse if the recipient lives off the reserve.

Corporate or Trust Income. Section 87 of the *Indian Act does not apply to corporations or trusts*, even if they are owned or controlled by an Indian. A corporation or trust is treated as a separate taxpayer and therefore neither would be considered an Indian for purposes of the exemption. If a trust has claimed a deduction for amounts paid to an Indian, the amounts must be added to income unless it can be shown there are connecting factors of the trust's income to a reserve, in the case of business or investment income.

THE ELDERLY. Canada has one of the three lowest death rates in the world, eclipsed only by Iceland and Australia. With longer living, however, comes more disease, more costs and potentially more tax assistance: note that two thirds of people age 75 and over report having major medical problems[13], some of which can hasten or exacerbate cognitive decline and dementias like Alzheimer's disease. The costs of care can be significant. From a planning perspective, consider discussing the following in your visits with your financial advisors to develop a plan for risk management in case of significant and long-term illness:

Checklist for Health Transition Planning

☐ **REQUIRED CASH FLOW:** Establish a new budget for anticipated income and new costs using after-tax dollars using inflation-adjusted dollars.

☐ **REGISTERED INVESTMENTS:** What do we tap first? TFSA? RRSP? RRIF? What are the tax consequences? Clawback consequences on refundable or non-refundable tax credits?

☐ **NON-REGISTERED INVESTMENTS:** What financial assets will be used? Tax consequences? Opportunity to leverage for short term expenses?

☐ **INSURANCE PLANNING:** Are there life insurance assets with cash surrender values? Blue Cross, Disability? Critical Illness? Will home insurance cover an unoccupied home in the case of hospitalization or a stay in a personal care home or long-term care facility?

☐ **CPP DISABILITY BENEFITS:** What is the amount of benefits available to client, spouse and children?

☐ **GUARANTEED INCOME SUPPLEMENT:** Is income low enough for application to be made for the GIS to supplement income? Is there an involuntary separation due to special care home needs? This can increase GIS benefits.

☐ **EI COMPASSIONATE CARE COVERAGE:** What is the amount of benefits available to caregivers?

☐ **TAX TREATMENT OF INCOME SOURCES:** What are the terms of annuities, should beneficiaries to company benefit plans, registered plans be changed?

---

13 Brondesbury Group Financial Life Stages of Older Canadians, Prepared for the Ontario Securities Commission, Spring, 2015.

☐ **INCOME TAX DEDUCTIONS AND CREDITS:** are there special tax preferences available to generate new funds to cover new costs:

- Home accessibility tax credit
- RRSP Home Buyer Plan
- Canada Caregiver Credit
- Medical expenses
- Disability tax credit
- Nursing Home and Attendant Care
- Medical Expense Supplement

☐ **WAR VETERANS:** what special allowances are available to war veterans?

☐ **PROVINCIAL DRUG PLANS:** what income levels/deductibles or senior's drug plans are available?

SEPARATION AND DIVORCE. When spouses or common-law partners have lived apart for a period of at least 90 days because of a breakdown of their conjugal relationship, then from the beginning of that 90-day period they are no longer treated as spouses. In the year of such a breakdown, there are significant tax rules to observe regarding the following:

- the division of assets
- the divisions of spousal or individually held RRSPs
- the claiming of child care expenses
- support payments made and received and legal fees paid
- federal non-refundable credits such as the amount for eligible dependants and refundable credits including the Canada Child Benefit and the Canada Worker's Benefit, and
- the effect of relationship breakdown on provincial tax credits.

Division of Assets. On the breakdown of a marriage or common-law relationship, where the terms of a separation or divorce agreement require that the funds from one spouse's DPSP, RESP, RPP, PRPP, RRSP, or RRIF be transferred to the other, the funds may be transferred on a tax-free basis.

Spousal RRSPs. Withdrawals from spousal or common-law partner RRSPs made by the annuitant are generally reportable by the contributing spouse if any RRSP contribution has been made in the current year or the previous two years. However, this rule is waived for separating/divorcing couples. The minimum holding period requirement does not apply to spousal RRSPs when the taxpayers are living apart for the required period of time due to a breakdown in their relationship.

Depreciable Assets. The transfer of depreciable property (such as a rental house) between spouses as a result of a relationship breakdown takes place at the *Undepreciated Capital Cost (UCC)* of the property. As a result, no recapture, terminal loss, or capital gain is incurred on the transfer.

Other Financial and Non-Financial Assets. For other capital property, the transfer takes place at the *Adjusted Cost Base (ACB)* of the assets, so again no capital gains or losses are triggered.

Attribution Rules. When one spouse transfers assets to the other, the Attribution Rules generally attribute any income earned by the transferred assets back to the transferor. However, the Attribution Rules do not apply to income earned during the period when the former spouses are living apart because of a breakdown in the relationship. Capital gains or losses, however, continue to attribute back unless the spouses elect otherwise.

Child Care Expenses. Child care expenses must normally be claimed by the lower-income spouse but may be claimed by the higher-income spouse during a period where the taxpayer was separated from the other supporting person due to a breakdown in their relationship for a period of at least 90 days as long as they were reconciled within the first 60 days after the taxation year. If the taxpayers were not reconciled within 60 days after the taxation year, then each spouse may claim any child care expenses they paid during the year with no adjustment for child care expenses claimed by the other taxpayer.

Alimony, Support and Legal Fees on Separation or Divorce. Alimony or support payments made to a spouse or common-law partner are taxable to the recipient and deductible by the payor. In the year of separation or divorce, however, the payer may claim either the deduction for support or the spousal amount, but not both.

> **ESSENTIAL TAX FACT** ▶ **Legal Fees to Obtain a Divorce or Separation Agreement are Normally Not Deductible.** However, CRA considers legal costs incurred to obtain spousal support relating specifically to the care of children (not the spouse) under the *Divorce Act* or under provincial legislation, as well as the costs incurred to obtain an increase in support or to make child support non-taxable, to be deductible.

Claiming Refundable Tax Credits. While most taxpayers in this situation will want to immediately supplement their cash flow with these credits, remember that since a separation is not recognized until 90 days after it begins, you should *not* notify CRA of your separation until you have been separated for a continuous period of 90 days.

However, if you marry or divorce, you must notify CRA immediately. Also, because the statute of limitations for recovery of missed or underpaid credits is generally only 11 months, it's important to notify CRA immediately after you have met the rules. Some leniency in the time frames may be available.

The *Income Tax Act* assumes that the eligible CCB recipient is the female parent. However, "prescribed factors" will be considered in determining what constitutes care and upbringing and who is fulfilling that responsibility.

For example, where, after the breakdown of a conjugal relationship, the single parent and child returns to live with his or her parents, the single parent will continue to be presumed to be the supporting individual unless they too are under 18 years old. In that case, the grandparents may claim the Canada Child Benefit for both their child and their grandchild.

Audit Check Point

- ✔ Where both parents share custody of a child, CRA now allows the parents to share the CCB and GST/HST Credit. However, the audit requirements are onerous. Be prepared to show CRA that you are indeed separated and to what extent you each are involved with the care of your children.

Provincial Tax Credits. Many provinces have tax reductions or refundable credits that are based on family net income. In most cases, in the year of separation, it is not necessary to include the estranged spouse or common-law partner's income in the family income calculation and normally no credits or reductions on behalf of the estranged spouse or common-law partner will be allowed. Each partner will claim the credits or reductions to which he or she is entitled based on their own income.

Tax Efficiency Checklist for Separating or Divorcing Couples

- ☐ *What is the estimated personal tax liability at the end of the first year of separation and each subsequent year based on your new income level?* Each person will be taxed as an individual after the separation and will be responsible for their own tax remittances. This must be carefully understood to properly manage any instalment remittance requirements and negotiate the right net cash flow required to manage family finances.

- ☐ *What are the individual net incomes?* Refundable and non-refundable tax credits will be allocated based on individual, not family, net income levels.

- ☐ *What is your unused RRSP contribution room?* Spousal RRSP contributions will no longer be allowed. Are you prepared to make your own contribution?

☐ *Are there new opportunities for family income splitting?* Income attribution becomes a non-issue, except for transfers to minor children or a new spouse.

☐ *Are there family trust structures or shares in corporate companies involved?* If so, review those structures and any change requirements with your professional advisory team. This will asset with income planning and income splitting.

☐ *Have all the transfer forms for private pension accumulations in RPPs, RRSPs, RRIFs, PRPP's, etc. been completed?* These accumulations can be split when the parties are living apart if the payments follow a written separation agreement, court order, decree or judgment. The transfer must be made directly between the plans of the two spouses and one spouse cannot be disqualified because of age (over age 71).

☐ *Have you transferred the TFSA?* TFSA accumulations can also be split on a tax-free basis. The funds from one party's TFSA may be transferred tax-free to the other party's TFSA. This will have no effect on the contribution room of either of the parties.

☐ *How will Canada Pension Plan accumulations be divided and when?*

☐ *Are there inheritances to consider?* Property brought into the marriage by one of the spouses will be considered owned by that person. Generally, the property is assigned to that person during the negotiation of the separation agreement. Have the transfer forms been completed?

☐ *Is a designation of principal residence required?* After separation, CRA recognizes two family units, and therefore it is possible for each to own one tax-exempt principal residence. Who will own each of those residences and what are their valuations?

☐ *Have valuations been completed for the transfer of other property?*

Transfers of Property on Relationship Breakdown. Property can be transferred at its Adjusted Cost Base, or Undepreciated Capital Cost in the case of depreciable property so that there are no tax consequences at the time of transfer. These rules effectively transfer any accrued gains on the property to the transferee.

By special election, assets may be transferred at their Fair Market Value. This could result in significant tax savings if, for example, the transferor had unused capital losses to apply to gains on the transferred property. Have the valuations been completed?

Where this election is made, the transferee receives a significant tax benefit in that future capital gains will be calculated based on the FMV at the time of transfer. Further, if the FMV of the property is less than its ACB, it may be advantageous to trigger the capital loss. This would allow the transferor to offset other capital gains of the year, the previous three years or capital gains realized in the future.

> **TAX FORM FACT.** Do you have a copy of the T664 *Capital Gains Election* form? Capital gains elections made in February 1994 may increase the adjusted cost base in calculating the tax consequences of property transfers resulting from the relationship breakdown.

DEATH OF A TAXPAYER. To everything there is a season, and for many, understanding the tax consequences of death on personal and family net worth is a crowning achievement that allows for a powerful wealth transition. This type of preparedness, unfortunately, is rare.

While no personal wealth management plan can be completed without a plan for transferring assets to the next generation, the majority of Canadians are reluctant to discuss the transfer of their assets with family members and many don't have a will. But to paraphrase Benjamin Franklin, death and taxes are perhaps the only two constants we can count on from the moment of birth... and it pays well to be prepared for the inevitable.

> **ESSENTIAL TAX FACT** ▶ **Deemed Dispositions at Death Can Be Very Expensive.** You can plan to transfer your assets on a tax-efficient basis throughout your lifetime, to take advantage of the highs and lows in economic cycles, and to preserve most of your wealth at your death. Without those plans, however, you could lose half of it.

A lifetime of complicated personal relationships makes the transition of wealth more difficult. That's why we look to significant legal documents—your will, power of attorney, and health care directives as well as your significant financial documents—the personal net worth statement, tax returns and your financial plans, for guidance. Whether you are already alone or preparing to be alone, protecting your assets at the time of death is an important obligation to your family as well as society. Consider the following checklist for starting an estate plan:

Checklist: Objectives for Starting an Estate Plan

- [ ] *Identify financial institutions.* Where are your assets held? Include key contacts.

- [ ] *Identify advisors.* Who are your professional advisors including banker, accountant, lawyer, stockbroker, insurance agent?

- [ ] *Identify proxies.* Who will exercise Power of Attorney if you become disabled or cannot direct your own personal affairs?

- [ ] *Identify heirs.* List exact contact information, as well as their relationship to you. In the case of singles, these heirs could include your favorite charity. Discuss options for the transfer of assets and funds during your lifetime and at death.

- [ ] *Identify gifts.* Sketch out what you wish for each of your heirs to receive.

- [ ] *Identify needs.* Will any of your heirs require assistance with ongoing income?

- [ ] *Identify executors.* Prepare a list of possible executor(s) and make approaches.

- [ ] *Identify guardians.* Prepare a list of those to whom you would trust the care of your minor children, as well as those who should not have that responsibility.

- [ ] *Identify business succession plans.* How should your business interests be distributed, and who should step in to run the show?

- [ ] *Plan for probate fees and capital gains taxes at death.* Review life insurance policies that may be used for those purposes.

- [ ] *Identify capital assets and their fair market value annually.*

- [ ] *Identify asset transfer instructions.* Which assets should be transferred during your lifetime, and which should be transferred only upon your death?

- [ ] *Make plans for safekeeping.* Keep all important documents in a safety deposit box and identify the location.

- [ ] *Deal with debt.* Cleaning up spilled milk is no fun for anyone... especially if it's been there for a while. List debt obligations and the order they should be repaid. Make a list of ongoing financial obligations that should be cancelled on death.

- [ ] *Draw up your will.* Tell your lawyer where it is to be kept.

Tax Filing Deadlines at Time of Death. When someone dies, one mandatory final return must be filed for the period January 1 to date of death, and this return must be filed by the later of:

- April 30 of the year immediately following the year of death
- six months after date of death

TAX FORM FACT. There are several "elective returns" that can be filed on death, which will allow you to claim against certain personal amounts, to result in a substantial tax benefit.

However, the final return from January to date of death is usually the only one most taxpayers will file. On that return, income earned up to date of death is reported. Certain income sources may have to be "prorated" to the date of death, including interest, rents, royalties, or annuity income. Offsetting expenses are accrued to date of death in a similar fashion.

Deemed Dispositions at Death. By far the most significant transaction on the final return could revolve around the disposition of capital assets. That's because a deemed disposition of your assets is considered to have taken place immediately before your death.

When you die, you are deemed to have disposed of your assets immediately before death, usually at Fair Market Value (FMV). However, the value of the deemed disposition can vary, depending on who will acquire the assets... your spouse (including common-law partner), child or another. Transfers to children or others are generally made at the property's FMV; transfers to spouse can be at the asset's adjusted cost base (or UCC in the case of depreciable assets) or FMV.

The use of "tax-free rollovers." The deemed disposition rules on death of the taxpayer therefore override the Attribution Rules that apply while living. That is, capital property transferred to the spouse on your death will not be taxed until your spouse disposes of the property. The spouse will use your adjusted cost base, and pay tax on the full gain from the time you acquired the asset, thereby completely postponing the tax consequences at the time of your death until your spouse dies or sells the property.

Depending on your taxable income at the time of your death, your executor may wish to roll over assets to the spouse on a tax-free basis or have them transfer at fair market value. Fair value may make sense if your income in the year of death is low or if you have unused capital losses from the past that have been carried forward. Such balances can often be used to offset income created by the higher valuations that have accrued to the date of death. It will also provide your surviving spouse with the opportunity to start with a higher adjusted base on the acquisition of your assets, which will save them money down t. line as well.

> **TAX FORM FACT.** Use the $100,000 Capital Gains Election to your advantage. Be sure to provide your executor with a copy of the 1994 tax return and, in particular, Form T664 *Capital Gains Election* upon which a capital gains election may have been made to use up your $100,000 Capital Gains Exemption. This will affect the calculation of the deemed disposition of capital properties on the final return.

In the absence of those plans, capital gains or losses resulting from the deemed disposition of your assets on death must be reported, together with any recapture or terminal loss on depreciable assets, with the resulting tax payable (if any) on that return.

> **TAX FORM FACT.** It is possible to postpone the payment of tax arising on the death of a taxpayer. Use Form T2075 *Election to Defer Payment of Income Tax, Under Subsection 159(5) of the Income Tax Act by a Deceased Taxpayer's Legal Representative or Trustee*

RRSPs and other pensions. Didn't spend it all? What happens when you die and leave unspent accumulations in your RRSP, PRPP or RRIF?

You are deemed to have received the fair market value of all assets in those plans immediately prior to death. If there is a surviving spouse or common-law partner the assets may be transferred tax-free to that person's registered plan. In certain circumstances, the accumulations can be transferred to a financially dependent child or grandchild, even when there is a surviving spouse. Speak to your tax advisors about these options.

If there is no surviving spouse or common-law partner, the assets are transferred to the estate and the full value of the RRSP or RRIF is included in income on the final return. Any decrease in value of RRSP assets while held in the estate may be used to decrease the income reported on the deceased's final return. Similar rules will apply to accumulations in PRPPs.

In recent years, we have also seen the introduction of several surtaxes and high-income tax brackets designed to "tax the rich." Unfortunately, those brackets also seem to catch the unspent accumulations in registered plans such as RRSPs and RRIFs and therefore represent a new estate tax. Be sure you plan your withdrawals carefully throughout your lifetime to generate your taxes on these accumulations at the lower tax brackets or risk losing half the amounts above the high-income bracket levels.

EXAMPLE ▶ Wilhelm was a widower, living in Ontario. When [he died] in May, the value of his RRSP assets was $400,000. In [addition he ow]ned a rental property with an accrued capital gain of [$50,000. He h]ad income for the year of $35,000.

Because Wilhelm had no spouse, the value of his RRSP assets plus the capital gain on his rental property are added to his other income for the year. The result is a taxable income of $485,000. Even though Wilhelm normally has a very modest income, he will be taxed at the highest rate: 53.53% on his final return. Over $220,000 of his legacy will go to the government in income taxes.

Tax-Free Savings Accounts. Accumulated earnings in your TFSA are not taxable, but earnings after death no longer accumulate tax-free. However, the assets may be rolled over to the TFSA of a surviving spouse or common-law partner.

Life Insurance Policies. Death generates numerous tax consequences which can be expensive, particularly for single taxpayers. To preserve wealth, however, the acquisition of a life insurance policy can make some sense and can lead to numerous tax advantages, especially if deemed dispositions of capital assets result in a hefty tax bill. Note, when an individual buys an insurance policy, the premium is not deductible. But, subsequent benefits or proceeds paid out to beneficiaries are tax exempt.

Income earned within whole life or universal life insurance policies will generally accumulate on a tax-exempt basis provided that the policies have a limitation on the size of the investment component. These features should be discussed with your insurance advisor. The proceeds from a life insurance policy can help to pay the taxes which arise on the deemed disposition of taxable assets as at the date of death.

 Tax Moves

Managing the financial well-being of your household and family with a collaborative, strategic, and tax-efficient approach to your wealth accumulations, is especially important for specific tax filing profiles. Be sure to see your tax, financial, and legal advisors for help to get the most of the tax system, and to enable a sound relationship with the CRA.

Tax Moves & Audit Buster

PART-YEAR RESIDENCY REQUIRES SPECIAL FILINGS. Taxpayers who immigrate to or emigrate from Canada during the year are required to file a Canadian tax return to report their world income during the period in which they were **resident** in Canada.

ASSET VALUATION ON IMMIGRATION IS REQUIRED. Those who immigrate to Canada must determine the Fair Market Value (FMV) of their assets at time of immigration. Canada is not able to tax any accrued capital gains before this; nor will Canada recognize accrued losses.

ABORIGINAL PEOPLE: DETERMINE TAX STATUS AND WHERE INCOME IS EARNED. A special provision under section 87 of the *Income Tax Act*, exempts income earned on the reserve from taxes for Status Indians.

A HEALTH CARE TRANSITION PLAN CAN PRESERVE WEALTH. For vulnerable seniors, the tax system can provide important support. However, the best time to plan for cognitive or physical decline is when you are healthy. Be sure to claim special tax preferences available to generate new funds to cover new costs, including the home accessibility tax credit, access new funds under the RRSP Home Buyer Plan to move to a home more accessible to the disabled, claim the Canada Caregiver Credit, Disability Tax Credit, medical expenses, nursing home and attendant care and in some cases, the Refundable Medical Expense Supplement.

TRANSFER CAPITAL ASSETS TO YOUR SPOUSE TAX-FREE. While most asset transfers result in a deemed disposition at fair market value and result in a taxable capital gain, court-ordered transfers and transfers at death to a spouse may be made on a tax-free basis.

PLAN DEEMED DISPOSITIONS ON DEATH OF SPOUSE CAREFULLY. It's possible to rollover assets on a tax free basis from the deceased spouse to the surviving spouse. But using fair market value may bring better results; to use up losses the deceased may have and to bump up adjusted cost bases so that the survivors pay less tax in the future. Professional help is important.

TRANSFER RRSP, TFSA OR OTHER REGISTERED ASSETS TO YOUR SPOUSE TAX-FREE. Either at death, or through a court-ordered transfer, registered accounts can be transferred to a former spouse on a tax-free basis. TFSA assets received from your spouse may be transferred to your own TFSA even if you don't have TFSA contribution room.

USE LIFE INSURANCE TO PROVIDE A TAX-FREE INHERITANCE TO YOUR CHILDREN. There is no tax on life insurance proceeds. Be sure to have enough life insurance to at least pay the taxes on your final return so that your assets do not have to be sold to pay the taxes. In some cases, taxes can be deferred until the sale of assets has occurred however; speak to your tax advisor about this option.

Tax Tools of the Trade

THE FOLLOWING TAX FORMS MAY BE REQUIRED BY PART YEAR RESIDENTS:

NR73 Determination of Residency Status (Leaving Canada)

NR74 Determination of Residency Status (Entering Canada)

Schedule A Statement of World Income for Non-Residents and Deemed Residents of Canada

Schedule B Allowable Amount of Non-Refundable Tax Credits for Non-Resident and Deemed Residents of Canada

Schedule C Electing Under Section 217 of the Income Tax Act for Non-Resident and Deemed Residents of Canada

THE FOLLOWING TAX FORM MAY BE REQUIRED AT DEATH OF A TAXPAYER:

RC240 Designation of an Exempt Contribution Tax-Free Savings Account (TFSA)

RC249 Post-death decline in the value of an unmatured RRSP or RRIF—Final distribution after 2008

T1-ADJ T1 Adjustment Request

T1090 Death of a RRIF Annuitant—Designated Benefit

T1255 Designation of a Property as a Principal Residence by the Legal Representative of a Deceased Individual

T2019 Death of an RRSP Annuitant—Refund of Premiums

T2069 Election in Respect of Amounts Not Deductible as Reserves for the Year of Death

T2075 Election to Defer Payment of Income Tax, Under Subsection 159(5) of the Income Tax Act by a Deceased Taxpayer's Legal Representative or Trustee

TX19 Asking for a Clearance Certificate

Audit-Buster Checklist

- ✓ **NEWCOMERS.** Be sure to get a fair market valuation of all assets on your date of entry in Canada. In addition, apply for your Social Insurance Number, the refundable tax credits your family may qualify for and file a tax return every year by the filing due dates. The Canadian tax system is based on self-assessment and the burden of proof is on you to justify what you claim on your tax return.

- ✓ **ABORIGINAL PEOPLE.** Be sure to report income that is earned off the reserve on your tax return to avoid tax trouble.

- ✓ **VULNERABLE PEOPLE.** CRA has been particularly tough on auditing those who claim the Disability Amount and medical expenses. Be sure you have the proper documentation.

- ✓ **SEPARATED PEOPLE.** Avoid tax trouble by reporting your taxable spousal support and alimony. Many make the mistake of thinking these payments, like child support, are not taxable. It's important to make quarterly instalments, too, if you have higher income levels without adequate tax withholdings.

- ✓ **OBTAIN A CLEARANCE CERTIFICATE FOR DECEASED TAXPAYERS.** It's an important rule for executors, who face personal liability for taxes payable.

Concluding Thoughts

MORE THAN HALF A CENTURY AGO, Finance Minister Edgar Benson, through a Royal Commission on Taxation, introduced a framework and guiding principles for a tax system we still follow. It was ground-breaking for its time, as it introduced, amongst other things, a tax on capital gains and other measures that would redistribute the tax burden and, along the way, raise 5% more revenues in the first five years. It was greeted with howls of protest and many changes in the ten years of deliberations that preceded implementation.

The ideals of this new tax system, importantly, set standards for fairness and equity[14] and a goal for greater simplification, which, as we all know, is the illusive challenge when it comes to anything tax-related. Specific goals were articulated:

- Fairness in taxation implies that people in similar circumstances should carry similar shares of the tax load.

- People with higher incomes should be expected to pay a larger share of their incomes than those with lower incomes.

- "Ability to pay" is embodied mainly in personal income tax as a progressive graduated tax.

- The tax system should be simple enough for the vast majority of taxpayers to willingly comply with the law, and understand it, while trusting an efficient and impartial tax department to administer it.

- The tax system should not interfere seriously with economic growth and productivity... while taxes cannot promote all economic goals, they should not interfere with incentives to work and invest.

---

14 Proposals for Tax Reform, Hon. E. J. Benson Minister of Finance 1969.

Since then, successive governments have indeed used the tax system to promote economic and social goals, as well as raise and collect taxes, and redistribute income. Most recently, the federal government has attempted a significant, and ultimately failed attempt at comprehensive tax reform for the taxation of private corporations. Have all these changes led to a better tax system for Canadians? One could argue, perhaps not. Here's why:

Things have gotten more complex. In 1917, the tax return was 6 pages long and contained 23 lines; today there are over 300 lines on the return, and it is estimated that it costs $500 a year for Canadians to comply with their tax system[15]. The mind-numbing complexity recently introduced for caregivers, and family business owners, is about to make compliance a lot more expensive for many.

If it feels like you are paying more, it's because you are. Back in 1918, the share of government revenues from the personal income tax was 2.6%; in 2019 it was the biggest revenue line item: 51% of all revenues collected by the federal government came from personal income taxes. In 1918 the average tax burden per tax filer was $14.

Efforts to help taxpayers are at an all-time low. Aside from significant service problems at CRA, Finance Canada has been deliberate in its release of complex legislation at inopportune times (mid-summer and right before Christmas). They have not made it easy to understand, analyze and interpret new legislation and its effect on your bottom line by limiting consultation periods and debate.

These are three big reasons to hone your tax moves to make sure you arrange your affairs within the framework of the law to pay only the correct amount of tax. Now, here are three action items to ensure they are audit-proof too:

1. **GET POINTS ON THE SCOREBOARD.** Always use your available tax deductions and credits to your maximum advantage, as soon as you can. Tax reforms of the future may limit the personal tax deductions and credits you can claim today. Stay up to date on tax change by subscribing to a complimentary copy of Knowledge Bureau Report at knowledgebureau.com. We will do our best to keep you up-to-date with tax change in real time and tell you what it means to you and your bottom line.

2. **HAVE A STRONG DEFENCE.** The government has invested close to $1 billion in the CRA recently to enforce the tax rules Canadians have been filing their returns under. Over $7 Billion is expected to be

---

15 The History and Development of Canada's Personal Income Tax, edited by William Watson Fraser Institute April 2017.

recovered through the tax collections department alone. The CRA, in other words, is armed to audit YOU. Be proactive, be audit-proof, and be prepared to establish and stand firm on your taxpayer rights. But, take responsibility, too. Play the game with respect, and make sure you file on time, with all documentation in order.

3. **BE A TAX-WISE INVESTOR.** Build your family's wealth by using all your TFSA, RRSP and RESP room; invest tax-efficiently in your non-registered accounts. Remember, too that the accrued gains on your principal residence may be completely tax exempt; however, there are new reporting requirements when you dispose of it. To avoid expensive penalties, always know your tax form facts.

Taxes do appear to be going up for most taxpayer profiles—from middle class earners to high earners and non-active shareholders in family businesses — and so is tax audit risk. For these reasons, how you play the tax game matters more than ever. This is, indeed, about your money and how much of it you get to keep. Knowing more about your tax system is going to pay off, in higher tax refunds, a more proactive relationship with your professional tax and financial advisors and in a more empowered relationship with the CRA.

I hope this book helped you to think about how to pay only the correct amount of tax and no more, but also to maximize your tax-efficient income and capital through planning and, finally, to better manage your relationship with the CRA, for your financial peace of mind.

Yours in tax savings,

Evelyn Jacks

ESSENTIAL TAX FACTS
Appendices

Appendix 1—Tax Acronyms

Appendix 2—Tax Trouble: CRA's Penalty Power

Appendix 3—Tax 360: Your Carry Over Periods

Appendix 4—New Moves: By Taxfiler Profile

All Taxpayers

Changes for Employees

Changes for Students

Changes for Families

Changes for Homeowners

Changes for the Sick or Disabled

Changes for Investors

Changes for Business Owners

Changes for Pensioners

Appendix 5—Summary of Personal Amounts

APPENDIX 1. TAX ACRONYMS

Acronym	Meaning
ACB	Adjusted Cost Base: used in calculating capital gains or losses
CCA	Capital Cost Allowance: a deduction for depreciation of income-producing assets
CCB	Canada Child Benefit: a refundable credit paid monthly to parents of children under 18. The amount of the benefits depends on the number and age of the children. The benefit is "clawed back" as income rises
CESG	Canada Education Savings Grant: an amount of up to $600 given to those who contribute to Registered Education Savings Plans for their children
CLB	Canada Learning Bond: an amount allocated to low-income children by government as a savings incentive to be transferred to an RESP
CPI	Consumer Price Index: used to calculate the indexing of tax provisions for real dollar terms
CPP	Canada Pension Plan: a contributions-based public pension benefit system
CRA	Canada Revenue Agency: formerly Revenue Canada
CSB	Canada Savings Bonds: a fixed rate interest-bearing investment backed by the Canadian government (No new bonds after November 2017)
CWB	Canada Workers Benefit: replaces the Working Income Tax Benefit for low earners in 2019. It is a refundable credit calculated as 26% of earned income in excess of $3,000 (25% in 2018). It is reduced as income rises above a threshold specific to individuals and families. Several provinces have variations
EI	Employment Insurance: a premium-based public insurance program for those who lose their source of employment income
GIC	Guaranteed Investment Certificate: an interest-bearing investment
GIS	Guaranteed Income Supplement: a supplement paid to low-income seniors to ensure a minimum income level. The GIS is reportable but not taxable
GST	Goods and Services Tax: a federal tax on goods and services purchased in Canada
GSTC	Goods and Services Tax Credit: a refundable tax credit for low income families to offset the Goods and Services Tax
HBP	Home Buyers' Plan: a plan to allow individuals to borrow from their RRSPs to assist in a home purchase
HST	Harmonized Sales Tax: a single tax which incorporates the federal GST and a provincial sales tax

Acronym	Meaning
LLP	Lifelong Learning Plan: a plan to allow individuals to borrow from their RRSPs to assist in full-time education
LSIF	Labour-Sponsored Investment fund: an investment fund which is registered in a province and qualifies for the Labour-Sponsored funds Tax Credit
MTR	Marginal Tax Rate: the tax rate that will be applied to the next dollar of income earned. for accuracy, we often include in this rate the federal and provincial taxes and surtaxes as well as the clawback of refundable and non-refundable credits
NR	Non-refundable: a credit that will reduce taxes payable, but will be lost if the credit exceeds the taxes. A refundable credit, by contrast, will be paid to the taxpayer if the credit exceeds taxes payable
OAS	Old Age Security: a universal government pension for Canadians who are 65 or older. OAS begins to be clawed back when income exceeds a certain threshold
PRPP	Pooled Retirement Pension Plans: a new retirement vehicle, introduced in November 2011 to provide a registered savings opportunity for small companies and their employees who do not have access to RPPs
RDSP	Registered Disability Savings Plan: a registered plan within which funds can be accumulated to provide a private pension option for the disabled
RESP	Registered Education Savings Plan: a registered plan for accumulating funds for a child's education. Contributions to such a plan may qualify for the CESG
RPP	Registered Pension Plan: a private pension plan funded by the employer and/or employee which is registered and qualifies for a tax deduction
RRIF	Registered Retirement Income fund: a registered fund which provides for the payment of an increasing portion of the funds in the plan each year until the taxpayer turns 90
RRSP	Registered Retirement Savings Plan: a contribution-based savings plan where contribution limits are based on earned income (to a pre-defined limit). Contributions to the plan are tax deductible, income earned within the plan is not taxed until withdrawn, and funds withdrawn from the plan are taxed at the taxpayer's current marginal rate
SDSP	Specified Disability Savings Plan: an RDSP where the beneficiary's life expectancy is less than five years. Special rules apply to allow faster withdrawal of funds
TFSA	Tax-free Savings Account: an account to which taxpayers over age 18 may contribute. Contribution room increases each year and both earnings and withdrawals from accounts are not taxable

APPENDIX 2. TAX TROUBLE: CRA'S PENALTY POWER

	Penalty
Failure to file a return on time	5% of unpaid taxes plus 1% per month up to a maximum of 12 months from filing due date
Subsequent failure to file on time within a three-year period	10% of unpaid taxes plus 2% per month to a maximum of 20 months from filing due date
Failure to provide information on a required form	$100 for each failure
Failure to provide Social Insurance Number	$100 for each failure unless the card is applied for within 15 days of the request
Failure to file a return or comply with a duty	For each such failure, the greater of $100 and the product obtained when $25 is multiplied by the number of days, not exceeding 100, during which the failure continues.
Gross negligence: false statement or omission of information in the return	50% of tax on understated income with a minimum $100 penalty. This penalty will also apply to a false statement relating to the GSTC.
Late or insufficient instalments	50% of interest payable exceeding $1,000 or 25% of interest payable if no instalments were made, whichever is greater.
Misrepresentation by a third party: penalty for tax planning arrangements or valuation activities	$1,000 and the total of gross entitlements from the plan or in all other cases, $1,000
Third-party participation in making of false statements	$1,000 and lesser of the penalty to which the taxpayer is liable to under S. 163(2) and the total of $100,000 plus the person's gross compensation
Failure to deduct or remit source deductions	10% of amount not withheld, or remitted
Second such failure in same year	20% of amount not withheld or remitted if this was done knowingly or through gross negligence.

APPENDIX 3. TAX 360: YOUR CARRY OVER PERIODS

Carry Over Period	Details
Preceding ten years	• To correct errors and omissions for most federal provisions. • To correct errors and omissions for GST/HST Rebates.
Preceding three years	• To apply capital losses to capital gains in those years. • To apply non-capital losses to income of prior years. • To adjust most provincial tax credits.
24-month period	Medical expenses can be claimed over this period ending on and including the date of death.
The current and immediately preceding year	• To apply previous net capital losses carried forward against other income in the year of death, after their application to capital gains in current and prior three prior years. • To claim charitable donations in year of death.
Preceding 11 months	To recover unpaid Canada Child Benefits and GST/HST Credits. Note: late applications may be allowed with sufficient documentation.
The following year	To use unclaimed medical expenses of the previous year to make a claim for the best 12-month period ending in the tax year.
The next three years	• To make or amend a joint election to split pension income. • To recover overpaid EI premiums in cases where employee did not qualify (e.g. significant or majority owner of a corporation).
The next five years	• To use any charitable donation tax receipts. • To deduct student loan interest.
The next seven years	• To minimum tax carry forwards. • To claim legal fees in excess of RRSP contributions in respect of job termination payments.
The next 10 years	To apply allowable Business Investment losses (BIL) against other income. Thereafter, unabsorbed loss becomes a capital loss.
The next 20 years	To apply unused non-capital losses to other income.
Indefinite time	• To use RRSP deduction when there is RRSP room. • To use capital losses against capital gains up to and including year of death. • To use unclaimed RRSP deductions, up to and including year of death. • To use tuition, education & textbook amounts carry forward.

APPENDIX 4. NEW MOVES: BY TAXFILER PROFILE

The following overview includes changes proposed in the March 19, 2019 federal budget, which were not passed into law at the time of writing.

A. ALL TAXPAYERS

TOP PERSONAL TAX RATES. Here are recent federal tax brackets and rates you need to know to plan the level of your taxable income sources.

	2018 Rates		2019 Rates
Up to $11,809	0	Up to $12,069	0
$11,810 to $46,605	15%	$12,070 to $47,630	15%
$46,606 to $93,208	20.5%	$47,631 to $95,259	20.5%
$93,209 to $144,489	26%	$95,260 to $147,667	26%
$144,490 to $205,842	29%	$147,668 to $210,371	29%
Over $205,842	33%	Over $210,371	33%

- Pay attention, especially, to the top tax rate of 33%, which will apply to several calculations on the return:
   a. **TAXES ON SPLIT INCOME WITH MINORS AND WITH ADULTS.** These calculations will reflect the 33% rate on all income.
   b. **TAXES LEVIED ON INTER VIVOS TRUSTS AND ESTATES** not including Graduated Rate Estates (GREs) and Qualifying Disability Trusts (QDTs).
   c. **ALSO SUBJECT TO 33% FEDERAL TAX RATES:** excess employee profit sharing plan contributions, and personal services business income earned by corporations, and calculations relating to charitable donations.
- **SOME GOOD NEWS ON CHARITABLE DONATION CALCULATIONS.** Claim:
   a. 15% on the first $200
   b. 33% on the lesser of the amount over $200 and taxable income taxed at 33%
   c. 29% of the remainder of the gift.

DIGITAL NEWS SUBSCRIPTIONS. Individuals will be eligible to claim a non-refundable tax credit for 15% of up to $500 paid for eligible digital news subscriptions in the tax year. This credit may be split between taxpayers.

CHARITABLE DONATIONS. Gifts of cultural property need not have "national significance" starting in 2019. Amounts given to Qualified Canadian Journalism Organizations will qualify for tax receipts starting in 2020. Recall that the First Time Donor's Super Tax Credit was eliminated for tax years starting in 2018.

PRINCIPAL RESIDENCE DISPOSITION RULES. The principal residence section on Schedule 3 of the tax return was simplified in 2017, but the data must be entered in complicated Form T2091—*Designation Of A Property As A Principal Residence By An Individual (Other Than A Personal Trust)* **anytime a principal residence is disposed of starting in 2017.**

HOME RELOCATION LOAN DEDUCTION—The value of a benefit that occurs when an employer provides to an employee a low interest loan to assist in a move to a new employment location has previously been offset through a home relocation deduction from taxable income. The value of the deduction was limited to the annual benefit arising on loans up to $25,000 if the employee moved at least 40 kilometers closer to a new work location. This deduction was **eliminated for the 2018 and subsequent years.** Existing home relocation loans will continue to have the taxable benefit but will not be eligible for the deduction

VOLUNTARY DISCLOSURE PROGRAM (VDP) RULES, MARCH 1, 2018. A taxpayer may voluntarily comply with the Income Tax Act to correct errors and omissions on previously filed returns or to file omitted returns and in some cases apply for relief from penalties and interest. However, those with spotty filing records may now be denied both interest and penalty relief, and after this implementation date, no one will receive 100% interest relief.

EXTENDED INFORMATION GATHERING TIME. Upon receiving Royal Assent for this provision, CRA will have more time to "stop-the-clock" on a tax reassessment period, in cases where a taxpayer contests its requirements for information and/or a compliance orders. The extension will be granted for the time it takes to contest the information requests and compliance orders, and will end on the final disposition of the application, including appeals.

B. TAX CHANGES FOR EMPLOYEES

CPP CONTRIBUTIONS. Above a basic exemption of $3500, employees must contribute 5.1% of their pensionable earnings to the Canada Pension Plan in 2019, (up to a maximum of $2,748.90, based on pensionable earnings of up to $57,400). The employer will match this contribution. If you're self-employed, you'll have to contribute 10.2% of your earnings, to a maximum of $5,497.80, but one half of this amount can be claimed as a deduction on the T1 return; the other half as a non-refundable tax credit.

The goal is to increase the pension available to the current generation of workers from the current 25% of pensionable earnings to 33%. To fund this, the CPP premium rate will increase annually over the period 2019 to 2023. Then, in 2024, the basic rate will remain the same but an additional premium will be required on the next $4,800 over the maximum pensionable earnings; and by 2025, on the first $10,200 over the maximum pensionable earnings. The premium rate on these enhanced pensionable earnings will be 4%, payable by both the employer and the employee. All of the additional premiums over 4.95% will be tax deductible and the self-employed will, of course, have to pay both the employer and employee premiums.

The following table shows the projected premiums to the year 2025 adjusted for known 2018 and 2019 pensionable earnings and indexed at 2.5% after 2019.

Year	Regular CPP Rate	Max. Pens. Earn.	Max. Reg. Premiums	Additional Pens. Earn.	Max. Pens. Earn.	Add. Rate	Add. Prem.	Total Prem.	Max. SE Prem.
2018	4.95%	$55,900	$2,593.80		$55,900	0%		$2,593.80	$5,187.60
2019	5.10%	$57,400	$2,748.90		$57,400	0%		$2,748.90	$5,497.80
2020	5.25%	$58,800	$3,087.00		$58,800	0%		$3,087.00	$6,174.00
2021	5.45%	$60,300	$3,286.35		$60,300	0%		$3,286.35	$6,572.70
2022	5.70%	$61,800	$3,522.60		$61,800	0%		$3,522.60	$7,045.20
2023	5.95%	$63,400	$3,772.30		$63,400	0%		$3,772.30	$7,544.60
2024	5.95%	$65,000	$3,867.50	$4,800	$65,000	4.0%	$192.00	$4,059.50	$8,119.00
2025	5.95%	$66,600	$3,962.70	$10,200	$66,600	4.0%	$408.00	$4,370.70	$8,741.40

Benefits are expected to accrue starting in 2019 but a full two-thirds of income replacement will not occur until the worker has contributed for 40 years. This means if you are currently approaching retirement, you will see no increase in your pension despite the higher premiums.

CPP Benefits for Pre-retirees: Taxpayers who elect to receive their CPP retirement pension before or after age 65 receive an adjusted pension amount. The augmentation for late pension take-up is 0.7% per month. This means that a pensioner who begins receiving their CPP retirement pension at age 70 would receive 142% of their age 65 pension entitlement.

The additional contributions made after the taxpayer begins receiving a CPP retirement benefit earn the taxpayer a post-retirement pension. This amount of the post-retirement pension earned each year will depend on the taxpayer's CPP contributory earnings in those years but could be as much as 1/40 of the current CPP "maximum" pension for each year they contribute premiums after they begin receiving their CPP retirement pension.

Employees under age 65 must continue to contribute to the Canada Pension Plan even if they are currently receiving CPP retirement benefits. Contributors over 64 who are receiving CPP retirement benefits and wish to stop contributing must file form CPT30 *Election to stop contributing to the Canada Pension Plan, or revocation of a prior election* with their employer. CPP contributions will cease the month following the submission of the form. For self-employed taxpayers the same rules apply except that the election not to contribute to CPP will be made on Schedule 8.

As the cost of the CPP is already quite high, the after-tax amounts received from the CPP benefits and the savings from the cessation of the premiums, may be better invested in a TFSA, which will earn tax free income for the future, and guarantee a return of contributions to survivors.

CANADA TRAINING GRANT. For 2019 forward, this is a new non-taxable credit accumulated at a rate of $250 per year to a lifetime maximum accumulation of $5,000. It will be shown on Notices of Assessment for those between the ages of 25 and 65 who earn at least $10,000 from employment, self-employment, or taxable scholarships. The non-taxable portion of income of volunteer firefighters or emergency service volunteers and the tax-exempt earnings of status Indians qualify in the threshold. Taxable income must not exceed the upper limit of the third tax bracket ($147,667 in 2019). When eligible tuition fees are paid, the taxpayer may claim the lesser of the available Canada Training Credit, and 50% of the eligible tuition fees paid to reduce tax otherwise payable; after this any excess credit is refunded. To make this more complicated, the Tuition Amount otherwise available is limited to the portion of tuition paid less the Canada Training Credit.

EI TRAINING SUPPORT BENEFIT. By late 2020, workers who go back to school may qualify to collect EI benefits while they do so, for up to four weeks (at 55% of weekly earnings) while training if they have at least 600 hours of insurable employment. This leave can be taken over a four-year period. This new EI benefit will increase EI premium rates. Businesses which pay EI premiums of $20,000 or less will be eligible for a rebate of an unspecified amount.

EMPLOYMENT INSURANCE RATES. Maximum insurable earnings for 2019 are $53,100, maximum premium is $860.22 for employees, $1,204.31 for the employer. The rate decreased to 1.62%.

EI BENEFIT CLAWBACK. If you become unemployed, you may be collecting EI Benefits, which are taxable, and reported to you on a T4E slip. A clawback of regular benefits may be required when net income exceeds $66,375 in 2019 and the taxpayer has received regular benefits at some time in the prior ten years.

ELIGIBLE EDUCATOR SCHOOL SUPPLY TAX CREDIT. This refundable credit was introduced in 2016 and subsequent years. It is available to teachers and early childhood educators; it is a refundable tax credit.

EMPLOYEE STOCK OPTIONS DEDUCTION. The March 2019 budget proposed to limit the availability of the stock option deduction of 50% of the benefit received to an annual maximum of $200,000 where options are granted to employees of "large, long-established, mature firms".

RRSP DEDUCTION LIMIT—Your additional RRSP contribution room earned each year remains at 18% of last year's earned income, but the maximum contribution for 2019 it's $26,500 and for 2020 it's $27,230. Make the contribution within 60 days of the year end.

MEMBERS OF LEGISLATIVE ASSEMBLIES AND CERTAIN MUNICIPAL OFFICERS. A portion of allowances received by these taxpayers to cover costs incurred in the course of carrying out the duties of office or employment will become taxable. Effective 2019, any non-accountable portion of these allowances will be fully taxable; accountable allowances will remain non-taxable.

C. TAX CHANGES FOR STUDENTS

EDUCATION AND TEXTBOOK AMOUNTS. These tax credits, based on the number of months of full time or part time attendance at a post-secondary school, have been eliminated for 2017 and future tax years on the federal tax return; but many provinces will continue on with them. In addition, starting in 2019, the federal government will require designated educational institutions to report to CRA the months of student enrolment, in order to calculate the Canada Workers Benefit, administer the RRSP Lifelong Learning Plan (LLP) and exemptions for scholarships, fellowships and bursaries.

TUITION FEE AMOUNT—The tuition fee amount has been extended, starting in 2017, to include fees paid to organizations that provide occupational skills courses that are not at a post-secondary level provided that the courses are taken for the purposes of providing skills or improving skills in an occupation. The student must also be at least 16 years of age. The claim is based on a calendar, not an academic year, and fees must be over $100.

EXAM FEES. Students can claim certain exam fees as tuition amounts if the exams are written to get a professional status recognized by the federal or provincial governments or required to qualify as a licensed or certified tradesperson.

FOREIGN STUDIES. For the purposes of claiming the tuition, education and textbook amount, the minimum qualifying time for a course of studies for full-time students studying abroad has been three consecutive weeks since 2011.

This will also be the minimum duration for the purposes of taking Education Assistance Payments under a Registered Education Savings Plan (RESP).

RESP SHARING WITH SIBLINGS. Tax free transfers will be allowed between individual RESPs for siblings without triggering a repayment of the Canada Education Savings Grant, so long as the receiving beneficiary is under 21 at the time of the transfer.

ROLLOVERS OF RESPS TO RDSPS. Beginning in 2014, the RESP rollover provisions to RRSPs apply to rollovers to Registered Disability Savings Plans (RDSPs). RESP investments, after Canada Education Savings Grants (CESGs) and Bonds (CESBs) have been repaid, may be rolled over to an RDSP so long as the plan holder has sufficient RDSP contribution room. These contributions will not generate government contributions (CDSB or CDSGs). Withdrawals of rolled over RESPs will be taxable.

PROVINCIAL TUITION AND REBATE PROGRAMS. The provinces of Alberta, Manitoba, Nova Scotia, Prince Edward Island, Newfoundland, Northwest Territories and Nunavut all have retained their full and part-time education and textbook amounts—at least so far. B.C.'s February 20, 2018 budget eliminated the amounts effective 2019.

In an effort to retain graduates, provinces had programs to reimburse tuition paid to post-secondary graduates if they remain in the province. However, in Manitoba this provision was reduced in 2017 and eliminated for 2018. Saskatchewan is the only province which has retained its program to rebate up to $20,000 of tuition fees.

NEW VETERANS EDUCATION AND TRAINING BENEFIT—Starting in April 2018, veterans who are honourably discharged will qualify for a taxable $40,000 benefit if they have 6 years of eligible service and $80,000 if there is 12 years of eligible services. Veterans will not be limited to post-secondary training. If university or college is not their choice, up to $5,000 of the total funding earned can be used for career and personal development courses. This could include small business boot camps, continuing education, etc. Living expenses, travel, and incidentals *will not be covered* by the career and personal development funding unless built into the course costs by the institution or organization.

D. TAX CHANGES FOR FAMILIES

INDEXATION OF CANADA CHILD BENEFITS. These benefits were indexed beginning in July 2018. Benefits will increase by 1.5% as will the clawback thresholds. This will amount to an increase of $9.00 (or less) per month per child, beginning in July 2018; the amount of the benefit depends on the age of the child, as below.

	July 2018 to June 2019	July 2019 to June 2020
Benefit for Children Under 6	$6,496 ($541.33/month)	$6,639 ($553.25 per month)
Children Between 6 and 17	$5,481 ($456.75/month)	$5,602 ($466.83 per month)

These benefits are clawed back as shown below:

	Family Net Income 2018			Family Net Income 2019		
Number of Children	Under $30,450	$30,450 to $65,975	Over $65,975	Under $31,120	$31,120 to $67,426	Over $67,426
1	0%	7.0%	$2,486.75 + 3.2%	0%	7.0%	$2,541 + 3.2%
2	0%	13.5%	$4,795.88 + 5.7%	0%	13.5%	$4,901 + 5.7%
3	0%	19.0%	$6,749.75 + 8.0%	0%	19.0%	$6,898 + 8.0%
4+	0%	23.0%	$8,170.75 + 9.5%	0%	23.0%	$8,350 + 9.5%

Foreign-born Status Indians. These persons, legally residing in Canada who are neither Canadian citizens or permanent residents will now be able to receive retroactively to July 2016, payments of the Universal Child Care Benefit (UCCB), Canada Child Benefit (CCB) and the National Child Benefit Supplement.

INDEXED GST/HST CREDIT. Here are the amounts receivable by those who are over 18. Note that since July of 2011, each parent who lives with the child can receive 50% of any GST/HST Credit and Canada Child Benefits. Each parent will want to invest these benefits in the name of the child to build up a great education fund, but also to avoid tax on investment earnings.

GST/HSTC AMOUNTS RECEIVABLE:	July 2018 to June 2019	July 2019 to June 2020
Adult maximum	284	290
Child maximum	149	153
Single supplement	149	153
Phase-in threshold for the single supplement	9,209	9,412
Family net income at which credit begins to phase out	36,976	37,789

CANADA WORKER'S BENEFIT. For 2019 the benefit will be 26% of earned income over $3,000 to a maximum of $1,355 for single taxpayers and $2,335 for couples and single parents. It will be clawed back at a rate of 12% for income over $12,820 for singles and $17,025 for families. Disabled taxpayers will receive an additional benefit of $700, subject to clawbacks that begin when at $24,111 for a single person and $36,483 when both spouses are disabled. Kinship care providers will be able to apply for this benefit retroactive 10 years. This newly enhanced benefit in part compensates low earners for CPP premium increases.

Optional Reporting of Tax Exempt Amounts. For the purposes of the Canada Working Benefit, certain taxpayers who receive tax exempt amount of money —tax exempt income earned on a reserve, for example, or amounts received by an emergency volunteer—may elect to report these amounts in order to meet the $3000 income threshold needed to receive this benefit, starting in 2019. Beginning in 2019, CRA will include the Canada Workers Benefit in the assessment of qualifying taxpayers even if they do not apply for it.

CLIMATE ACTION INCENTIVE. In the provinces of SK, MB, ON and NB all families should file tax returns to claim the Climate Action Incentive rebate to offset the cost of carbon taxes. The amount of the credit varies by province and family size but does not depend on family income. For families who reside outside a census metropolitan area, the credit is increased by 10%. One claim is made for the taxpayer, their spouse, and their dependent children who are under age 18. Taxpayers who are age 18 or over at the end of the year should file their own return to claim this credit.

E. TAX CHANGES FOR HOMEOWNERS

THE RRSP – HOME BUYER'S PLAN (HBP) INCENTIVE. *Starting on March 20, 2019,* tax-free withdrawals from an RRSP is increased to $35,000; $70,000 per couple. The money must be repaid in 15 years or added to income, as per existing rules. Starting in 2020, separating couples may participate in the HBP as first-time buyers. To qualify the taxpayer must be living apart from their former spouse or common-law partner at the time of the withdrawal. The separation must begin in the current or four preceding years. But individuals are disqualified if they move into a home owned and occupied by a new spouse or common-law partner. Also the former principal residence must be disposed of no later than two years after the HBP withdrawal. Taxpayers who have an existing HBP balance may not make a new HBP plan withdrawal until the former plan withdrawal is repaid.

CMHC FIRST-TIME HOME BUYER INCENTIVE. First-time home buyers whose household income is $120,000 or less may qualify for a CMHC shared equity mortgage of 5% of the cost of an existing home or 10% of the cost of a new home. To qualify, the CMHC insured mortgage plus the CMHC shared equity mortgage must be less than four times annual income. There will be no payments or interest accruing on the shared equity mortgage, but it must be repaid when the home is sold.

F. TAX CHANGES FOR PEOPLE WITH MEDICAL ISSUES

QUALIFYING MEDICAL EXPENSES. This is a non-refundable amount in which qualifying expenses in excess of the lesser of a threshold amount ($2,352 in 2019) and 3% of net income can be claimed for the patient and/or family members. For these reasons, it is generally the taxpayer with the lower net income that claims the medical expenses. There are three recent additions:

Medical Cannabis. As of October 17, 2018, no prescription is required. A medical document signed by a medical or nurse practitioner will suffice to claim in.

Psychiatric Service Animals. Starting in 2018, the costs of animals that have been specially trained to provide assistance to people with severe mental impairments, such as guiding a disoriented patient, searching the patient's home if the patient has severe anxiety, or applying compression to patients who have night tremors, may be claimed. The animal must be trained by a person or organization whose main purpose is this specialized training. Eligible expenses include cost of care and maintenance for the animal, including food, veterinary costs, reasonable travel costs for the patient to attend training at a facility that teaches how to handle the animal.

Reproduction Therapy. Couples experiencing medical infertility issues have previously been allowed to claim prescribed fertility medication and in-vitro fertilization procedures and their associated costs as a medical expense under the medical expense tax credit.

What's new is that taxpayers may elect to claim the costs of reproductive technologies even where the treatment is not medically indicated because of a medical infertility condition. In addition, the taxpayer may elect to claim the expenses in any of the immediately preceding ten tax years.

DISABILITY TAX CREDIT (DTC)—There has been significant controversy around the audit activities extended to those who apply for these credits, especially, diabetics, who must verify that they require at least 14 hours of life-sustaining therapy per week in order to claim the DTC. It is a non-refundable tax credit which translates to a federal real dollar amount of over $1,200, plus the value of the provincial tax saving. Nurse practitioners have been added to the list of qualified professionals who may certify the T2201 *Disability Tax Credit Certificate* form, effective March 22, 2017. Note that medical doctors can certify all types of conditions; others as below:[16]

---

16 Source: March 2017 budget documents

Basis of Disability Tax Credit Certification		Type of Medical Practitioner
Vision		Medical doctor (MD) or optometrist
Marked restriction:	Speaking	MD or speech-language pathologist
	Hearing	MD or audiologist
	Walking	MD, occupational therapist or physiotherapist
	Elimination of bodily waste	MD
	Feeding or dressing	MD or occupational therapist
	Mental functions	MD or psychologist
Life-sustaining therapy		MD
Cumulative effects of significant restrictions		MD (all restrictions) or occupational therapist (walking, feeding and dressing only)

Disability Tax Credit Certificate (Form T2201). A *disabled dependant* for this credit is one who has a "severe and prolonged impairment in mental or physical functions." To qualify as disabled, a *Disability Tax Credit Certificate* (Form T2201) must be completed and signed by medical practitioner to certify that the individual is disabled. In addition, CRA must accept the certificate. Other provisions that require form T2201 are summarized below:

IS THE DISABILITY TAX CREDIT CERTIFICATE (FORM T2201) REQUIRED?

TAX PROVISIONS	T2201	Considerations:
Disability amount	Yes	Type 1 Diabetes: all applications previously refused in 2017 by CRA will be reviewed.
Enhanced child care expenses for disabled person	Yes	File form T778 to claim up to $11,000 in child care
RDSP	Yes	Claim up to $70,000 CDSG and $20,000 CDSB; Go back 10 years for unclaimed entitlements
RESP	Yes	For disabled, maximum lifespan for plan is extended from 35 to 40 years for a single beneficiary. Amounts can transfer to RDSP
RRSP Home Buyer Plan	Yes	Up to $35,000 may be withdrawn tax free for a DTC-eligible relative (blood, marriage, common-law, adoption) for more accessible home. Must occupy in 1 year; needn't be first home.

TAX PROVISIONS	T2201	Considerations:
Attendant care expenses claimed as medical expense	No/yes	Both disability amount and medical expenses can be claimed, if only a limited amount of the attendant care expenses are claimed: $10,000 or $20,000 in year of death; but no disability supports deduction.
Disability supports deduction	No	Medical expenses cannot be claimed for the same amounts. File Form T929
Canada Caregiver Credits	No	
Refundable Medical Expense Supplement	No	Limited by 25% of any disability support deduction claimed.
Qualified Disability Trust	Yes	A testamentary trust that will continue to qualify for graduated tax rates. Elect this treatment by using T3 QDT Form.
Preferred Beneficiary Election	No	Income in inter vivos trust is treated as capital and not taxed. Election must be made in writing 90 days after trust year end.
Lifetime Benefit Trust	No	A testamentary trust which acquires a qualifying trust annuity to defer taxation of a registered plan if spouse, child or grandchild has cognitive impairment
Henson Trust	No	A discretionary trust for a disabled child will ensure income from invested capital will not affect social assistance payments

Rules When Claiming Attendant Care Expenses and the Disability Amount. When a taxpayer claims expenses for an attendant or the cost of nursing home care for a patient as a medical expense, neither that individual nor any other person may claim the Disability Tax Credit (DTC) for that person or transfer it from that patient. But, the DTC can still be used if the claim for an attendant is less than $10,000 ($20,000 in the year of death).

Expenses claimable for these purposes can include fees paid for nursing home residence, full time care in a personal residence, or care in a group home plus costs for a special school or detox centre, which may qualify as both medical expenses and tuition fee credits. This generally does not include "stop smoking" treatment unless part of a medical treatment prescribed and monitored by a medical practitioner.

Note that when attendant care expenses are claimed as medical expenses, the same expenses cannot be deducted for the *Disability Supports Deduction* on Line 215 of the T1 return.

CANADA CAREGIVER CREDIT. In 2017, the (CCC) replaced the Family Caregiver Tax Credit, the Caregiver Tax Credit, and the Credit for Infirm Dependants. This credit comes in two parts:

- A *"Mini" CCC of $2,230 in 2019*, which must be claimed for an infirm minor child or someone for whom you are claiming a spousal amount. The term spousal amount also includes an "eligible dependant" or a someone you are claiming as "equivalent to spouse".

- A *"Maxi" CCC of $7140 in 2019*, or a portion thereof, may be claimed if you are supporting a spouse or eligible dependant over 18 whose net income is over $12,069 in 2019. You may also claim this amount for infirm adults who are considered "other dependants." *But this larger credit, is never claimed for a minor child.*

Infirm spouses, common-law partners, and eligible dependants over 18. This Canada Caregiver Credit is complicated for spouses because you may be able to claim the Mini CCC of $2,230 in conjunction with the spousal amount. However, if you can't claim the spousal amount then you may be able to *claim part (or all)* of the Maxi amount of $7,140. Two questions are important:

- *Can you claim partial spousal amount for a low-income earner?* Generally, that's for your spouse who has net income under $7159. If so, then you can add the Mini amount of $2,230. There may be an additional claim for a partial Maxi CCC if you have a small spousal amount. That is, a top-up of your total combined CCC claim (Mini and Maxi) to $7,140 is possible, as follows: claim the spousal amount; claim the Mini CCC; and then claim $7,140 minus the spousal amount minus $2,230.

- *Is your dependant's income too high to claim the spousal amount?* If your spouse's income is between $12,069 and $16,766, claim the full Maxi CCC of $7,140. If your spouse's income is between $16,766 and $23,906 claim the Maxi CCC minus the dependant's net income over $16,766.

Only one claim may be made for the *Canada Caregiver Credit* for your spouse or eligible dependant. No claim may be made for a dependant for whom the taxpayer is required to make spousal support payments except in the year of marital change when the taxpayer may claim either the dependant or the support payments made. Note: these figures are indexed annually.

Other Infirm dependants age 18 and over. Your dependant can be your parents/grandparents, brothers/sisters, aunts/uncles, nieces/nephews, or adult children or that of your spouse or common law partner. Only one claim will be allowed for the Canada Caregiver Amount for this class of dependant although the claim could be shared amongst two or more taxpayers so long as the total amount claimed does not exceed the allowable claim.

Infirm or Disabled—What's the Difference for Tax Purposes? CRA may contact you to verify your claim for the Canada Caregiver Amount or the Disability Amount. For these reasons, it's important to draw the distinction between "infirm" and "disabled," for different provisions on the tax return. A disabled person is markedly restricted.

An *infirm dependant* is one who has "an impairment in physical or mental functions." A child *under 18* will be considered to be "infirm" only if they are likely to be, for an indefinite duration, dependant on others for significantly more assistance in attending to personal needs, compared to children of the same age. This person can be claimed for the Canada Caregiver Credit.

Audit-Proofing. With the new Canada Caregiver Credit there is no longer a requirement that the dependant reside with the taxpayer. Nor does the CRA have any specific documentation requirements. But, CRA may ask for a signed statement from a medical practitioner verifying when the impairment started and how long it is expected to continue. In the case of children under 18, CRA will want to know whether the child will be dependent on other adults for a specific or an indefinite period of time.

NEW CAREGIVER RECOGNITION BENEFIT FOR VETERANS—A new non-taxable $1000 monthly benefit will be paid directly to informal caregivers of ill and injured veterans including family members. Close to $190 million has been set aside over 6 years starting April 1, 2018. The benefit will be indexed to inflation.

EI COMPASSIONATE CARE BENEFITS FOR CAREGIVERS are available for up to 6 months starting in 2017.

G. TAX CHANGES FOR INVESTORS

CARRYING CHARGES. Note that effective 2014, Safety Deposit Box fees are no longer deductible as carrying charges.

CANADA SAVINGS BONDS. These investments were phased out in 2017. Annual interest rates on existing premium bonds have been set at .80% and .5% for other unmatured CSBs in 2019.

CORPORATE CLASS FUNDS. Fund switches in non-registered accounts will trigger taxable capital gains (or losses) starting in 2017.

ETF AND MUTUAL FUND REDEMPTIONS. Certain redemptions by fund holders may result in higher taxes, depending on the structure of their holdings effective March 19, 2019. Details were scarce at the time of writing. Check with your financial advisor.

H. TAX CHANGES FOR BUSINESS OWNERS

INCREASED CCA CLAIMS. First-year capital cost allowance claims will increase for assets acquired after November 20, 2018. The claim will be 150% of the normal CCA claim until December 31, 2023. For purchases in years 2024 to 2027, the half-year rule will be suspended and where the half-year rule does not apply, the claim will be 125% of the normal claim. For purchase after 2027 the usual rules with the normal half year claims will apply.

In addition, for cars purchased on or after March 19, 2019 and before 2028, a new depreciation rate will be allowed for a zero-emission car with a maximum cost of $55,000 plus taxes, unless a federal purchase rebate of $5000 for electric battery or hydrogen fuel cell vehicles under $45,000 is received. A 100% CCA rate will apply for purchases up to December 31, 2023 and 75% for purchases in 2024 and 2025; then 55% for purchases in 2026 and 2027. For purchases after 2027, the normal CCA rates will apply.

SMALL BUSINESS TAX RATE—for *private* corporations that earn active income eligible for the $500,000 Small Business Deduction (SBD), tax rates will go down to 9% for 2019 and future years. The 10.5% rate in effect for 2016/2017 was reduced to 10% for 2018.

DIVIDEND TAX CREDIT CHANGES. As a result of the tax rate reductions on active business income eligible for the small business deduction, the taxation of dividends that are distributed into personal hands of the shareholders will also change as follows:

Year	Small Business Tax Rate	Dividend Gross Up Rate	Dividend Tax Credit Rate*	Dividend Tax Credit Rate**
2015	11.0%	18%	11.0%	13/18
2016	10.5%	17%	10.5%	21/29
2017	10.5%	17%	10.5%	21/29
2018	10.0%	16%	10.03%	8/11
2019	9.0%	15%	9.03%	9/13

*as a percentage of the grossed-up dividend   ** as a fraction of the gross-up

PASSIVE INVESTMENT INCOME EARNED BY PRIVATE CORPORATIONS. Two new measures were introduced in the February 27, 2018 budget that curtail the advantages of investing inside a private corporation, starting in 2019.

Reduction of the Small Business Deduction. The Small Business Deduction, which is also known as the business limit is currently reduced on a straight-line basis when there is between $10 million and $15 million of taxable capital employed in Canada. Taxable capital is calculated on Schedule 33 of the T2 corporate tax return and includes retained earnings, share capital, certain forms of debt and advances and declared by unpaid dividends. The Small Business Deduction is not allowed when taxable capital exceeds $15 Million.

In addition, for tax years after 2018, private corporations that earn more than $150,000 in passive investment income that is not incidental to an active business, will be taxed at the general tax rate, currently 15%. If both restrictions apply to the corporation, the greater of the two will apply.

More specifically, the business limit of $500,000 will be reduced, also on a straight-line basis when Canadian Controlled Small Business Corporations (CCPCs) have passive investment income between $50,000 and $150,000. The reduction in the business limit is calculated as $5 for every $1 of "adjusted aggregate investment income" above $50,000 and will be calculated annually based on the prior year's passive investment income.

The calculations focus in on three things, as illustrated below: the adjusted aggregate investment income, the small business deduction available and the amount of active business income earned. The active business income of the CCPC must remain below the reduced business limit, for all the income to continue to be taxed at the small business tax rate.

A. Adjusted Aggregate Investment Income over $50,000	Reduction in Small Business Deduction (A x 5)	Reduced Business Limit
$1	$5	$499,995
$20,000	100,000	$400,000
$40,000	200,000	$300,000
$50,000	$250,000	$250,000
$75,000	$375,000	$125,000
$100,000	$500,000	$0

The calculation of the adjusted aggregate investment income will *not include:*

- Taxable capital gains and losses on the disposition of property used principally in an active business, carried on primarily (50% or more) in Canada by the CCPC or a related CCPC.
- The disposition of a share of another connected CCPC where all or substantially all of the fair market value of the assets are used primarily in Canada in an active business of the CCPC

- Net capital losses carried over from other tax years

But, the following sources must be included in the calculation:

- Dividends from non-connected corporations
- Income from savings in a non-exempt life insurance policy if it is not otherwise included in the aggregate investment income.

These changes will require some strategic thought regarding the deployment of capital retained in an active business, as corporate taxpayers will experience a 6% corporate tax hike on active business income in 2019, should passive investment earnings exceed $150,000. However, integration of the personal/corporate tax system has been retained with the refundable tax mechanism on passive investment income.

REFUNDABLE TAXES ON INVESTMENT INCOME. Corporations must pay taxes at the top rates applied to individuals on their passive investment earnings held in the corporation. When that income is distributed as dividends into personal hands, some or all of the corporate taxes are refunded through the Refundable Dividend Tax on Hand (RDTOH) account at a rate of $38.33 for every $100 of dividends paid. Personal taxes are then assessed at the personal level on the dividends distributed, based on the taxpayer's marginal tax rate. These rules allow for the integration of the personal and corporate tax system, so that the same income is not taxed twice.

Dividends paid are classified into two categories:

- "Eligible dividends" originate from active income above the small business deduction, which is taxed at the general rate of 15%, including any eligible portfolio dividends.
- "Non-eligible dividends" stem from active income taxed at low small business tax rates and passive investment income earned in the corporation (however this excludes eligible portfolio dividends, and the non-taxable portion of capital gains, which may be distributed as tax-free capital dividends.)

Effective after 2018, the RDTOH account will feature the pooling of two categories of RDTOH that will correct an unintended advantage corporate shareholders were receiving: they could recover full RDTOH whether either low-taxed eligible or higher-taxed non-eligible dividends were paid out to the shareholder personally. Now the government will limit the recovery of RDTOH for non-eligible portfolio dividends included in active business earnings, normally paid out as a non-eligible dividend:

- The *"eligible RDTOH"* account will track Part IV taxes paid on eligible portfolio dividends (38.33%). A refund from the eligible RDTOH is possible on distribution of *any taxable dividend—eligible or non-eligible.*
- The *"non-eligible RDTOH"* account will track refundable taxes paid under Part 1 (15%) on investment income plus Part IV taxes (38.33%) on non-eligible portfolio dividends from a non-connected corporation. *Refunds are possible only on payment of non-eligible dividends.* These refunds must be obtained before those from the eligible RDTOH account.

TAX ON SPLIT INCOME. Significant changes have been made on distributions of income from private corporations and related businesses to non-active family members starting in 2018 to curtail income sprinkling.

The previous rules that required certain income source sprinkled from a corporation to related minors be taxed at the highest personal tax rate, have been expanded to taxpayers who are over age 17. The new rules apply the tax on split income to all family members unless they fall into an exception. Exceptions include:

- Family members age 25 to 64 who own shares that represent at least 10% of the voting shares and value of the company;
- Spouses of business owners who are age 65 or older;
- Family members who are over age 17 if they averaged at least 20 hours per week working in the business in the current year or any of the five previous years.

PROFESSIONALS—WORK-IN-PROGRESS. For business years that begin after March 21, 2017, professional taxpayers may no longer exclude from income their work in progress. A phase-out of the provision was implemented over a period of years to soften the effects of this change. These professionals include accountants, dentists, lawyers, medical doctors, veterinarians and chiropractors.

INCORPORATION COSTS. Effective January 1, 2017, the first $3,000 of incorporation costs will be deductible as a current expense rather than being added to a new CCA class for eligible capital property as described below.

ELIGIBLE CAPITAL PROPERTY. A new class of depreciable property for CCA purposes applies starting in 2017. Expenditures that were previously added to the Cumulative Eligible Capital account at 75% will be added at 100% with an annual 5% depreciation rate (instead of 7% of 75% of costs and a 7% amortization rate). Existing recapture, capital gains rules and the half year depreciation rules will apply.

Small balances of eligible capital property carried over to the new classes will be allowed to be deducted more quickly. Specifically, on expenditures incurred before 2017, the greater of $500 per year and the amount otherwise deductible for that year will be allowed. For existing properties, the amortization rate will be 7% until the property is disposed or until the last taxation year ending before 2027.

GOODWILL. Special rules will apply for goodwill. According to the Budget, every business will be considered to have goodwill even if there was no expenditure for it. An expense that does not relate to specific property will increase that capital cost of this class. Transitional rules will apply.

I. TAX CHANGES FOR PENSIONERS

As a result of a significant pension reform, the way Canadians contribute to and access their public and private pensions has changed recently:

DEFERRING OAS. Since July 1, 2013, Canadians have had the option to defer receiving their OAS pension for up to five years. If you elect to do so you will receive a proportionately larger pension when you do start to receive it. This may also enable you to withdraw other taxable amounts first, like deposits in an RRSP, in a more tax-efficient manner. You would want to do this if your net income is always going to be high in the 5-year period, and OAS, as a result, will be clawed back.

The OAS is clawed back. You will start receiving reduced benefits when individual net income reported on your tax return exceeds $77,580. Your benefits will stop completely when income exceeds about $125,696 (est) in 2019. Assuming no clawback, the amount that is receivable differs quarterly with an indexing factor.

INCREASED INCOME EXEMPTIONS FOR GIS RECIPIENTS. Starting in the July 2020 benefit year, seniors will be allowed to make $5000 from employment or self-employment before their GIS benefits are reduced. Only 50% of active earnings between $5000 and $15,000 will reduce the GIS received.

CANADA PENSION PLAN CHANGES. CPP can be split between spouses so long as both spouses are at least age 60 and the non-recipient spouse has never contributed to the CPP. This can be an important way to reduce instalment payments and clawbacks of the Old Age Security for the higher income earner.

Collecting CPP and Working. Since 2012, it has been necessary for those between age 60 and 64 to continue to contribute to CPP if they are working and drawing benefits from the plan. As mentioned, those benefits are taxable. From age

65 to 69, recipients of the CPP retirement benefits who are still working may elect to opt out of paying premiums by filing a new form *CPT30 Election to Stop Contributing to the CPP.* The self-employed can opt out on Schedule 8 of the T1 return.

In either case, additional contributions made in this period for those who don't opt out will be saved in a *"Post Retirement Benefit"* (PRB) account to bump up your monthly pension benefits—albeit slightly—beginning the following year. The PRB cannot be split with the spouse.

New CPP Enhancements for 2019. Further enhancements to the CPP began on January 1, 2019:

*Child rearing drop-in provision. For each year in which a child is under age 7, an annual amount will be "dropped in" to the CPP retirement benefit calculation equal to the parent's average earnings during the five years prior to birth or adoption of the child if that amount is higher than the actual earnings in this period.

Disability drop-in provision. A drop in amount of 70% of earnings will be made for the years in which someone was receiving the CPP disability pension for a severe and prolonged disability. This will increase retirement benefits for both the disabled person and their spouse.

Elimination of reduction benefits for young survivors. Widows/widowers under the age of 45 will no longer have their survivor's pension reduced as a result of their age; about half of young survivors will also become eligible to receive survivor's pensions before age 65. In addition, recipients of CPP retirement benefits who develop a severe and prolonged disability while under the age of 65 will now be able to receive a top up to the level of the CPP disability benefits, which are larger than the retirement benefits.

Lump sum death benefits. A one time lump sum death benefit of up to $2500 has been payable to the surviving spouse or estate of a CPP contributor who has passed away. A flat rate amount will now be paid, regardless of actual contributory earnings of the deceased. Regrettably the government did not take this opportunity to index the lump sum benefit.

Electing to Start CPP Early or Late. Taxpayers who elect to receive their CPP retirement pension before or after age 65 receive an adjusted pension amount. The augmentation rate is 0.7% for 2014 and subsequent years. A pensioner who begins receiving their CPP retirement pension at age 70 would receive 142% of their age 65 pension entitlement.

Beginning in 2012, the reduction for **early pension take-up** was increased to 0.6% per month. This means that a pensioner who began receiving a CPP retirement pension in 2019 would have received pension that is reduced to 64% of the amount they would have been entitled to at age 65.

Should an Individual Elect to Begin CPP at Age 60, Age 65, or Age 70? This question is not as simple as one might think. The answer depends on a number of factors, including:

1. Is the taxpayer currently receiving a CPP survivor pension? Any survivor pension will likely be reduced or eliminated once the taxpayer begins receiving the retirement pension as the maximum pension applies to the sum of the survivor and retirement pensions.

2. How long will the taxpayer live? For taxpayers who have a shorter than normal life expectancy, it may make more sense to begin receiving a reduced pension at age 60 as the total received during their lifetime will be less if they wait. For those who will live longer than normal, the increased pension received by waiting 'til age 70 could result in a larger amount being received over the taxpayer's lifetime. In addition, a postponement of the benefits could allow for room to add other taxable amounts into income—RRSP or RRIF withdrawals for example—with the affect of "averaging down" the tax on combined pension income.

3. Will receiving an enhanced CPP pension result in an OAS clawback once the taxpayer starts receiving CPP and OAS?

4. Remember that combined survivor and retirement benefits will not exceed the maximum retirement benefit of one contributor; which means there is zero benefit to the surviving spouse with a maximum benefit entitlement.

The above will impact on the role of other retirement income funding opportunities and should be compared to other joint-last-to-die funding options.

POOLED RETIREMENT PENSION PLANS (PRPP). This new type of pension plan was passed into law by the federal government in 2012 and provincial legislation has since followed for most provinces. The plan provides a voluntary and affordable alternative for small employers to offer an employer-sponsored pension plan at work, with contribution levels that will mirror those available under the Registered Pension Plan (RPP) defined contribution or money purchase rules.

INDIVIDUAL PENSION PLAN (IPP) RULES. Individual Pension Plans are established for an owner-manager who is an employee of his or her own corporation. Annual minimum amounts are required to be withdrawn from the IPP once the plan member is 72, similar to the rules under the Registered Retirement Income Fund (RRIF). Also, contributions related to past years of employment will now have to come from RRSP or RPP assets or by reducing RRSP contribution room, before deductible contributions to an IPP can be made. As of March 19, 2019, taxpayers may no longer transfer funds from a defined benefit plan from a former employer to a new IPP.

ALDAS AND VARIABLE PAYMENT LIFE ANNUITIES. As of 2020, Advanced Life Deferred Annuities will be allowed in an RRSP, RRIF, deferred profit-sharing plan (DPSP), pooled registered pension plan (PRPP) and defined contribution registered pension plan (RPP). The ALDA pays a pre-determined monthly income at a pre-determined age until the annuitant dies. No more than 25% of the plan assets may be used to invest in an ALDA. The income must start no later than the end of the year in which the annuitant turns 85. There is a lifetime contribution limit of $150,000 (indexed in increments of $10,000 starting in 2020).

A variable payment life annuity (VPLA), pays a variable amount based on performance investments in the annuity fund and the mortality of VPLA annuitants. Payments must begin by the later of the end of the year the member turns 71 years and the end of the year in which the VPLA is established. These annuities will be allowed under a PRPP and defined contribution RPP.

CHANGES TO GERMAN PENSION FILING RULES. If you receive German social security pension it's reportable in Canada, but you may qualify to claim a partial exempt portion. You will have filing obligations in Germany. Taxpayers have had trouble getting Canada to recognize the allowable foreign tax credits; but they are properly claimable on income that is taxed both in Canada and Germany.

REGISTERED DISABILITY SAVINGS PLAN (RDSP) RULE CHANGES. First established in 2008 the RDSP is used to accumulate private pension funds for the benefit of a disabled person. RDSPs function in a similar fashion to RESPs, in that contributions are not tax deductible, earnings accumulate on a tax deferred basis and the government contributes grants and bonds to enhance savings. Any person eligible to claim the Disability Amount can be the beneficiary of an RDSP and the plan can be established by them or by an authorized representative. Until the end of 2023, a plan holder may be a family member if the beneficiary's capacity to enter into a contract is diminished.

APPENDIX 5. SUMMARY OF PERSONAL AMOUNTS

		2017	2018	2019
Basic Personal Amount	Maximum Claim	$11,635	$11,809	$12,069
Age Amount	Maximum Claim	$7,225	$7,333	$7,494
	Reduce by net inc. over	$36,430	$36,976	$37,790
Spouse or Common-Law Partner Amount	Not infirm	$11,635	$11,809	$12,069
	Infirm	$11,635	$11,809	$12,069
Amount for Eligible Dependants	Not infirm	$11,635	$11,809	$12,069
	Infirm	$11,635	$11,809	$12,069
Pension Inc. Amt.	Maximum Claim[1]	$2,000	$2,000	$2,000
Adoption Expenses	Maximum Claim	$15,670	$15,905	$16,255
Canada Caregiver Credit	Infirm spouse, eligible dependant or child	$2,150	$2,182	$2,230
	Other infirm dependants	$6,883	$6,986	$7,140
	Reduced by net inc. over	$16,163	$16,405	$16,766
Disability Amount	Basic Amount	$8,113	$8,235	$8,416
	Supplementary Amount	$4,733	$4,804	$4,910
	Base Child Care Amount	$2,772	$2,814	$2,875
Tuition and Education Amounts + Textbook Tax Credit	Minimum Tuition[1]	$100	$100	$100
Medical Expenses	3% limitation	$2,268	$2,302	$2,352
Refundable Medical Expense Supplement	Maximum	$1,203	$1,222	$1,248
	Base Family Income	$26,644	$27,044	$27,639
	Minimum earned income	$3,514	$3,566	$3,645
Donation Credit	Low-rate ceiling[1]	$200	$200	$200
First-Time Donations	Rate[1]	25%	N/A	N/A
	Maximum Donation[1]	$1,000	N/A	N/A
Canada Employment Amount	Maximum	$1,178	$1,195	$1,222
Home Buyers' Amount	Maximum[1]	$5,000	$5,000	$5,000
Volunteer Firefighters, Search & Rescue	Maximum[1]	$3,000	$3,000	$3,000
Home Accessibility TC	Maximum[1]	$10,000	$10,000	$10,000

[1] These amounts are not indexed

Index

ADDITIONAL FINANCIAL EDUCATION

knowledgebureau.com

CERTIFICATE COURSES ONLINE

5. Introduction to Personal Tax Preparation
6. Intermediate Personal Tax Preparation
7. Advanced Family Tax Preparation
8. T1 Professional Tax Preparation— Proprietorships
9. Final Returns on Death of a Taxpayer
10. Use of Trusts in Tax & Estate Planning
11. T3 Basic Tax Preparation
12. Bookkeeping for Small Business
13. Debt and Cash Flow Management
14. Advanced Payroll for Small Business
15. T2 Tax Preparation for Small Business
16. T2 Tax Preparation for Professional Businesses
17. Tax Efficient Retirement Income Planning
18. Portfolio Risk Management in Retirement
19. Fundamentals of Succession Planning
20. Business Valuation
21. Cross Border Taxation